Stationed at Westhampnett, Air Vice-Marshal Sandy Johnstone commanded 602 Fighter Squadron during the critical time of the Battle of Britain.

D1369098

By the same author

Air Vice-Marshal
SANDY JOHNSTONE CB, DFC, AE

Spitfire into War

GRAFTON BOOKS

A Division of the Collins Publishing Group

LONDON GLASGOW
TORONTO SYDNEY AUCKLAND

Grafton Books
A Division of the Collins Publishing Group
8 Grafton Street, London W1X 3LA

Published by Grafton Books 1988

First published in Great Britain by
William Kimber & Co Ltd 1986

Copyright © Sandy Johnstone 1986

ISBN 0-586-20066-5

Printed and bound in Great Britain by
Collins, Glasgow

Set in Times

To Nigel Fieldman

Contents

Contents

ILLUSTRATIONS IN THE TEXT

Foreword

I was too young to remember much about the Great War, not being born until 1916. Nevertheless I still have a few childhood memories of the time, not least that of scampering behind the coal scuttle in the living room in great terror whenever an airship from nearby Inchinnan flew over the house.

As I grew older, however, the many stories of excitement and gallantry about those grisly days stirred my imagination, until I began to feel somehow deprived of the opportunity of playing a part in those stirring events. But one learned to live with it and I went on to enjoy my schooldays, managing to win colours for rugby, but failing to do so at cricket in spite of having been a regular member of the First Eleven for two whole seasons. Indeed, mine was a very ordinary progression into adulthood, taking life as it came and not worrying overmuch about what was going on in the world around.

Becoming a member of the local Auxiliary Air Force squadron soon after leaving school changed all that, however, for it gave me an entirely new purpose in life and I henceforth devoted most of my spare time to trying to justify my inclusion in such elite company. At the same time I became involved in a much wider orbit and, by the time the Auxilaries were called up for Active Service in August 1939, I had passed my twenty-third birthday, was the holder of a commercial pilot's licence and had well over 1,000 hours' flying experience tucked under my belt.

Remembering how stirred I had been by the tales of

excitement from World War One, it was reasonable to expect more to arise in the next. I decided therefore to record as much as possible about the daily doings of those serving with me so that I, too, could be in a position to regale the next generation with tales of derring-do, just as my elders and betters had done in the past hoping, of course, that I would survive long enough to tell them. Thus I began to make notes, often no more than jottings on the backs of envelopes, about our experiences during the first two years of World War Two, but it was not long before I was assiduously chronicling everything in a proper diary.

No 602 (City of Glasgow) Squadron, AAF, was a household name long before WWII began. It had been the first Auxiliary squadron to get into the air in 1925; two of its members, Lord Clydesdale and David Mac-Intyre, were first to conquer Mount Everest in 1933; the squadron swept the board in gunnery and bombing in 1935, beating the regular squadrons at their own game, and it was the first Auxiliary squadron to be equipped with Spitfire fighters as far back as March 1939. And 602 was to continue clocking up 'firsts' in the years to come and, in view of its outstanding record throughout a regrettably short history (1925–57), I am more than glad I maintained a diary throughout the first two years of its war service.

With the benefit of so much first-hand material to draw from, plus additional information extracted from official documents held in the Public Record Office, I have done my best to re-create, in diary form, the story of a pilot's life in this fine squadron during its early days on active service. It is essentially a personal account, inevitably embodying material from *Enemy in the Sky – My 1940 Diary*, but written in a form which, hopefully, will take

the reader behind the scenes and carry him along as part
of our team.

S.J.

London,
July 1985.

1939

August/September

August 23rd Sandy Mackay was expecting me for an early lunch and I drove into Largs shortly before half past eleven with prospects for good sailing ahead – frequent breaks of sunshine and a stiff breeze blowing from the south-west. It still feels strange to have a day off in mid week, but since being appointed to run the Volunteer Reserve section of the Civil Navigation School at Prestwick two months ago, I am required to be on duty at weekends and allowed to take time off in lieu. Fortunately Sandy is now in charge of the Largs branch of his father's bakery firm, so has no difficulty arranging his own leisure time.

The weather really blew up during the afternoon and we got thoroughly soaked as the lugsail kept shipping water during three hours' cruising round the Cumbraes. Consequently, by the time we had dried out and dined well at the Queen's Hotel, it was after ten before I fetched up at my parents' flat. I had told them I was visiting Sandy before coming on to Glasgow, but never thought to mention he had moved from Greenock to Largs, an omission which caused no end of bother, as I was soon to find out.

I had been expecting a mild ticking-off from Mother for being late, but was hoping to be forgiven as I would be able to spend some time with her the following morning, not being required to report back at Prestwick until lunchtime. I was certainly not expecting to find both parents so worked up as they were for, as soon as I set foot in the flat, they started bombarding me with questions about my recent whereabouts. 'This came for you early this afternoon and we've been moving Heaven and Earth to trace you ever since!' Dad finally got round to telling me, handing over a strange blue envelope bearing the legend ON HIS MAJESTY'S SERVICE – URGENT, EMBODIMENT, the last two words being heavily underlined. That the missive reached me at all is a testament to the efficiency of the Post Office, for it is addressed to the digs I left eighteen months ago, my rank is incorrectly stated and name wrongly spelt. But the message itself is plain – it seems I am called up for Active Service although, if past experience is anything to go by, it will probably turn out to be another mobilization exercise.

August 24th Cranking up the old Vauxhall, I arrived at Abbotsinch shortly after eleven to find the place ablaze with lights and a frenzy of activity with people milling in all directions, presumably trying to find out what was going on. I made straight for our squadron headquarters to find the CO and Vivian Bell helping the Orderly Room staff to cope with a mountain of paperwork when, after signing on, was told curtly to push off and report back at the aerodrome before eight o'clock next morning, bringing back sufficient clobber to last me for at least a week. '. . . Don't bother about civvies . . .' they added, '. . . you'll be wearing uniform from now on!'

Turning up at Abbotsford House to claim a room in the Mess, I was surprised to be told we would be sleeping rough in tents which were even then being put up round the perimeter of the airfield. This seems like taking the exercise a bit too far if you ask me, an opinion shared vociferously by others I've spoken to. However it appears to be a fait accompli and I find B Flight will occupy an area along the southern boundary whilst A flight beds down in the corner of the field beyond the old buildings. Bully for them, for they will have the use of a rickety old farm shed in which to store some of their gear.

George Pinkerton, my flight commander, was looking more worried than usual when I came upon him beside a tent, notebook in hand, apparently trying to make out a list of immediate requirements and allocating the tentage among key personnel. It seems I will be sharing a tent with George, although what we were to sleep on was the first thought that came to mind. 'Nip over to Stores and draw a camp kit . . .' he ordered, '. . . and bring one for me while you're at it.' By the time the beds were put up I was ready to use mine, for I hadn't slept much the previous night and was feeling depressed at having left without first explaining things to Margaret, my fiancée. Hopefully the exercise will be called off before next weekend, as she has promised to spend it at Prestwick.

After I had parked my Spitfire close to the tent, George then sent me to the Mess to put my head down for an hour or two, but after what seemed no more than a few minutes of fitful slumber, a batman woke me to say I was to report to the CO. Douglas Farquhar was wanting me to deliver some important operational documents to 269 Squadron, our resident squadron of Coastal Command Ansons, which had up-sticked that afternoon and gone off to Turnhouse without them. 'Make a note of the mileage and we'll ensure you're paid for the petrol . . .' was his parting shot before I hastily downed a plate of bacon and eggs and set out for Edinburgh at seven in the evening. Reporting to the Station Adjutant at Turnhouse two hours later he told me that 269 Squadron had never been there, nor was it expected but, after telephoning back to Abbotsinch, established its destination to have been Donnibristle, which entailed going over to Fife. He said I might just catch the last ferry from South Queensferry if I hurried but, when I rolled up the slipway there, the boat was already half way across the Forth, leaving me no alternative but to take the long route via Kincardine Bridge.

Apart from a dim glow showing through the curtains of the main guardroom, RAF Donnibristle was shrouded in darkness by the time I got there around midnight. The erk on duty went off to find the Duty Officer, but when that dignitary eventually turned up, heavy with sleep, it was only to inform me that the plans had been changed and 269 Squadron had gone on to Montrose. No, the Tay ferry did not operate after ten o'clock, he replied to my query. So, first scrounging a mug of cocoa from the duty watch, I once more drove into the night and headed for Perth, where I fortunately came across an all-night garage. My petrol was running low.

Lack of sleep was beginning to overtake me by the time I reached Montrose, where at least something seemed to be going on. I found the CO in his office and handed over the wretched documents. 'Sorry you've had all this trouble, Johnstone,' he said, briefly scanning the top page. 'These instructions have been superseded and should have been destroyed before we left Abbotsinch!'

I am two days late with this entry as I was just about all in when I finally got back to base, having driven throughout the night, once falling asleep at the wheel somewhere near Auchterarder and only waking up when a noisy lorry passed by. The car was nestling into a grassy bank at the side of the road. However the CO had the decency to let me stand down yesterday.

* * *

August 29th   The news is not good and it appears there is a real threat after all. Rumour has it that we are soon to move to our 'War Station', wherever that might be, and we have been told to remain on the airfield in case orders come through. I have done very little flying lately as most of the Spitfires are required for the new boys (RAFVR) who have been sent to us from Prestwick with no experience on modern fighters, and need all the training they can get. Sergeants McDowall, Lyall and McAdam arrived yesterday to join the queue whilst some of our more elderly members have yet to be converted to the type and also make demands on the operational aircraft. However, Vivian Bell and Andrew Rintoul reckon they have outgrown their ability to master Spitfires and have applied for transfer to the Administrative Branch.

I took Hodge for a spin in the Magister this morning to get his hand in before tackling a Spitfire, but he thinks he needs more time on the basic types before taking the plunge. However I was allowed into Paisley this afternoon to stock up with essential domestic supplies, and paid the penalty. Until being called up we were never allowed to wear uniform off the station, so the unaccustomed sight of a young flight lieutenant walking up High Street soon became the focus of attention from a number of passers-by, whose audible comments ranged from, 'Maw, is yon a Jerrman?' from one small urchin to 'Jings, It's a corporal!' from a mill girl returning from work at Coates' Mill further up the street. I wasted no time purchasing soap and toothpastes and returning to the sanctuary of the airfield.

September 3rd   All those not on duty were summoned to the big hangar this morning to be addressed by the station

commander. He was accompanied by Farquhar and
Donald Fleming, the sector commander from Turnhouse,
and it was immediately clear from their expressions that
we were to hear grave tidings. The Group Captain wasted
no time coming to the point: barring a miracle, he told
us, we were about to go to war and the Prime Minister
would be broadcasting to the nation at eleven o'clock.

Farquhar sought me out afterwards and asked me to
accompany him to Grangemouth as he wanted to look at
the airfield there as a possible new location for the
squadron. Apparently Fighter Command wants us to
operate from a base on the East Coast to be nearer the
scene of action when it comes, but Drem, our designated
war station, is still in the hands of Flying Training
Command and Turnhouse 603 Squadron. Douglas chose
me to accompany him as I was intimately concerned with
the development of Grangemouth during its construction
by Scottish Aviation Ltd while I was employed by that
company. In fact, I landed the first aircraft there earlier
this year.

He said we would take the dual-controlled Hart, but
would wait to hear what the Prime Minister had to say
before setting out.

I climbed into the front cockpit, wondering whether we
would be the first RAF aircraft to take off after the
declaration of war. However I didn't like the look of the
weather, as heavy thunder clouds were building up all
around. Nevertheless Douglas let me take the controls
and we were soon airborne and climbing round the
northern boundaries of Glasgow to avoid the balloons,
before setting course for Grangemouth. Maybe we should
have gone south-about, for in next to no time we were
swallowed up in a massive Cu Nim and subjected to a
battering the like of which I have never before experi-

enced and, at one point, I wondered whether the old crate would hold together. I heard nothing from my CO in the rear cockpit but suspected he was going through the same trauma of emotion as I had endured four and a half years ago when our positions had been reversed and I was in the rear cockpit, with Douglas at the controls. On that occasion we had been caught out by a severe snowstorm, eventually running out of fuel and forced to make an emergency dead-stick landing on the beach at Portobello. This time we were more fortunate and broke into the clear just short of our destination, where I put the Hart down and taxied towards the large semi-circular airport building. But no one was about; the place appeared deserted. We climbed out and were walking towards the main entrance when I caught sight of three airmen slowly emerging from a nearby air raid shelter.

'Och it's you, Mr Johnstone . . . The sirens went off and we thocht you was a German!'

Having completed the inspection we returned to base where we discovered our flight had triggered off an alert throughout a wide area of Central Scotland, during which a barrage balloon was struck by lightning over Glasgow and came down in flames, thus lending an element of realism to the occasion. Douglas thought it was very funny, but I can't help wondering what might have happened if it had been the real thing.

September 7th   Air tested one of the reserve aircraft this morning but had to report it unserviceable as the engine is running rough. Thankfully the weather was good, as the balloonatics have now pushed their barrage up to 12,000 feet and I reckon their charges are more of a menace to ourselves than to our enemies.

I managed to get off the station this afternoon and

drove into Glasgow to see Margaret and my parents,
when I found Mother cock-a-hoop because a balloon unit
is parked in the gardens outside her front door. She says
she feels a lot safer now, although she still rebels at the
need for putting up blackout every night. I too am finding
the lighting restrictions a bugbear, for darkness had fallen
before I set out for the return trip to Abbotsinch and my
headlight masks have reduced forward visibility to near
nought.

The chaps have been reacting to the new circumstances
in very different ways. Archie McKellar's comment on
hearing we were at war was, 'Christ, I didn't join up to
fight – I only came in for the dancing!' whilst Dunlop
Urie, not wanting to be caught on the hop, has wangled a
forty-eight hour pass and gone off to get married, resulting in B Flight being kept on the Readiness state to allow
his pals in A Flight to join the celebrations. I have also
been detailed to be first off tonight, so am sleeping at
dispersal.

September 8th   Life is gradually settling into a regular
pattern as we accustom ourselves to being at war. The
flights have been split into two sections, each section
comprising three aircraft. Furthermore, the squadron
code letters ZT have been changed back to the pre-war
code of LO, so I now find myself allocated Spitfire K9973
bearing the letters LO-Q.

The pessure is still on to give priority to training our
inexperienced pilots during daylight hours, with emphasis
on night flying for the rest of us. I can't say I like the
latter, for the exhaust stubs emit a lot of flame which
tends to blind one when the throttle is closed during the
final approach. The problem is already beginning to
manifest itself for, not only did George bend his undercar-

riage a couple of nights ago, but we have had two prangs tonight, one, alas, fatal. Sergeant McDowall had a long walk back to dispersal after depositing his Spitfire in a boundary hedge a few hours ago whilst young Sergeant Bryden, who has only been with us for a week, must have become totally disorientated on his first night take-off, for he has just flown straight into the ground at full throttle, creating a fireball which must be visible for miles around.

In spite of these problems Sector Control still insists on maintaining unnecessarily high states of readiness, thus keeping us on perpetual tenterhooks even though nothing much seems to be happening. We have also had a few false alarms, including one tonight when I spent a fruitless three-quarters of an hour being vectored all over Perthshire in pursuit of nothing in particular. However I was able to give the searchlight boys some practice before landing back at Abbotsinch and it also appears I have clocked up the RAF's first night operational patrol of the war!

Donald Jack has also got himself married and, following Dunlop's example, has dragged a small caravan on to the dispersal, so creating a miniature married families area. No doubt they will be expecting us to drop calling cards on them before long!

September 14th   Although difficult to spot in their previous condition, most of the drab buildings on the aerodrome have now been daubed with dull green and brown camouflage paint. Indeed the camouflage craze is apparently here to stay for I am told they are even thinking of painting the airfield surface itself to look like a series of hedgerows and, with this in mind, I today flew a Mr Campbell from the Ministry of Works round the area in our Tiger Moth to size up the prospects. I doubt whether an application of tarry paint will ever transform our airfield into a scene of pastoral beauty.

Smith and Wesson .38 revolvers have been issued to all officers, although we have little opportunity to try them out. However McKellar and Ferguson have set up a target against the sandbagged revetment guarding one of the Spits and vie regularly with one another for a pint of beer. Of course we were issued with gas masks a few days before war broke out and are under strict orders to carry them with us wherever we go and, to emphasize how seriously we view the threat of poison gas, most have been able to scrounge small quantities of a special gas-detecting paint to put on our private cars. The Vauxhall now sports a small blob of puke green paint on top of its bonnet. However, in an attempt to add a little sparkle to the scene, B Flight has decided to name its Spitfires after Walt Disney's Seven Dwarfs, with the result that LO-Q is now 'Bashful'. George's aircraft bears the legend 'Grumpy' but we haven't yet decided to whom we shall allocate 'Dopey'.

September 25th   We are rapidly becoming bored with the war, for we seem to do little but sit around at dispersal these days, with occasional practice flights thrown in or, even less often, doing a spell on the Link Trainer. However we had a brief moment of excitement this morning when a three-engined Junkers 52 circled overhead prior to lining up for a landing on the neighbouring airfield at Renfrew. We thought it odd that no warning had been given, until a call to the controller elicited the information that it was one of a batch British Airways had purchased from Lufthansa some months previously. They will be sticking their necks out if they persist in flying them in these parts for we have enough trouble already trying to identify the tri-motor Spartan Cruisers in service with Scottish Airways.

However I managed to break the routine this afternoon when I flew a replacement cowling panel to Sealand. Jimmie Hodge, who had flown down to Cheshire to pick up a new Spitfire earlier in the day, had shed one on take-off and had had to land back at the airfield.

September 29th   George and I have just been interviewed by the police about a complaint from a farmer on the Mull of Kintyre who reports that one of his greenhouses has been damaged by a hail of bullets raining down on it from a cloudless sky. It is possible we are the culprits for we both tested our guns off the Ayrshire coast this morning, although we must have been at least twenty miles away when we fired. However Douglas has managed to mollify the arm of the law by taking him to the Mess for a drink and doubtless charging the cost to our respective bar accounts.

1939

October

October 1st   The month has begun for me in an unorthodox and decidedly painful manner. Murky conditions severely curtailed the dusk flying programme yesterday evening and, by the time darkness fell, Abbotsinch and the surrounding countryside were enveloped in a blanket of fog. Having first checked with the Met people that there would be no improvement throughout the night, Douglas scrubbed the rest of the flying detail and ordered the flarepath party to stand down. Nevertheless our friends at Sector Control insisted on their pound of flesh and ordered one Spitfire to remain at readiness and, of course, the Joe Soke happened to be me.

By the time George and I were ready to turn in around eleven o'clock the visibility was so poor we had to peer hard to make out the silhouette of even the nearest Spitfire, which happened to be George's. 'You might as well have a decent night's rest,' he said. 'No one's going to be sent off in this clag!' So, taking advantage of my flight commander's solicitude, I was not slow to don pyjamas and climb into the dubious comfort of the camp bed.

The Ops telephone woke us about two o'clock. 'One aircraft to patrol Dumbarton at five thousand feet . . .?' George repeated incredulously into the instrument, at the same time making signs to me to get moving. So, hastily pulling on a pair of sheepskin flying boots and my service greatcoat, I staggered into the murky gloom in search of LO-Q. By now the alarm had been sounded and ghostly shapes hustled past me as they sped to their allotted tasks. Corporal Burnett was already standing by my aircraft when I reached it and helped to strap me in before jumping off the wing to remove the chocks as soon as the old Merlin coughed to life. Appreciating the difficulties pilots had in seeing ahead at the best of times on account of the Spitfire's long nose, to say nothing of the distracting exhaust flames, he used his loaf and set off at a trot, torch in hand, to guide me across the airfield until I was able to distinguish the outline of one of the windsocks which was hanging like a discarded sack in the windless night. But at least I now had some idea of my whereabouts, and lined up towards the west preparatory to taking off.

George too used his loaf and, knowing the flarepath remained unlit, whipped the headlight masks off his Morris and drove it to the far end of the airfield and turned it in my direction. I now had the bonus of two pinpricks of yellow light to aim for so, having set the gyro compass, opened the throttle and sped towards them.

The futility of it all hit me as soon as I was airborne. There was no horizon, the ground was out of sight below and the R/T set failed to answer when I called up for assistance. Indeed the best I got from it throughout the trip was some faraway dance music played by a foreign band. To hell with the Bogey, or unidentified aircraft, thought I. The saving of Johnstone's skin was henceforth of much greater importance!

Mindful of the balloon barrage possibly flying as high as 12,000 feet a few miles to the east, I concentrated my climb in a westerly direction until reaching 14,000 feet, without yet breaking into the clear. So, believing that if any clearance was to be found, it would be in the area around Prestwick, I turned towards the south-west. Fifteen minutes later, and still having to concentrate on instruments, I gave it up as a bad job and headed back in the direction of Glasgow, with a degree of panic now setting in as I continued to shout for help with nary a word of comfort in reply. Neither was there moon nor friendly star to guide me. Then I remembered the emergency sodium flare stored in the belly of the Spitfire. If I let if off, I might just be able to recognize some features on the ground.

Descending to 3,000 feet, I let off the flare and dived beneath it to get the benefit of the light and was startled by the brilliance when it suddenly burst into life. Now, in spite of the conditions, I could make out open countryside below and then, to my even greater relief, spotted a large open field, large enough to land a Spitfire on, and swung towards this unexpected haven. Realizing the flare would not last forever, I wasted no time lowering the undercarriage and flaps as we swept towards it, praying I could get down before the light went out. I suppose we were down to a few hundred feet before the awful truth dawned on me. It was no flat field I was aiming at – it was a ruddy great reservoir and it was coming up at an alarming rate.

I have only vague memories of what followed. However I remember pumping frantically at the undercarriage lever, during which the flare burnt out, thus leaving me once more in Stygian darkness, and I remember too the fiendish noise of tearing metal and of being pelted with large clods of earth and stones as the Spitfire ploughed up the slope of a hill: I also have a hazy recollection of receiving a blow on the face when the aircraft slewed to a standstill and ended up facing the direction from which it had come. Then there was a frantic scramble to get out of the plane followed by a period in limbo, until I came to, sitting on a grassy knoll, gently probing my left cheek, feeling very cold and wondering why anyone should be blowing a motor horn so insistently into the night air. There was no sign of my aeroplane.

I have no idea for how long I sat there, pulling up the collar of my greatcoat to fend off the bitter chill and trying to take stock of what had happened. The noise of the motor horn kept insinuating itself on my consciousness and it was this which eventually pulled me to my senses for, by making towards the sound, I was led back to the aircraft which seemed surprisingly undamaged and very accessible without its undercarriage extended. In my fuddled condition, however, I couldn't think of a way to stop the racket and was becoming increasingly alarmed about the possible consequences of blowing a motor horn after eleven o'clock at night. Indeed it was only after splitting several fingernails in a desperate attempt to remove a cowling – although goodness knows what I was to do once it was off – it suddenly dawned on me that I only had to push forward the throttle lever to quieten things down. It was the undercarriage warning system merely reminding me I had landed with my wheels up. So, clad only in greatcoat and pyjamas, I climbed gratefully into the comparative warmth of the cockpit to work out what to do next.

I had no sooner got used to my new-found sanctuary when I became aware of someone moving outside and, pulling back the sliding canopy, was startled to find myself looking straight down the barrels of a shotgun held only a few feet from my face. A gruff voice behind it demanded to know who I was but, in my thoroughly rattled state, I couldn't remember my name. 'It's me! It's me! Don't shoot . . .' was the best I could do, whereupon the man lowered his gun and helped me out of the cockpit.

I have now identified my saviour as John McColl,

warden of the local reservoirs. On our way to his home
further down the slope he told me he had watched the
shenanigans from the moment I let off the flare but, as
the sirens had been sounded, had assumed it was a
German raider who had been shot down. He added that
he was surprised to find me alive for it sounded as if my
aircraft was being smashed to smithereens as it ploughed
into the hillside.

McColl and his family were kindness itself. They made
me tea and gave me cigarettes – albeit Woodbines, but
tasting exquisite in the circumstances – and, best of all,
access to a telephone. George sounded quite pleased to
hear me, for he had apparently given me up as a goner.

Although able to visit the scene in daylight, when I also
called on Mrs McColl to thank her for her hospitality, I
have now been taken off flying for the time being, a
sensible precaution in the circumstances. As soon as
Archie McKellar, who drove up to fetch me, brought me
back around five o'clock, Doc Allan whipped me off to
the Paisley Royal Infirmary for an X-ray and thorough
check-up, but nothing more serious than a bang on the
head was diagnosed. I have been lucky to get off so
lightly.

Ops tell me I was sent off after a Bogey which later
turned out to be one of our own bombers which had
strayed off course.

October 8th   I have been allocated a new 'Q' (L1004),
but George won't let me re-christen it 'Bashful', maintaining the name is too indicative of the condition in which I
left K9973. Instead I found a pot of paint in workshops
and have painted a large red coiled cobra on the port
cowling, adding the title 'Kedoying' in white. I think it
looks virile but George considers it vulgar, and says so.

We arrived at Grangemouth this afternoon, presumably the first stage in the squadron's move to the East Coast, so can now bed down in the comparative luxury of the airport building instead of having to suffer the discomforts of a leaky tent. I managed to fly my Spit across, although confess to a certain amount of apprehension in doing so, the approach and landing being more reminiscent of a pupil making a bog of his first solo. Burnett is driving my bits and pieces over in the Vauxhall.

October 10th   Paid my first visit to Prestwick that fateful day in August when I set out to sail with Sandy Mackay. George Reid collected me in an Anson to save me the bother of having to drive sixty-odd miles, and I found the place much changed. Many erstwhile colleagues have been called up and gone to other units whilst both the Flying Training and Navigation Schools have been augmented with many more aircraft, the latter even boasting the large four-engined Fokker for which McIntyre had been negotiating with KLM when I left. Reid tells me it can carry up to forty students at a time – a big improvement on the two I was accustomed to flying around in the Ansons. Most, too, are back in RAF uniform and David McIntyre is resplendently dressed as a group captain. I was given a warm welcome back, albeit for a few hours only.

Having arranged with the Mess steward to forward my civilian clothes to the parents' flat in Glasgow, I gathered up the rest and settled my outstanding dues before Reid flew me back to Grangemouth. I can't help feeling he would prefer to be back with his old unit, 603 Squadron.

October 13th   I am not normally superstitious, but today is Friday the thirteenth and it took on a special significance when I noticed that thirteen of us sat down to breakfast and realized we were later to fly thirteen aircraft across to Drem. Furthermore, not only do we operate as a unit in No 13 Fighter Group, but Drem itself is the home of No 13 Flying Training School. Some wag had the impertinence to wonder aloud what would be happening at 1300 hours.

We were thoroughly briefed about our destination before leaving Grangemouth and I well remember being warned about the slope at Drem, not that I could see any sign of it from the air when I circled the field preparatory to landing; it looked like any other grass airfield of its type. However I realized I was travelling too fast as soon as we crossed the threshold and, in spite of much fish-tailing and side-slipping, the aircraft seemed to take an unholy delight in leaping into the air whenever its wheels made contact with the ground. If I had any sense I would have swallowed my pride and gone round again: As it was we were well down the slope before becoming properly glued to the ground, with the result that the aircraft ran full tilt into a patch of marshy ground at the bottom of the hill and ended up with its prop buried in the mud and its tail stuck high in the air.

A fire tender came bounding down the hill while I was clambering from the striken aircraft and I was just in time to prevent its eager crew from spraying me with a tankful of foam. The NCO was grinning as he turned off the tap. 'We've never had one down here before, sir,' he announced, and I can well believe it, having seen how easily our most junior pilots were coping with their landings. The tender gave me a lift to the Watch Office where I was greeted by Rupert Watson, whose brother Irvine is one of my colleagues at Prestwick and whose parents own the ground on which Drem airfield is built.

'Irvine told me to expect you,' he greeted, 'but didn't say you'd be arriving on a fire engine. Come to the house later if you haven't been locked up!'

True to his word, Rupert rang up to confirm his invitation and I walked the short distance to the big house after coping with the inevitable paperwork arising from my latest indiscretion. I was hoping to meet his father, Dr Chalmers Watson, having heard much of how he had produced the first accredited herd of TT-test milk cows in the country, but he was visiting elsewhere. However Rupert introduced me to his stepmother who had been Lily Brayton before her marriage. It is not difficult to see why this charming old lady captured the hearts of London's theatregoers during World War I during which she played the leading role in *Chu Chin Chow*. The old charm is still there. However, in spite of the doctor's absence, it was not long before the legendary Watson hospitality was in full swing and I returned to the Mess without a care in the world.

October 15th   I was lucky to get off with nothing worse than a gentle reprimand from the CO who was kind enough to take account of an understandable twitchiness after my narrow escape earlier in the month. The servicing crews also came up trumps and, by working through the night, had LO-Q back on the line the following morning, resplendent with a new propeller.

We are quickly settling into our new surroundings. Drem sits on top of the hill about two miles south of Gullane, which is near enough for the lads to visit on their time off. Nor is North Berwick much further away. On the airfield, a number of wooden huts, hitherto occupied by the Flying Training chaps until they moved away last week, will make excellent dispersal sites and there is plenty of room available in the armoury, stores and maintenance sections. We are lucky to have the place to ourselves.

October 16th Farquhar decided to come on the detail this morning and chose to lead my Section (Green) with myself and Ian Ferguson. Before being called on, both the A Flight Sections had carried out search patrols during which both reported a higher than normal level of R/T chatter. Indeed Marcus Robinson said he felt it in his bones that 'something was afoot', a feeling we too experienced when ordered off shortly after eleven and told to patrol May Island, where visibility was good with a little broken cloud around 5,000 feet.

After circling the island for ten minutes I realized something was amiss with the CO's R/T, as he kept ignoring Control's instructions to stop orbiting May Island and instead to Vector 360. I waggled my wings at the same time pointing to my headphones, and he must have got the message, for he signalled me to take over and immediately assumed station on my port quarter. We continued on a northerly course, encouraged by the controller's frequent references to 'Bogeys' believed to be in our vicinity, but after a long and fruitless search over a wide area, we were ordered to return to base. A strong southerly airstream had carried us far north and I reckoned we were flying about forty miles to the east of Peterhead when the order came through. Now we were to nose into the wind during the ride back.

Coming up to Leuchars at 7,000 feet, I saw Drem clearly visible on the south bank of the firth, but I was now concerned about the fuel states, having been airborne for almost an hour and with at best another fifteen minutes' worth left. Therefore, having first checked with Ferguson that he too was running low (Douglas was still incommunicado) I landed the section at Leuchars.

The fellows there are only used to servicing Coastal Command Hudsons, so we reckoned there would be a delay whilst they refuelled the Spitfires. Douglas therefore rang Operations at Turnhouse and got permission to nip over to the Officers' Mess to grab a bite to eat. We had no sooner sat down to lunch when the air raid sirens sounded and the dining room cleared as its occupants hastily made for the shelters. Our hosts suggested we follow for, although it was probably just another practice alert, the station commander was a stickler for the drill being carried out to the letter. So, quickly grabbing a morning roll from the table, I followed Douglas and Ian outside only to find the nearest shelter already full but, rather than risk offending the susceptibilities of the worthy group captain by returning indoors, we compromised by climbing on top of the grass-covered mound. I settled down to munch my roll.

We chatted idly for five minutes or so, during which there was not much to do except watch a number of Blenheims flying in and out of the clouds overhead as they made their way up the river towards Edinburgh. 'Hang on while I ring Ops to find out what's happening,' announced Douglas, sliding down the bank and disappearing into the Mess, only to re-emerge seconds later as if catapulted from a gun. 'For Christ's sake get a move on – these aren't Blenheims – they're ruddy Germans!'

All credit to the Leuchars boys for their efforts in getting us back into the air. A van was already at the Mess to take us to our aircraft, which themselves had been started up by the time we reached them. Brian

Baker, the station commander, was also standing by, fulminating loudly about the ineffectiveness of Fighter Command in general and of us in particular. Unfortunately my aeroplane had been started first so that, by the time I was strapped in and ready to go, the engine temperature was off the clock and, as soon as I opened the throttle, the only response was a massive backfire and a cloud of dense black smoke. Douglas and Ian were more fortunate and got away safely, but I wasted precious time coaxing the engine back to life. When I too finally got off, they were but two small specks in the distance.

Belting over the Forth towards the bridge I suddenly experienced severe turbulence and noticed I was being circled by numerous puffs of dark smoke and looking over the side saw it was coming from the aircraft carrier *Furious* which was clearly living up to her name and letting fly at me with everything she'd got! From the amount of excited shouting going on in my earphones it was also clear that the boys had got stuck into a real fight and I was anxious not to be left out of it. However by the time I had extricated myself from the unwelcome attentions of the Royal Navy and reached the Forth Bridge, the sky was empty except for one twin-engined aircraft I spotted climbing rapidly towards a bank of cloud to the east of Edinburgh. I managed a short burst at extreme range just as it was disappearing from view, praying inwardly it was not one of ours, as it still looked awfully like a Blenheim.

There was an atmosphere of great excitement when I returned to dispersal. Harry Matheson, standing in as Intelligence Officer, was doing his best to take statements from the group of pilots gathered round him, arguing among themselves whilst depicting their part in the action with exaggerated gestures of hands and arms. Not unnat-

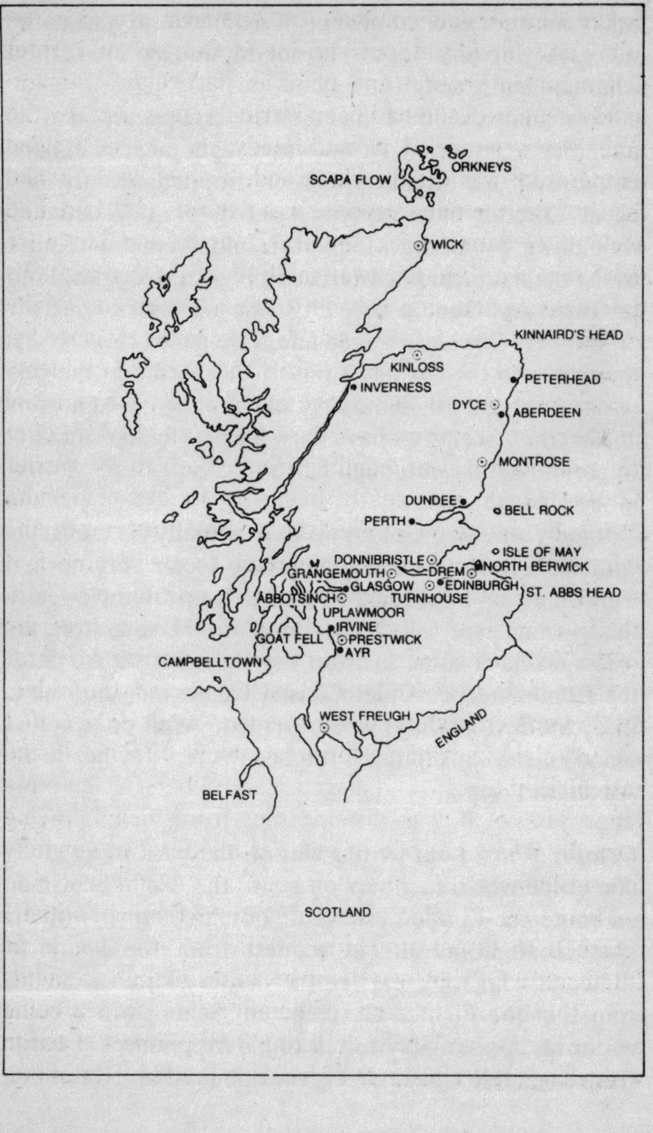

ORKNEYS

SCAPA FLOW

WICK

KINNAIRD'S HEAD

KINLOSS

PETERHEAD

INVERNESS

DYCE

ABERDEEN

MONTROSE

DUNDEE

BELL ROCK

PERTH

ISLE OF MAY

DONNIBRISTLE

DREM

NORTH BERWICK

GRANGEMOUTH

GLASGOW

EDINBURGH

ST. ABBS HEAD

ABBOTSINCH

TURNHOUSE

UPLAWMOOR

IRVINE

GOAT FELL

PRESTWICK

AYR

CAMPBELLTOWN

WEST FREUGH

ENGLAND

BELFAST

SCOTLAND

urally another excited group, this time of ground crews, was gathering outside, and it took Mathie ages to sort out what had happened.

Now that the dust had settled it appears that an unknown number of Ju88s was caught near the Forth Bridge and that bombs have been dropped. So far, three enemy aircraft have been accounted for, one definitely shot down by George Pinkerton and Archie McKellar, whilst others, including Marcus Robinson, Douglas, Findlay Boyd and Dunlop Urie all claim successes of one sort or another. Certainly a Ju88 and a Heinkel 111 were seen to crash into the sea and I have just heard that the pilot of one has been fished out and taken to the Naval hospital at Rosyth. It seems we have been the first fighter squadron to go into action, although I hear 603 Squadron was also in the air at the time.

It feels unreal to be told we have actually been engaged with the enemy, for everything now seems very normal. Yet it must be true, for the AOC flew up from Newcastle this evening especially to congratulate the squadron, and messages have come in from the Chief of the Air Staff, the Commander-in-Chief Coastal Command and our C-in-C, Stuffy Dowding, who signalled, 'Well done – First blood to the Auxiliaries!' It's been a real feather in the Auxiliaries' cap.

October 17th I am writing this on the back of an envelope in the wee sma' hours on board the 'Night Scotsman' en route for London. News of our first brush with the Huns brought an urgent request from the South for someone who took part in the action to join a tactical course at the Fighter Development School which began yesterday, presumably to tell of his experiences. I hardly seem a suitable choice, being the one least involved in the action, but I was nevertheless summoned to report to Douglas at nine o'clock and told to get going. They must be really anxious to get me there, for the night express was halted at Drem especially to pick me up.

October 26th   The past week has been a bit of an anti-climax. I reported to Air Commodore Tiny Vasse on arrival at RAF Northolt, where the FD School is to be found, and was straightaway directed to the course itself. Once installed, no one seemed particularly interested in either myself or the recent action over the Forth and, apart from answering a few unrelated questions from time to time, I might as well not have been there. Indeed the rest of the week consisted mostly of theoretical lectures on fighter tactics, interspersed with occasional pearls of wisdom from such an acknowledged expert as Harry Broadhurst who, as CO of 111 Squadron, went to great pains to advise us how best to synchronize the guns on a Hurricane. In fact I came away from the course with the impression that Spitfires were of little account and that the Auxiliaries who flew them of even less consequence.

However I nearly got a ride in a Messerschmitt. Apparently the Air Ministry bought a Me109 from the Luftwaffe some time ago for evaluation purposes and had based it at Northolt. So, coming across it sitting outside a hangar on my way to lunch last Thursday I asked if I might be allowed to fly the machine later in the day. The OC Flying was very decent about it and told me to borrow flying kit whilst he first gave it an air test. An hour later, standing on the tarmac, helmet in hand, I waited for him to land but, as soon as the Messerschmitt joined the circuit, it was obvious something was amiss, for it was being put through some very unorthodox manoeuvres overhead.

One of the ground crew reckoned the undercarriage had jammed and the pilot was trying to shake it loose. The diagnosis must have been spot on, for the machine made a belly-landing in the middle of the field, thus ending my chance of clocking up another type in my flying log book.

On the domestic side, my cousin Edward allowed me to live in his flat at St John's Wood during my sojourn in London, so was able to wangle a living-out pass and commute to Northolt by Underground. I find the atmosphere much changed in London since my last visit, with most public buildings protected by sandbag emplacements and their windows either boarded up or covered with paper strips. Service personnel and civilians alike are assiduous about carrying gas masks, although I'm told many ladies prefer to remove the innards and use the cases as handbags.

Am now trying to catch up with news of what went on in my absence. Apparently the German victims of the Forth raid were given a proper military funeral at Portobello, conducted by Padre Sutherland, with the coffins even draped with Nazi flags. Not to be outdone in the matter of entente, George went a step further and called on one of his victims in hospital, only to find Hauptmann Ernst Pohle had lost his front teeth in the ensuing crash. Nonetheless, George insisted on handing him the bag of toffees he had brought as a peace offering.

It's good to be back in harness.

1939

November

November 3rd   I had not appreciated how much freight is transported by sea around our coasts until seeing the shipping assembling in Methil Bay. These small coasters are loaded to the gunwale with coal, machinery and farm produce destined for ports up and down the East coast but, having learned the hard way during World War I, the Admiralty won't allow them to sail unless in convoy and escorted by units of the Royal Navy. To add to their protection, the Powers that Be now also require a measure of air cover to be afforded them, with the result that we have the added chore of maintaining standing patrols whenever they sail within our area of responsibility.

No doubt those manning the escorting frigates and destroyers are trained to identify the silhouettes of all enemy warships likely to be encountered on their voyages, but we wish their training could be extended to include identification of friendly aircraft, for we are finding that as soon as the first patrol of the day nears its charge, it is likely to be met by a barrage of anti-aircraft fire which continues unabated until the sailors are fully convinced of our friendly intentions. So far no harm has been done but, remembering my own frightening experience at the hands of HMS *Furious* three weeks ago, I am delighted to hear that a Royal Air Force officer will henceforth sail with the commodore to help him identify all aircraft whether friendly or otherwise. One of our ops officers, Cairns Smith, has just been detailed for the job, although none too eager to take it on until reminded that pink gins cost only twopence a glass on board His Majesty's ships.

But our flying is not solely confined to the role of guardian angel. I was sent off this morning to patrol May Island in company with Paul Webb, when there was much heavy cloud in the area, unbroken from a height of 1,000 to 12,000 feet. We were not very hopeful of finding anything worth while as most earlier patrols of this nature have ended up chasing our own plots, the result, I suppose, of delays occurring between the time a flicker is detected by the CH Station and its ultimate interpretation on the Controller's table. Because of this, one's own plot tends to become confused with that of the target so that we often end up chasing our own tails. We call this 'Ogo-Pogoing' after the bird of the same name which has a propensity for flying up its own fundamental orifice, from which advantageous position it continues to throw abuse in the face of its pursuers!

This time, however, the controller was insisting there were two distinct plots, one a bogey, and continued vectoring us eastwards just above cloud tops, when I sent Paul well out to the right to widen the area of visual search. We both spotted the target at the same time; a small black dot streaking in and out of the clouds at high speed, travelling in a north-easterly direction. We banked steeply, giving chase, Paul now a few miles astern, but the Heinkel (I was now able to identify him) must have seen us for he suddenly stuffed his nose down and high-tailed it for the nearest cloud cover. But our controller was on the ball and warned us the bandit was turning southwards, thus giving Paul a chance to swing round on an intercepting course, whilst I too turned in hot pursuit, continuing to fly above the clouds from where I'd have a better chance of seeing the Heinkel if he should break cover.

Then Paul suddenly reported he had seen the blighter between breaks in the cloud and I was just in time to catch sight of his Spitfire some way ahead, diving fast into a bank of cloud. That was the last I saw of either aircraft until Paul caught up with me as we were crossing the coast near Dunbar. Control had previously reported that the plot had faded and had ordered us to pancake at base.

Webb had managed one long burst at our adversary, but unfortunately lost sight of him before able to assess the results. However he insists he registered a number of hits and is claiming a probable.

November 17th   Cairns Smith has returned from his stint with the Navy, full of nautical jargon and affecting an exaggerated rolling gait for our benefit. Nevertheless he reckons his trip was worth while as he found his naval colleagues very trigger happy whenever anything appeared in the sky, invariably dealing with the matter on the principle of shooting first and identifying it later. However he's grumbling about being done out of his full quota of cheap gins due to a bout of sea-sickness on the first two days at sea, although he admits it was not surprising, as previously he had a tendency to turn green even at the mention of going for a row on the boating pond at Great Western Road.

Indeed the entire question of identifying friend and foe is currently under the official spotlight. Firstly a system embodying different coloured Very cartridges has been evolved for fitting to our Spits, different colour sequences to be used at predetermined times of the day. Thus, when challenged in future, we can respond immediately by shooting off a double red flare, a red-yellow, two greens or whatever combination with which we've been fitted for a particular time of day. In fact all operational aircraft of

Bomber and Coastal Commands are soon to follow suit
which should save all manner of problems when interceptions are made at night or in conditions of poor visibility.
And secondly, our intelligence factor is about to be tested
still farther by a requirement to learn the morse code:
Henceforth we are to identify ourselves to the Watch
Office when joining the circuit at night by flashing the
letters of the day in response to a morse challenge from
the ground.

November 24th   This has been a red letter day. George
Pinkerton's promotion to squadron leader has just been
promulgated and he is being posted to command No 65
Squadron at Northolt. Naturally I am delighted, because
I've been appointed flight commander of B Flight in his
stead.

Not surprisingly the celebrations carried on well into
the night, during which George became progressively
maudlin at the thought of leaving his old pals. However
he cheered up somewhat when I reminded him about the
Me109 at Northolt, as it will probably have a new undercarriage fitted by now.

November 26th   George's guardian angel has been working overtime recently for, to top all, he had been awarded
a DFC for his part in shooting down the first enemy
aircraft over the Forth last month, the first decoration of
its kind to be won by a pilot of the Auxiliary Air Force. I
too have had a share in the bounty, but only in the shape
of a replacement to fill George's vacant slot. Pilot Officer
Glynn Ritchie has arrived straight from his Flying Training School and posted to B Flight, a welcome newcomer
indeed as Glynn and I were schoolmates at Kelvinside

Academy. Roger Coverley has also turned up at Drem, but is destined for A Flight.

November 30th Our good fortune was bound to run out sooner or later, and today our franchise at Drem was violated by the arrival of a regular squadron of Hurricanes. No less a unit than 111 Squadron from Northolt; *la crème de la crème*, as Harry Broadhurst would have us believe, has managed to wangle its way here, doubtless hoping there are better pickings to be had at Drem than in the fastness of the South. But we have had one small crumb of comfort in return; the only Spitfire in the country which is fitted with cannons has been attached to 602 Squadron so that its Hispano-Suizas can be given a proper try-out under operational conditions. By coincidence, the machine belongs to 65 Squadron, but I don't think George had anything to do with its venue. At all events, we now have a valuable addition to our fleet for George Proudman, a pilot trained in the use of cannons, has also put in an appearance, thus augmenting the squadron's effective strength to the tune of one complete unit.

1939

December

December 6th The Jerries have been forsaking this neck of the woods recently, so giving us time to squeeze in a lot of much-needed training. Ferguson, Donald Jack and Paul Webb are already fit to take their share of the night states, thus easing the pressure on those who have been carrying the burden until now, whilst some of our newer arrivals, including Lyall, Moody, Ritchie and Coverly, have become sufficiently fledged to play a part in daylight operations. Also we have been somewhat hampered by the lack of a suitable dual-controlled aircraft since the Fairey Battle was taken away some months ago, a state of affairs now partially rectified by the recent allocation of a Harvard Trainer.

I am keen to improve the standard of instrument flying in the flight, so have been using the present lull to get as many as possible conversant with the new machine and, besides putting Sergeants Bailey, McAdam and Babbage through the hoop under its hood, have also succeeded in scaring the living daylights out of Marcus Robinson when showing him how to work the taps on the new Trainer. He apparently means to put his flight through the same hoop.

December 11th RDF Stations have already proved their worth in the air defensive system for, without them, we would never have been able to make the interceptions we have. Being comparatively new, however, they have gone through a number of teething troubles but, in spite of these, their value has been inestimable and we would be lost without them. At present the coverage afforded doesn't extend northwards beyond Forfar, but there are rumours of additional stations in the offing. In the meantime it is important that those we have are adequately defended, for the Germans must know of their existence and realize their importance. Consequently a number of Bofors anti-aircraft guns have been deployed for the defence of our latest RDF Station, situated at Drone Hill just north of Dundee, and we were ordered to carry out a mock attack on the site to give the new defences a thorough work-out. I took B Flight to carry out the task this morning.

Weather conditions were poor when we took off: cloud base at 1,000 feet with visibility less than half a mile in frequent rain squalls. I was leading Green Section with Archie McKellar in charge of the other but, as soon as we were airborne, I began to doubt the wisdom of the sortie, particularly as we had with us a couple of pilots not yet fully trained. However, having been told that a number of Staff Officers had gone to Drone Hill especially to witness the test, I decided to press on, hoping the weather would improve nearer the target area. But it was not to be.

Arriving at the south end of the Tay Bridge, it was just possible to distinguish the general outline of Dundee ahead, but conditions were clearly too bad for carrying on the exercise with our full quota of aircraft. I therefore told Archie to peel off and take his lot back to Drem, at the same time ordering Webb and Ferguson, who made up the rest of my section, to close up while we tried to make a dart for Drone Hill. But wisps of rain clouds were already clinging to the hills behind the city so, rather than

trying to force a way through from the south, I decided to
fly up the coast and approach from the east.

Flying low and skirting the shoreline beyond Carnous-
tie, we eventually turned inland near Arbroath, crossing
the coast at virtually nought feet and startling a number
of passers-by in the process. Thus we drove inland, flying
in and out of clouds, tossing hither and thither in the
turbulent air with only intermittent glimpses of the ground
flashing below. Suddenly we were confronted by an
enormous steel mast, its top hidden in the clouds, and I
barely had time to shout 'Break!' before we had to haul
frantically on our controls to scrape past with little to
spare. It was a close call.

Having each found our own way back to base, we were
discussing the near miss at dispersal when the ops officer
came in with a signal. 'Did they not tell you the exercise
had been cancelled?' he queried, handing me the message. 'The narks from Group never got to Drone Hill.
Their car broke down!'

December 21st The weather has remained overcast for
the past few days and a slight haze beneath cloud level is
reducing visibility even further. It was certainly not
weather in which to practise a full squadron formation,
the exercise Douglas Farquhar suggested we carried out
while he and Marcus attended a sector commanders'
conference at Turnhouse. In fact I had already decided to
limit practice flying to pairs of aircraft at most, and
arranged for A Flight, under Dunlop's able control, to
provide the required Readiness state whilst the B Flight
fellows caught up with their ground training. We were
thus employed when, out of the blue, the whole squadron
was ordered to scramble.

Chairs, maps and chessboards went sprawling as, to a

man, we dived for flying kits and dashed outside to our
aircraft. Ground crews came running from all quarters,
some still carrying magazines and newspapers they were
reading when the alarm sounded, whilst from the top of
the hill we could already hear the noise of Dunlop's
Spitfires starting up. Not pausing to assemble on the
ground before taking off, aircraft left willy nilly as soon
as they were ready to go. 'Twelve plus Bandits approaching from the East – Angels two,' I heard the Controller
say as soon as I switched on my radio, 'Buster! Buster!'

Through the gloom I saw several Spitfires grouping
around me as they got airborne one after the other whilst,
about a mile to the east, I could just make out the gaggle
of A Flight travelling eastwards as fast as it could go. We
swung after them, throttles open, alarmed at the sudden-
ness with which we had been ordered into the air. Never
before had the entire squadron been scrambled together.
Clearly the Germans must be making another raid on the
Navy at Rosyth, but this time at low level, which would
account for the lack of adequate warning. 'Bandits now
ten miles east of Dunbar.' The Controller's voice reflected
the urgency of the moment. 'Now turning west at Angels
Two.' We leant on the throttles, urging every ounce of
speed out of our trusty aircraft.

Dunlop's shout of 'Tally-ho' suddenly electrified the air
when, simultaneously, I caught sight of A Flight's six
Spitfires making towards a formation of what appeared to
be twin-engined Dornier bombers looming indistinctly
through the haze. The oncoming formation suddenly
broke apart, aircraft swooping in all directions, trying to
dodge the withering fire of the attacking fighters. We
ourselves were now closing the scene and, just as I was
about to wade into the mêlée, one bomber pulled up
ahead of me in a steep climbing turn, presenting a full

plan view of his underside. I was about to press the firing
button when, to my utter horror, I saw RAF roundels
clearly visible on the mainplanes. 'Don't fire!' I shouted
into the radio. 'Don't shoot. They're friendly! They're
friendly!'

But it was too late; the damage was already done.
Under the initial onslaught, delivered from more or less
head-on, two Hampdens – for that was what they were –
were already on their way down, one crashing into the sea
off North Berwick and the other in the shallower waters
of Aberlady Bay. The remainder followed us back to
Drem.

There was an uncanny silence when we came face to
face with the Hampden crews whose feathers had been
ruffled, and our attempts to explain what had happened
met with scant success. You could have cut the atmosphere with a knife. We can understand their feelings,
however, particularly as one of their colleagues has been
drowned. He was the navigator in the aircraft which came
down in the Bay although his pilot managed to swim
ashore. The crew of the other Hampden was rescued
unhurt by the North Berwick lifeboat.

Feelings were running very high by the time Douglas
and Marcus got back from their conference and, presumably because of their senior positions in our squadron,
instantly became the principal targets for the bomber
crews' venom, although we did our best to convince them
that neither had had anything whatever to do with the
tragedy. A Court of Inquiry is to assemble here tomorrow
to delve into the whole affair.

December 22nd I have spent most of the day hanging
about Station Headquarters waiting to give evidence to
the court, which comprises a group captain, a wing

commander and a squadron leader. The Hampden boys
were kept apart from us in a separate waiting room for
obvious reasons and, after giving my statement, I was
stood down and told to get on with my job. Although I
had not opened fire, I nevertheless came away from the
hearing with an underlying feeling of guilt. Such a question as, 'Surely you could have recognized a Hampden
when you saw one?' seems obvious enough in the fullness
of time and with hindsight to call upon, but it was a
different kettle of fish when unexpectedly confronted by
a gaggle of twin-engined aircraft of a type hitherto unseen
in our sector of operations, in conditions of poor visibility,
having been warned by Control they were Bandits and
still very conscious of the Huns' recent attempts to go for
naval units moored near the Forth Bridge. In fact I am
told that the Hampdens, which were returning from a raid
on the island of Sylt, were supposed to have landed at
Lossiemouth but, through an error of navigation, had
found themselves flying up the estuary of the Forth
instead of the Moray Firth. We will have to wait until
tomorrow to hear what the court makes of the evidence.

While all this was going on, a section of 111 Squadron,
doubtless relieved that it is the Auxiliaries, and not them,
who are in the doghouse, was scrambled after a Bogey
reported in the vicinity of Bell Rock. Our own Red
Section, comprising Dunlop, Hector MacLean and Fumff
Strong, was ordered into the air just after them. Weather
conditions were still far from good and they reckoned
they were in for a difficult search, although Control was
pumping out firm information about the target's position
and seemed to know what they were about. In the event,
the visibility improved once they reached the patrol area,
so much so that Dunlop could now see the Hurricanes of
111 Squadron several miles to his north.

From the tone of the controller's voice, Red Section soon realized they were on to something positive, particularly when told there were two Bogeys, and not just one, in the vicinity. But it was Treble-one which spotted the quarry first and, as soon as Dunlop heard their 'Tally-ho', he set off at full throttle to join the fray. It was not long before he too caught sight of the Heinkels and, indeed, now found himself better placed than 111 Squadron to make the interception and it was clear that the superior speed of the Spitfires was going to get him to the target first. The He111s, now alerted to the danger, sped towards the nearest cover but Red Section was too quick for them and managed to set the nearer intruder well alight before it disappeared into the cloud. Then the Hurricanes arrived on the scene.

A great old hullabaloo is now going on, with Broadhurst complaining that 602 poached Treble-one's prey from under their noses. Be that as it may, Dunlop has justifiably claimed his victim, particularly as four parachutes were seen descending in the area, a fact grudgingly confirmed by the Hurricane boys. However much the victory has done to lift our spirits, I fear it has done little to boost the popularity of 602 Squadron hereabouts!

December 23rd   Strange to relate, we have been cleared of blame for the Hampden incident. It appears the bombers were largely responsible for their own misfortune by being so far off course. Furthermore they should have been flying with their wheels down – a prudent instruction laid down for occasions when friendly multi-engined aircraft must operate within defended areas – and they failed to let off the correct Very signal reply when first challenged. Now it has been brought to my attention, I seem to remember seeing a yellow-yellow flare in the area when, of course, a red-yellow was the order of the day.

At all events, the bomber boys wasted no time getting off home as soon as the court delivered its findings, and we were much relieved to see them taxiing out for take-off. Most of us came out to watch the departure. We continued watching while the Hampdens took off and climbed towards the north, forming up as they gradually gained height before turning back preparatory, we imagined, to treating us to a good old bullshit flypast. And flypast we certainly got for, as the ten bombers dived towards us at full throttle, we watched in disbelief their bomb doors swinging open, whereupon hundreds upon hundreds of lavatory rolls rained down on us to spread far and wide all over the station. We'd got the message all right, although Charles Keary, our station commander, was not in the slightest amused and promptly gave us the job of clearing up the mess. At least the Hampden boys should be home in time for Christmas.

A message has just come in from the Navy to say that the Heinkels intercepted yesterday were of the mine-laying variety and that the parachutes seen coming down had mines at the ends of them, and not people. Apparently a Royal Navy frigate had been in the area and saw one aircraft crashing into the sea, but was unable to trace any survivors.

December 25th   We hear a lot about shortages from our friends in the south, but am glad to report that no such dearth is apparent here. Indeed, apart from a noticeable shortage of petrol, now rationed through a system of coupons, we have not been deprived of much else. If any commodities are in short supply, however, news of them can't have permeated to our kitchen staff, for they put on a Christmas lunch which would have graced the tables of the best restaurants in the land. There was even a boar's head, with an apple bunged in its mouth, as the centrepiece.

Margaret has wangled a few days off work and is staying at nearby Bisset's Hotel in Gullane, so I was able to pack up early and join her there in time for afternoon tea. We had lots to discuss, for our wedding has now been fixed for the twenty-seventh of next month, so let's hope the Germans will take note of the date and take some time off. As it is, Control must be bitten by the bug, for they are finally showing a little compassion by reducing the station's commitment to one section only at readiness for the next two days. This is no great burden as we are able to share the chore with Treble-one.

December 28th   The weather has turned very cold and the ground frozen solid, so one has to watch one's step when running out to aircraft parked on the slippery tarmac. I myself went for a burton when on my way to take the dusk patrol this evening but fortunately suffered nothing worse than a grazed knuckle.

The boys are drifting back in penny numbers after the Christmas break, but Sergeant McAdam has so far failed to report for duty. Maybe the spirit of Christmas is still with us, for Dunlop has just overshot the airfield after a night landing, putting his aircraft on its nose in the boundary hedge. But for me Christmas is definitely over. Margaret has gone back to Glasgow.

No 72 Squadron (Spitfires) has just flown in from Church Fenton to relieve 111 Squadron, which is destined for Wick. It is commanded by our old friend Ronnie Lees.

* * *

December 30th Both A Flight Sections were told to remain at dispersal throughout the night to cover the arrival in the Clyde of a large troop convoy from Canada. However their services were not required and no one was called upon to fly. Now B Flight is going to be needed on state for the next twelve hours and I hope they are not called on to operate, for the weather has turned really nasty, with frequent falls of sleet and snow.

As it was, I couldn't take my place on the line, as I woke this morning with an aching groin and reported to sick quarters for the quack to run the rule over me. After much humming and hawing, he has ordered me into the Station Hospital, where he says I will have to remain for the next few days under observation. He thinks I've got mumps, although I assured him I'd already suffered the disease as a child. On that occasion, however, I only had sore glands; this time I'm stricken in a much more vulnerable spot and finding it infinitely more painful.

The only other occupant of the ward is Pilot Officer Lees, who is here with a swollen knee, but we both have another complaint, this time in common, the cold. It is freezing in here and even the provision of two hot water bottles has done nothing to stop the shivering. However the CO and Findlay Boyd popped in to see me this evening, bringing with them a panel off one of the Heinkels we shot down recently. It seems Farnborough wants us to have it as a memento of our accurate shooting! Alas, they were also the bearers of sadder tidings: Sergeant Bailey was killed this afternoon when the starboard wing of his Spitfire broke off during practice aerobatics and his machine crashed into a field on the outskirts of Haddington. It is a shame, for he was beginning to show a great deal of promise.

1940

January

January 1st There must be better ways of bringing in the New Year than sitting on a loo! But maybe I've broken some sort of record, for there can't be many who have managed to prolong such a session from 1939 through to 1940! But I was just as lonely on returning to the ward, for Lees was discharged yesterday and I had the place to myself. In fact it would not have surprised me to know I'd had the entire hospital to myself for, apart from the duty orderly, who had been conspicuous by his absence when I rang to let him know where I was going, the rest of the staff had pushed off to celebrate Hogmanay on other parts of the station.

However, I had just managed to drop into a fitful slumber around two o'clock when the door swung open with a fearful clatter and Cairns Smith was dumped unceremoniously on the bed next to mine. Needless to say I assumed he was the first party victim of the Hogmanay celebrations, but it turned out to be less conventional than that; apparently Cairns had parked his car in a friend's garden in the blackout and set off in a direct line for the front door, completely forgetting there was an empty swimming pool between him and the entrance. He was claiming he'd broken his leg at the very least.

Several chums called to see me throughout the day, but did little to raise my spirits. Archie McKellar took a ghoulish delight in warning me about the possible dire consequences of contracting adult mumps, at the same time rubbing in the fact that I'm due to be married in a

few weeks' time, whilst Findlay brought the news that
Harry Moody's undercarriage folded up on landing this
morning and his aircraft is badly bent, making it the
squadron's sixteenth breakage since war began. The one
bright spot was to learn that Harry himself is unhurt.

Cairns is in a brighter mood at last, for he was taken
for an X-ray this afternoon to find he is suffering nothing
worse than a bruised kneecap. However, he is to lie up
for a day or two, so at least I'll have someone to talk to.

January 4th   This is no place to come for a quiet rest.
During daylight hours the boys, bless their hearts, come
in in droves and fill the room with tobacco smoke whilst,
at night time, the combination of a freezing temperature
and Cairns's snoring do little to encourage restful slumber. It really is cold now and, apart from finding my
sponge and toothbrush frozen solid in my spongebag, I'm
wearing two pullovers, a pair of woollen mittens, have my
greatcoat spread over the bed and two hot water bottles
inside it, and still feel cold. Besides the food is hardly
appetizing, for it has to be brought from the Officers'
Mess and is generally congealed on the plates by the time
it reaches here.

But Cairns seems to be enjoying his enforced lie-up and
is reluctant to be discharged, though the MO says he is fit
to go. Until now he has avoided expulsion on the pretext
that his trousers were torn when he fell into the empty
pool and had not been returned from the menders, but
they were delivered back this afternoon and I was sorry
to see him limp away. However I must be on the mend
myself, for the pain is much less and I am allowed to sit
in a chair for several hours at a time.

I had several visitors today. Firstly Fumff Strong looked
in to borrow my greatcoat to wear at Sergeant Bailey's

funeral, although I was reluctant to let him have it until being assured that the Met man was forecasting warmer weather. Then Harry Broadhurst came by with news that he has been promoted to wing commander, and he was followed by Nick Nicholson of 72 Squadron to say his outfit is due to return to Church Fenton within the next few days. I should have asked him whence he got the information, for the barmaid at the Royal Hotel is usually first with intelligence of this nature, and is generally quite accurate. Indeed she could probably tell us which squadron will be coming to replace them.

January 10th   Have become progressively more mobile throughout the week and have, this morning, managed to persuade Doc to let me out of his igloo for a couple of nights, so that I can drive through to Glasgow. Before leaving, however, I stopped off at the Flight Office for a session with Findlay, who has been running B Flight in my absence. I find the squadron as a whole has done very little flying and, apart from signing a few log books and checking the training schedules, there was little else to do. Findlay has introduced a modified filing system for the flight while I have been away by reducing the files to two. These are marked 'Miscellaneous' and 'Mysterious' respectively, and anything which does not fit easily into either category goes straight into the wastepaper basket!

However it seems our lads are doing more than their fair share of the readiness states, with many having to stand by for days on end, only getting off to snatch quick meals in the Mess before having to rush back on the job. Many too are being made to sleep at dispersal, which is no fun in the present cold spell. The ground crews are being similarly victimized, so I rang the sector commander at Turnhouse to complain and he assures me 602 Squadron would be stood down whenever 609 Squadron arrives to take over from 72. At least we got that bit of information straight from the horse's mouth, and didn't have to visit the Royal Hotel to find out!

I was anxious to reach Glasgow before nightfall because of the poor state of my headlights, so was pleasantly surprised when the car started up without much difficulty in spite of having sat out in the cold for so long. It says a lot for the old £30 Vauxhall. However I found my fiancée laid up with a heavy cold when I finally reached Glasgow.

Spent this morning making arrangements for our forthcoming wedding, first calling on the minister before accompanying my future mother-in-law to the Central Hotel to order essential stocks for the reception. Twelve dozen bottles of Veuve Cliquot seems a reasonable quantity to meet the needs of our 140 invited guests and it is good to know Mr and Mrs Croll intend to launch their daughter into the wedded state with such aplomb. I also purchased the ring.

Am now back at Drem where the boys are still maintaining the states and grumbling like billyo. Unfortunately 609 Squadron has not yet turned up, although expected this morning. I was no sooner back in the chair than the cracking sound of a Spitfire landing made me glance through the window, when I was just in time to see Alastair Grant tip his aircraft on its nose on the hard ground. I don't think Alastair is yet completely comfortable on Spits.

January 14th Am pleased to report that I passed my medical with flying colours and, as B Flight was stood down for the morning, went straight on to the Mess to read the daily papers. Had no sooner settled down when we were called back to readiness as Red Section was being scrambled to intercept an unidentified plot. The A Flight boys were already airborne when we reached dispersal and a message was waiting for us to come straight to stand-by and sit in our cockpits. Before we were ordered into the air, however, Red Section returned, streaking low across the airfield to show their ground crews that the gun patches had been shot off, thus alerting them that they had been in action and would need re-arming. It is vital to get this done without delay, otherwise Jerry might follow up and catch us on the ground with the proverbial trousers down.

Red Section has had a kill! They intercepted a Heinkel 111 twenty miles off the Fife coast and brought it down in the sea, after which Marcus said he saw at least one crew member take to his dinghy. In fact Leuchars has been on the telephone to let us know they have picked up this fellow and now have him safely under lock and key. The blighter must be trying to curry favour, for he apparently asked that a message be passed to Marcus to congratulate him on his fine shooting! However we ourselves didn't get off scot free, as Hector MacLean came back with a bullet hole in his windscreen and, although our cannon-armed Spitfire took part, its guns jammed before any assessment of their worth could be made.

B Flight is being left out of the glamour stuff these days, for the most we've done lately is to carry out a number of tedious patrols over convoy 'Alice', now approaching the Northumberland coast. Nevertheless we have been included in several parties to celebrate this and that: Douglas threw one to say farewell to Harry Broadhurst and some well-off neighbours invited a few of us to dine at the De Guise, in Edinburgh, ostensibly to celebrate A Flight's recent success. However, as Carl Brisson, the film star, was also a guest, the party was more likely given in his honour.

January 15th The temperature has dropped again and more snow is falling which, hopefully, will keep the enemy away. Sadly however it hasn't stopped convoys from sailing and I began the day leading the dawn patrol over a large assembly of shipping about to sail from Methil Bay. Paul Webb and Glyn Ritchie made up the section and we were with our charges before daylight, but no sooner had the ships set sail than we were diverted to investigate an X-raid approaching from the east at 25,000 feet.

Our windscreens and canopies became completely frozen over as we climbed through the snow-filled clouds, causing me to lose visual contact with the others, so I ordered them to sheer away left and right for a couple of minutes before resuming their original courses. We broke clear at 23,000 feet when I called Glyn, who was some distance off to port; but Paul was nowhere to be seen and repeated calls on the R/T failed to elicit any response. So Glyn and I continued the search alone until told by Control to pancake, as the plot on their table had been taken off.

We had a hairy ride down again, Glyn only able to maintain station on me by continually scraping frost off his canopy with the back of a penknife, until we broke cloud around 2,000 feet directly over Leuchars, where a Hudson was about to start its take-off run. We watched it rapidly gathering speed, expecting it to become airborne at any time, but something went wrong for, instead of climbing away in the normal fashion, the aircraft continued to career straight ahead and into a pine forest where it seemed to disintegrate in a cloud of dust before being

enveloped in flames and dense black smoke. We continued watching, fascinated, whilst crash vehicles and ambulances sped towards the scene when, suddenly everything
went up in the air together as depth charges, bombs,
ammunition and Very cartridges exploded in the intense
heat. To us, however, it was like watching a Brock's
benefit on the silent screen for, although privileged spectators, we could hear nothing of the inferno on account of
the noise from our Merlin engines.

I was much relieved to find Paul already on the ground
when we got back to Drem. He had had trouble with his
R/T set and oxygen supply, so wisely decided to abort the
sortie and find his own way back to base. I am also
relieved to hear that the crew of the Hudson got away
with nothing worse than minor injuries.

January 18th So much snow has been falling that we've
been told to keep our aircraft in the hangar. Yesterday,
however, we were sent for again to investigate an unidentified plot in the vicinity of one of the convoys and I took
the patrol, accompanied by Paul and George Proudman
with his cannon Spitfire. Whenever possible we try to fly
this machine as part of the first section off in order to give
it the most opportunities to show what it can do. So far,
however, it has achieved damn all for, every time it has
had a go, the guns have jammed as soon as a few rounds
are fired. But we are preservering, and who knows what
would become of this particular sortie.

In the event nothing happened and, after stooging in
and out of snow-laden clouds up to 25,000 feet for over
an hour with nothing to show for it, we were ordered
back to base to find the squadron had been released from
operations for the next twenty-four hours. This was too
good an opportunity to miss, so Archie offered to drive

me through to Glasgow, reckoning his Jaguar would have
a better chance of getting there than my Vauxhall. I was
glad to accept and was duly dropped at my parents' flat,
where I found the local balloon was also grounded with
eighteen inches of snow pressing on its envelope.

Margaret and I went to see *The Lion has Wings* in our
local cinema this evening.

January 23rd   We are still able to operate in spite of the
airfield being under a blanket of snow and, with occasional bursts of sunshine adding to the brilliance of the
scene, some spectacular results are created whenever
Spitfires take off, for they leave behind lengthy plumes of
powdered snow which seem to hover for ages in the still
air before falling back to ground like miniature
snowstorms.

The brighter weather has apparently inspired our station commander too. Charles Keary is one of the old
school who loves a bit of spit and polish, although it is not
easy to keep up with his high standards, operating as we
do from a grass airfield which alternates between being a
sea of mud and frozen solid, as it is now; besides we often
have to spend days on end with few opportunities to clean
up properly, living at dispersal more often than in the
Mess. So no one took very kindly to the notice in station
routine orders calling for a CO's inspection on the tarmac.
Nonetheless we were given no option but to comply, in
spite of Douglas's last-minute appeal to have excused
those who had been at readiness through the night. 'They
can turn in after the parade is over,' was his answer. 'I
insist on having a hundred percent turnout!'

An area large enough to accomodate the personnel of
two squadrons, plus the Headquarters staff, had been
cleared outside No 1 hangar and everyone was dutifully

lined up in their best blues and shivering like mad. Soon
the highly polished staff car swept round the corner and
skidded to a stop in front of the saluting dais, whereupon
the parade was called to attention in anticipation of the
General Salute. All eyes were now on the Group Captain
as he stepped gingerly from his car but, instead of making
a majestic appearance on the platform, his heels went
from under him and he landed with an almighty thump on
the frosty ground, leaving us nothing better to salute than
a pair of highly polished size nines! The parade was
cancelled there and then and we returned to the business
of fighting a war.

We have been having our share of misfortunes lately.
Sergeant McAdam has been causing further bother for,
not only did he put a Spitfire on its back at Acklington
two days ago and another on its nose here yesterday, but
would have landed with his wheels up this afternoon if the
duty ops officer hadn't been on his toes and managed to
fire a red Very flare across his bows to draw his attention
to the omission. As if that wasn't enough, one of our
lorries skidded into Hannibal, the pride of the Imperial
Airways fleet, which had just landed to deliver the ground
crews and equipment for 609 Squadron. However her
skipper, Captain Peacock, was remarkably philosophical
about the damage to his leading edge and showed me
over this extraordinary machine. It is truly impressive,
being capable of carrying forty-two passengers in considerable comfort, even to the extent of giving them a loo.

January 26th George Reid, my colleague from Prestwick, has undertaken to be Best Man at my wedding, so I
took myself off to Edinburgh the other morning to buy a
present for him and the Maid of Honour. I also took the
opportunity to call on my bank manager to ensure suf-

ficient funds are available to cover the cost of a honeymoon. It was as well I did, for last night's Burns Night celebrations have left me with a monumental hangover and I would never have been able to talk finance if I'd left the visit until today. Furthermore they tell me I gave Donald Jack a black eye when he, and others, tried to throw me into a cold bath at the conclusion of the party.

I am also glad I got away from Drem when I did, for a sudden thaw has set in, resulting in three 609 Squadron aircraft coming to grief in the mud whilst landing off the dawn patrol: Clearly I would never have managed to cope with such conditions in my fragile state of health. As it is, I had better have an early night, for the big day is set for tomorrow.

January 31st The knot is now truly tied, although I cannot yet claim to feel the responsibilities of marriage weighing heavily on my shoulders. Naturally Margaret was disappointed to be done out of a white wedding, but she nevertheless looked stunning in her costume with furry bits round it. Padre Sutherland assisted in the ceremony and nearly deafened us with the lustiness of his singing, for I fear neither Margaret nor I are accustomed to standing face to face with a burly Highland parson bellowing at full throttle. Furthermore, George's liberal ministrations with the champagne bottle immediately prior to the ceremony, although providing a modicum of Dutch courage, also played havoc with my innards and had me bursting to spend a penny throughout the proceedings.

I am blessed with an untold number of family relations, most of whom I only meet at funerals and weddings, and this wedding was no exception. However another heavy fall of snow prevented many other guests from getting

there, with the result that the ratio of champagne per
head increased significantly, and it was not long before
uncles, aunts and cousins, usually quite well behaved and
demure, were letting down their hair in most unseemly
fashion. However I was glad to see Donald Jack had
managed to force his way through the snow, for he evoked
considerable sympathy from my female relatives who
naturally assumed his discoloured eye was part of a
legitimate war wound. When the time came for Margaret
and me to leave the party, I was carried from the hotel
shoulder high, before being unceremoniously dumped on
the roof of the taxi whilst a number of classier inebriates
managed to climb inside along with the bride. I was only
permitted inside myself after falling off the roof as we
swung into Bothwell Street.

We had decided on Troon for the first night of the
honeymoon, but nearly didn't make it. Snow had been
falling throughout the day and, by the time we had sorted
ourselves out and collected the old Vauxhall from a
nearby garage, we had great difficulty making progress
through the storm, in spite of help from an unmasked
spotlight. By the time we reached Kilmarnock, however,
I realized I'd forgotten to switch on the windscreen wiper,
after which it was much easier going although our troubles
weren't completely over, as Margaret got a bit over-
excited and signed the hotel register in her maiden name.
By great good fortune, our photographs appeared in next
day's newspapers, after which we were treated with less
disdain and more befitting an honourably married couple
– albeit of only a few hours' standing.

When we looked out next morning, it was clear we
were in for a lengthy stay in the Marine Hotel, for the
snow was at least nine feet deep in places and our car was
presumably somewhere under it. In fact we heard later

that several cars and buses were still missing on the Fenwick Moor, over which we had blindly motored on our wedding day, whilst the crack LMS express Royal Scot was stranded on Beattock with several hundred passengers on board. Indeed we were stuck in Troon for two more days, and only got away by digging a route across some fields and driving as far as Prestwick, when we discovered that George Reid was still snowbound in Glasgow.

We were no sooner established in the Orangefield Hotel at Prestwick than I went down with a bout of flu and now Margaret is smitting for something else, as yet undiagnosed. I feel sure there are more orthodox ways of starting one's married life!

1940
February

February 6th The influenza bug kept me in bed for the next four days during which I ran a temperature and felt like death warmed up and, to make matters worse, later developed a hacking cough which drove Margaret to seek sleeping accommodation elsewhere. However her complaint, I am glad to say, never came to anything. But I felt better yesterday and risked taking a stroll on the airfield, well wrapped up against the elements, where I bumped into one of my pre-war colleagues who told me that another Nav School Anson had just crashed in Northern Ireland with the loss of four lives. His reference to 'another' makes me wonder if 602 Squadron is not alone in writing off aircraft in considerable numbers.

My leave is due up tomorrow, so we decided to make a start today in case road conditions still made driving conditions hazardous; and it is as well we did, for we found the route over the Fenwick Moor quite impassable, with much of it under drifts of twenty feet and more and, indeed, from one of which the body of a motorist was only recovered yesterday, having been missing since the day we ourselves came down that way. As it was, we had a devil of a time negotiating the coastal road as there are many sections still badly affected. However we finally got as far as my parents' flat in Glasgow, tired, cold and hungry, and have decided to call it a day.

In deference to my revised marital state, Mother has installed a new-fangled divan bed which opens up to make room for two. Margaret is happy enough with her side of

it, but mine was most uncomfortable until I discovered
that Dad had erected it upside down.

February 9th   I left Margaret in Glasgow and drove back
to Drem only to find that Findlay had taken B Flight to
Acklington as added protection for a particularly important convoy passing through that area. So I had to wait for
their return before resuming command, although I was
very pleased to find that Findlay has been made a flight
lieutenant in my absence. I just hope it won't mean his
being posted elsewhere as he is a real tower of strength in
the flight and we can ill afford to lose him, particularly as
half our lads are presently down with 'flu.

Got really back into harness this morning when ordered
to take Yellow Section to investigate a plot approaching
the coast. Douglas Farquhar was already airborne with
Red Section and, before we had gone far, I heard his
'tally-ho' and immediately went after him to see if we
could lend a hand. In the event Douglas's victim was
already streaming smoke and one engine was well afire by
the time we caught up, when it was also clear that the
Heinkel was on its way down. Like bees round a honey-
pot, other Spits were attracted to the scene and, by the
time the stricken bomber crossed the coast near North
Berwick, it was being escorted by no less than five
fighters, all of which continued circling overhead while
the Heinkel landed, wheels up, on the hill behind the
town. We watched three crew members clambering out
and dragging a fourth after them; the rear gunner, it
turned out to be. This poor fellow had been badly injured
in the attack, but died later in our station hospital whence
he was rushed by ambulance.

Douglas and I visited the scene later to find scores of
interested spectators milling round the crashed bomber,

although efficiently kept at arms' length by a small force of burly bobbies. In these circumstances it is important to prevent souvenir hunters from getting their hands on anything for fear they will remove something of vital intelligence value, although in this instance our trophy appears to be more or less intact.

Not surprisingly the incident has attracted a lot of interest from the press, but I confess the real significance didn't sink in until I was reminded by a reporter that this was the first enemy aircraft ever to be brought down on British soil. It is certainly the closest I have been to one and there is something very unreal about having a machine bearing the familiar iron crosses parked at one's back door. It also looked small and fragile sitting on a Scottish hillside, the incongruity further emphasized when one examined the undercarriage tyres and found printed on them, in English, the words 'Made in Germany'!

February 18th Surely the Germans have not given up already! They have certainly been leaving us very much alone recently and, apart from one or two minor scrambles after a number of indeterminate plots, the squadron has hardly been called on at all. Mind you, it is just possible our adversaries are taking a short breather to lick their wounds, for the ratio of their losses must be considerable. 602 Squadron itself has already accounted for six and several others probably destroyed, whilst 603 and the other squadrons operating within the 13 Group area have not exactly been idle. As a result we have been living a more settled life, doing a lot of training and taking advantage of the lull to give more time off to the hard-pressed air and ground crews. Indeed it's turning out to be a funny sort of war altogether for we find ourselves grappling with the enemy one minute, and the next enjoying a near-normal life style in the bosom of our families. Goodness knows what our Army and Naval colleagues must make of it, for in their cases, once they've joined their regiment or their ship, they become isolated from normal life until their next official spell of leave comes round. But we are not complaining!

As luck would have it, Margaret was able to scrounge another few days off (one of the advantages of working for one's father!) and I was able to drive into Edinburgh to pick her up at Waverly Station. Douglas and Bobbie Farquhar have invited us to stay with them in North Berwick, where they have taken a small house for a few months. The AOC has also rented a cottage in Gullane to get his wife and small daughter away from the vulnerable area around Newcastle, so we found ourselves dining in the somewhat exalted company of my commanding officer and the AOC on our first night there.

But it has not been all beer and skittles. Besides pressing on with a normal training programme, the squadron continues to provide regular cover for the coastal convoys, sometimes two convoys at the same time, and also diverting whenever possible to act as targets for our gunner friends and, at night, for the searchlight boys. We now find that some ships have taken to towing small barrage balloons astern, although I cannot see them doing much to deter a determined low-level attack; rather they will make the enemy's job of spotting ships from a distance that much easier.

February 21st   Findlay Boyd went on leave this morning and gave Margaret a lift back to Glasgow, so Archie McKellar will take over Green Section while he is away. However, shortly after they left, news reached us that there was a Hurricane down in the sea near May Island,

and Douglas and I went off to look for it. A Hudson from
Leuchars was already at the scene when we got there yet,
although the sea state was moderate and the visibility
good, we found nothing and returned to Drem when our
fuel threatened to run out. Unfortunately no one had
thought to tell us that a thaw had set in in our absence
and both Douglas and I just avoided digging our noses
into the ground when we touched down on an unexpected
sea of mud. However the cause of our search is something
of a mystery for, although a nearby ship first reported the
incident through the medium of a coastguard station, no
squadron has reported a Hurricane missing.

Later, after taking Blue Section on a convoy patrol
which passed without incident, I went back with Douglas
to pack my things and had no sooner sat down to
afternoon tea when the AOC rang to let him know he had
been awarded a DFC. So, instead of having to face a
dreary meal in the Mess, I was treated to a celebratory
dinner at the Marine Hotel. Margaret will be furious
when she hears what she's missed!

February 22nd Awoke this morning with a man-sized
hangover thanks to Douglas's generous hospitality, and
was none too pleased when called to readiness at half past
five. Douglas, presumably stimulated by his recent award,
also came on the early state, this time to fly with A Flight,
whose turn it was to operate the cannon Spitfire. Operations rang to say there was an unidentified plot appearing
on the table, so it was not long before Green and Red
Sections were both ordered into the air.

We had been ordered to a patrol position off the Fife
coast, but were not long there before I heard Red Section
being vectored towards St Abb's Head and Douglas
calling to say he had made contact with a Bandit and was

closing for an attack. Ferguson, Moody and I immediately
shot off at full throttle to join in and reached the spot just
in time to see a Heinkel 111, smoke streaming from its
port engine, making a forced landing in a remote field
near the Head itself and with three Spitfires circling
overhead. One suddenly detached itself and lined up on
the same field, undercarriage down, as if to land beside
the downed bomber. And land it did, bouncing alarmingly
down a steep slope before suddenly somersaulting into
the air and coming to rest flat on its back and wheels in
the air. From what we could gather on the R/T this was
our CO who had ended up in such an undignified posture.
However I'm glad to relate that Douglas is now back at
Drem with three Luger automatics, a stiff neck and a very
fascinating tale to tell.

Having succeeded in silencing the Jerry rear gunner,
Douglas left it to the cannon aircraft to show its paces
but, as was to be expected, the guns stopped firing after
letting off a few dozen rounds. But Douglas suspected a
few might have struck home and was very anxious that
the experts should have an opportunity to size up the
effects. However the Heinkel was down in a very remote
area and no one was there to stop the Germans from
setting light to their machine, so Douglas took it upon
himself to do it. The Heinkel crew watched in disbelief as
the Spitfire landed alongside at high speed before trundling down the slope and cartwheeling into a bog at the
bottom; they first hauled out their injured rear gunner,
then set fire to their aircraft, before running down the hill
to help Douglas extricate himself from the crashed Spitfire. They found him suspended by his safety harness,
unable to move, and had to put their combined weight
under one wing to give him enough room to release the
straps and crawl out from under. During this manoeuvre

he dropped on his nut; hence the stiff neck. Grateful as he was for their help, Douglas now found himself at the mercy of his victims, who were pointing their automatics at him and looking extremely disgruntled.

All four then climbed back to the Heinkel which was now well alight and Douglas helped the Germans to move their injured companion further from the flames. However he suddenly spotted a number of khaki-clad figures cresting a nearby hill and drew his captors' attention to them, at the same time pointing out, in his best schoolboy German, that it would be better for them to be taken unarmed, whereupon they grudgingly surrendered their Lugers to Douglas, who secreted them in the wide pockets of his flying overalls. The three Germans then approached their captors with their hands above their heads but, unfortunately, these Army fellows had not yet seen the Spitfire lying at the foot of the hill and assumed our CO was a member of the Heinkel crew. According to Douglas, the situation became quite ridiculous with Douglas himself trying to explain what had happened on the one hand, whilst the Germans tried to drag their captors towards the edge to show them the crashed Spitfire. Indeed the situation was only resolved when Douglas was able to produce an OHMS envelope bearing his latest Income Tax demand, after which he was grudgingly transferred to the side of the goodies.

We are much relieved to have our CO returned relatively unharmed, although Douglas is furious with himself for breaking his aeroplane. It is his first serious accident after more than thirteen years' experience.

February 25th Spring-like weather has burst upon us unexpectedly and it has become quite a treat to spend time with the convoys and be able to see clearly for miles around. We hope we've seen the last of the appalling conditions of the past seven weeks.

Douglas and I drove to Coldingham this afternoon to take a look at the Heinkel but were unable to take the car the whole way. Indeed we were faced with a two-mile trudge over the moors, which says much for the stamina of the LDV fellows who turned up so promptly. Once there, however, it was apparent that the Germans had made a good job of destroying their aircraft for, although it had not been much damaged in the actual crash-landing, it is now completely burnt out with only the tail section remaining intact. There are many bullet holes in this part, all made by .303 ammunition but, search as we did, we could find no trace of any holes made by anything larger. We then descended the hill to look at Douglas's Spitfire, but this is surely a write-off as it has already sunk deep into the bog and seems to have broken its back.

Was surprised to find Findlay at dispersal when I got back as he wasn't expected until tomorrow. On discovering his mistake, however, he packed up immediately and drove off in a high dudgeon to rejoin his wife for a further twenty-four hours. Maybe he was confused by today's change to summertime, which the Government says will remain in force for the duration of the war. Although we will have the benefit of an extra hour of darkness in the mornings, I doubt if many farmers will take kindly to the arrangement.

The Group Captain is on the warpath again. The whole station is to be given a thorough clean-up for a 'Very Special Parade' tomorrow.

February 28th   Great excitement this morning when told the King was coming to Drem. Everyone was on parade, unfamiliarly tidy in best blues and shining shoes; even our gas masks were specially buffed up and, after a quick briefing from the station adjutant on how to bow from the neck if lucky enough to be presented, we stood in serried ranks to await the big moment.

The C-in-C Fighter Command, Stuffy Dowding, and our AOC, Birdie Saul, were in attendance when the King came down the lines and spoke to each of us in turn although, by the time he came to me, I was too overcome to remember what passed between us as I shook the royal hand, although I remember thinking HM must also be visiting the Navy as he was wearing the uniform of an Admiral of the Fleet. The inspection completed, Douglas was called before the entire parade when the King pinned a DFC on our CO's tunic. We all felt immensely proud at that moment.

Dowding stayed on after HM had departed and spent some time discussing things with us at dispersal before making for the AOC's cottage where Birdie and Claire Saul were throwing a small party for their distinguished visitor. There I had a further opportunity for a chat with the C-in-C who had many nice things to say about our efforts so far. All in all it has been quite a day!

February 29th   Few have remembered it is a leap year, not that it much matters as most of us are already bespoken! Nevertheless the world seems a humdrum sort of place after the excitement of yesterday's Royal visit and we feel it somewhat beneath our dignity now to be ordered off merely to play nursemaid to a convoy chugging up the coast of Northumberland. Not only that, but the weather has turned nasty again, with frequent showers of heavy rain and sleet, this time accompanied by very strong easterly gales, and a new type of 'flu virus which is taking its toll. Thus, with Findlay, Ritchie and Moody already in the hands of the medicos and Archie away on leave, it has been left to Ferguson, Babbage and me to man the fort as best we can.

Although not officially on state today, we were unexpectedly scrambled this evening to take over the convoy protection from 609 Squadron as their flight had been diverted to deal with an X-raid reported nearby. The Yorkshire boys had already gone before we got there, but I hear they got their man. So another Heinkel 111 bites the dust of the North Sea!

1940
March

March 2nd It seems the continual traffic up and down our coastline is keeping Jerry busy for, even when no shipping is passing through the area, at least one German recce puts in an appearance every day, obviously on the lookout for nice juicy targets. Not that we mind, for it keeps us on our toes even though they only provide fleeting targets which are usually difficult to track down in the ever-prevailing cloud cover. It is certainly preferable to hanging about crew rooms, kicking one's heels, playing interminable games of chess or having to listen to Paul Webb's new gramophone record 'In the Mood' so often that one is ready to grab it off the machine and break it over his head! However things began livening up during last night.

I was ordered into the air shortly after four o'clock, followed shortly after by Archie McKellar and George Proudman with his cannon-armed aircraft. A convoy was reported to be under attack to the south of St Abb's Head but, although we saw a number of bright flashes as we raced towards the area, the fun was over by the time we got there. The intruder apparently failed to score any hits, although doubtless reported to its masters that an entire British convoy was now mouldering at the bottom of the North Sea. Ops had had no RDF warning of the raid, so presumably the marauder had slipped in at low level.

We had no sooner returned to base and refuelled than we were sent off again, this time to investigate a plot over

Perthshire, but again we were unlucky. However, instead of being given the expected order to pancake, we were told to go back to the convoy to make sure it was all right and set off southwards, where the weather had worsened considerably since we had left the area two hours previously. As a result it took ages to re-locate the ships in the dark; so long, in fact, that our fuel was running dangerously low by the time we finally did so. Dawn was breaking as we started back for Drem, now flying as a section of three, when the engine of George's aircraft cut without warning, forcing him to make a wheels-up landing in a ploughed field behind Dunbar and severely damaging his machine in the process. Thus ended the brief, but none-too-glorious, career of the only cannon-armed Spitfire on operational service.

We were much too tired to bother about breakfast and took ourselves straight off to bed.

March 6th The amount of time we are having to put in over convoys is taking its toll of the maintenance schedules as we are using up flying hours at an alarming rate. Not everyone appreciates that aircraft, whether operational or trainers, must undergo regular inspections, sometimes requiring airframes to be stripped down or engines removed, depending on the type of inspection being done. Now we are beginning to run out of serviceable aeroplanes. As 609 Squadron is experiencing the same problem, we made a joint approach to Group and Sector Headquarters and have been given permission to reduce the strengths of our sections from three to two aircraft from now on. So there will now be three sections in each flight instead of two, which means we'll have to find two more colours to call them by. Black and White seem the obvious choices.

Fred Wheeldon, our adjutant, has gone on leave and I am detailed to sit in his chair for the next ten days. I can't say I relish the prospect, although the experience will probably stand me in good stead later on. However one look at the filing system had me recoiling on the first day, when I would have liked to replace it with our two-file B Flight procedure, although I doubt whether Fred would approve. At all events, the highlight of today was holding an Orderly Room to take a charge against one of our MT drivers who had accidentally set fire to a refuelling bowser. I hope I've dealt with it correctly as I let off the culprit with a caution, at the same time telling him to be more careful in future.

Douglas called in to see how I was getting on and showed me a letter he'd got from our Honorary Air Commodore, Lord Stonehaven, in which he mentioned having met the King who, he wrote, was highly amused at the story of Douglas's foray with the Germans at St Abb's Head. Alas, those in slightly less exalted circles have a different opinion apparently, for Douglas got a hell of a rocket from Their Airships for jeopardizing the safety of his aircraft!

March 10th Operating from Dyce, our Edinburgh colleagues have just clobbered a Heinkel off Wick. Good old 603! However things are less active down here, thus giving me more time to concentrate on office chores without constant interruptions, although I could have done without having to attend the Station Commander's weekly conference yesterday. I cannot help feeling Charles Keary has his knife out for us, for he was like a bear with a sore head throughout the meeting and seemed to be picking on us whenever the opportunity arose. '602 Squadron – trouble; nothing but trouble!' he kept repeating and I got a fair old roasting about all manner of misdemeanours supposedly perpetrated by our lads, ranging from scruffy turnouts, bath plugs missing from the airmen's ablutions even to being blamed for a dented dustbin which he claims was run into by one of our drivers. It appears the Group Captain is not over-fond of Auxiliaries, for 609 also came in for a fair amount of criticism and it was noticeable that nothing of an operational nature was on the agenda.

Proudman has been to Catterick to pick up another cannon-armed Spitfire, but thinks nothing of it as it leaks oil all over the place. But let us hope he does better with this machine than he did before, for the pressure is again on to step up cover for the convoys. I think Group was somewhat shaken by the events of last week; indeed they must have been, for we are now being asked to patrol on a twenty-four-hour basis. I am glad we pressed on with our night-flying practice.

The AOC and his wife have invited Margaret to stay for a few days and, as a token of appreciation, I undertook to pluck their Sealyham terrier. But it was a bad move, for it will take many weeks to brush the dog's hair out of my tunic.

March 15th   Was relieved when Wheeldon came back off leave and I could hand back to him and return to a more orthodox existence. The enemy is still giving us a wide berth, it seems, and apart from the continuing chore of convoy patrolling, little has been happening on the operational front. So I was able to take a number of our ground crews for a trip in the Harvard to give them a change of scenery. These fellows do a grand job and have few opportunities to get into the air these days, although most would like to do so. It was different when the squadron was equipped with the two-seater Harts and Hinds and they could frequently scrounge flights, but these opportunities ceased when we converted to a single-seater fighter role. It says much for their loyalties that they accepted this change without rancour, although many must have been sorely disappointed at the time. At all events, most have now had a chance to see what Drem looks like from the air.

Because of the lull I have been able to squeeze in a spot of leave, so Margaret and I have come through to Glasgow to stay with my brother-in-law and his wife, as the former has been called up for active service. Alas we found him in a foul mood for he has just put a large dent in the front of his brand new Alvis Silver Eagle, having run into an inebriated reveller in the blackout.

The air raid sirens sounded while we were shopping in town this afternoon, but no one took a blind bit of notice and continued with what they were doing. I heard later it had been only a practice alert, but I hope Johnny Citizen will mend his ways, for next time it could be the real thing.

Douglas's promotion to wing commander appeared in *The Glasgow Herald* this morning, so I suppose he will be leaving us soon. I wonder who will take over from him.

March 20th   Left Margaret in Glasgow and returned to Gullane alone to find Douglas still firmly in the driver's seat, although he now knows he will be moving to Martlesham Heath as station commander. But there is still no news of his successor.

The AOC's weekend with his family was rudely interrupted yesterday when his ADC, Micky Mount, called to tell him there had been a heavy raid on Scapa Flow, so I drove him to Drem to find out the score. Happily the raid failed to achieve its objective and, apart from some minor damage to shore installations, nothing else was hit. As Saul wanted to spend some time with the lads at dispersal, I took the opportunity to go for a spin in his Vega Gull with Micky for I had never flown in one before. It was more like travelling in a private car and a pleasant change to be able to carry on a conversation whilst airborne.

Drem was thrown open to the press today and we have been inundated with reporters and cameramen, all intent on ferreting out the stories most acceptable to their particular readership. Hopefully they got what they wanted although I couldn't help overhearing one or two interviewees laying it on a bit thick when describing their heroic pasts! At any rate the gentlemen seemed satisfied with their day out and were particularly loud in their praise of the set piece attack by Red Section on a couple of visiting Blenheims, which they described as 'most exhilarating'. Exhilarating my foot; it was out and out foolhardy!

The gentlemen of the press were not long gone when a Hampden appeared out of the gloom and landed at Drem without so much as by your leave. It had apparently taken a wrong turning somewhere, for he was completely lost and nearly out of petrol, so much so that he had to ask us where he was. Nevertheless this unexpected arrival set us thinking about our own vulnerability for there is nothing to prevent enemy aircraft from following such lame ducks back and being led straight to a first-class opportunity target. So we have decided to disperse our aircraft further afield at nights from now on.

Something will have to be done about McAdam, for he has just taxied his aircraft into LO-Q while parking it for the night. It's as well for him that the damage to my aircraft is slight!

March 25th   Having taken to heart the need for better dispersal, we've been sending the off-duty squadron to Grangemouth, whilst the 'available' flight of the duty squadron sees out the night at Turnhouse. It was Marcus's turn to look after things at Drem last night so, after a most uncomfortable night in a disused hut on the Edinburgh base, I took my lads straight on to the dawn patrol from there, landing back at Drem in time for breakfast. We had to fly cover for a particularly large convoy assembling in Methil Bay during which we made three interceptions but, regretfully, they turned out to be nothing more menacing than a Coastal Command Anson and two Naval Swordfish.

Archie McKellar was sent off in the middle of the previous night to go to the aid of a convoy reported to be threatened off Montrose. He remained with his charge to the limit of the Spitfire's endurance, but had no sooner landed to refuel when word came through that the convoy was under attack, with one ship already going down. I have seldom seen anyone reacting so angrily and I fear Archie's comments are quite unprintable.

Intelligence tells us that more German navigation beacons are being activated, making us wonder whether they intend to step up activity in this area. At all events we don't intend to be caught napping and, apart from resting as many pilots as possible while the lull lasts, we are taking another look at how best to disperse our reserves overnight. The current business of using Grangemouth and Turnhouse is unwieldy and unpopular, so Douglas and I drove to the Edinburgh Flying Club field at Macmerry to size up its possibilities. We found it in the hands of Works and Bricks who are extending the landing area but, once that job is completed, consider it might provide the answer. The clubhouse would certainly make an excellent dispersal.

However the most significant news of the day concerns George Pinkerton who, after an absence of only four months, is coming back to 602 Squadron to take over from Douglas Farquhar. If this is true, we'd better have 'Grumpy' polished up and ready for his use again!

March 27th   There has been a lot of early morning frost recently and Sergeant Moody came a frightful cropper yesterday when jumping on to the wing of his Spitfire. He sustained a broken collar bone but I'm glad to say the doc has managed to patch him up sufficiently to allow him to accompany Pat Lyall to Group Headquarters where both are due to be interviewed for a commission by the AOC. They are excellent fellows and we all hope they pass the test. At the other end of the scale, Sergeant McAdam has been found guilty by the Court of Inquiry over the taxiing incident and will be leaving the squadron.

I flew on the dawn and dusk patrols today, on both occasions over ships entering or leaving the Firth of Forth, but, during the latter patrol, we had occasion to carry out a sweep in the vicinity of May Island where we saw a couple of frigates testing their armoury. It was not long before they turned their attention to us, of course, although on this occasion they had the decency to ring up later and apologize!

March 31st   Everyone seems to have a bee in their bonnet about the need for adequate dispersal of aircraft and the pros and cons of all manner of suggestions are still being bandied about. The main stumbling block centres on the ancillary equipment for, although it is easy enough to move the aeroplanes to wherever you want, they cannot be kept at an operational state unless backed up by a sufficient number of refuellers, armourers, starter batteries and so on, and the bulk of these must be retained at base to support the readiness flights. So we are going to try a compromise by spreading all our machines round the airfield perimeter, realizing of course that it will entail long walks for these crews whose aircraft are parked at the far end of the field. I am exercising my prerogative as a flight commander and will have LO-Q parked nearest the dispersal hut!

I flew Donald Jack to Turnhouse in the Magister this morning to pick up one of our aircraft which had developed a fault during one of the night dispersals and took the opportunity to have a closer look at the Heinkel shot down near North Berwick which is still languishing in one of the hangars there. I believe we are to be given one of its panels as a souvenir once the boffins have finished with it. However, on my return to Drem I found that George Proudman had managed to fly into a windsock whilst taking off on a patrol, fortunately doing more damage to the windsock than to his precious aircraft. It seems our cannon-armed Spitfires are destined to be preys of constant misfortune.

Later in the day I tested a replacement aircraft, when the undercarriage pump-handle almost came away in my hand. I wish someone would find an alternative means of raising and lowering a Spitfire's wheels as the wretched pumping action is a constant source of irritation and creates all manner of problems for the uninitiated. A long lever is positioned on the pilot's right-hand side which means that, during take-off, it is necessary to transfer one's left hand from the throttle to the control column in order to free the right hand for pumping up the wheels and, until one becomes conversant with the unusual transportation of hands, it is all too easy to forget which hand is doing what, and the control column comes in for its share of the pumping action. Take-offs by new pilots are easily recognizable by their see-sawing progression into the air.

A number of pilots are showing distinct signs of fatigue and I have sent Paul and Archie to see the MO who has ordered both to have a rest from flying for the next two days. It is not surprising, for B Flight has flown in excess of 300 hours this month.

1940
April

April 4th   April Fool's Day passed without any pranks,
which makes me think the boys must be more weary than
I thought. Indeed the only person in a frivolous mood
these days appears to be the Almighty as he is again
calling the changes and subjecting us to a series of storms
with much heavy rain and gale force winds up to 60 mph.
Archie and I were sent on patrol in the dead of night
whilst one of these storms was at its height and were
relieved when ordered back after fifteen minutes. As it
was, our landings were hairy, to say the least, with the
paraffin landing flares looking like a row of welders'
blowlamps in the high wind. We could even hear their
flames roaring once we got out of our aircraft.

The Germans mounted another attack on Scapa Flow
two nights ago, this time with a sizeable force of Do17s.
The local ack-ack boys managed to shoot one down and
damage another so severely that it crash-landed on a
nearby dummy flarepath, known as a Q-site, evidently
mistaking it for a standard one laid at sea for use by flying
boats. When the soldiers arrived to pick up the German
crew they found them, severely shocked and sitting on the
moor in their rubber dinghy, believing they had come
down in the sea. They must think Scottish water is *very*
hard!

No 29 Squadron is coming to bolster up the night
potential with long-range, twin-engined Blenheims, each
carrying a crew of two when, hopefully, we will be

relieved of much of the night vigils. However their ground crews and equipment were flown in ahead of them this afternoon in another Imperial Airways giant, 'Scylla', which was to stop at Drem overnight. They had some difficulty refuelling her in the gusty conditions and the ground staff had no sooner finished the job and were about to secure her with stout picketing lines, when a particularly strong gust hit the giant side on, causing Scylla to roll slowly on to her back with fiendish sounds of tearing metal and snapping bracing wires, as two crew members still inside scampered up the inside walls and on to the ceiling as she came to rest upside down. The airfield immediately resembled The Charge of the Light Brigade as everyone grabbed tins, bowls, jars, teapots – anything which would hold liquid – in a frantic attempt to catch the petrol which was now pouring from the recently filled tanks. It was an opportunity to augment their petrol rations not to be missed and the boys were quick to seize it, even although most of the precious fluid was being blown away in the high wind. I even caught sight of a large oil drum being hastily wheeled from the maintenance hangar, although I doubt if its enterprising owners got much out of the deal. At all events no one gave up trying, and it was not until the last drop had drained from the tanks that anyone thought of fetching a ladder to release the two blokes trapped inside.

George Pinkerton turned up at lunchtime and immediately disappeared into handover discussions with Douglas, who emerged in time to join me on the dusk patrol, his last sortie with 602 Squadron. Alas we were unable to add anything to his score, which would have made a very fitting farewell present. Douglas has been a member of 602 since 1927, and there were many heavy hearts sitting down to dine him out this evening. Unfortunately Ian

Ferguson and Paul Webb missed the occasion as they
have gone to Montrose for the night to bolster 603's duty
flight which has run out of serviceable aircraft.

April 9th   I was airborne chasing a suspect plot when
Douglas drove out of Drem, so missed his actual departure. What was even more annoying, I didn't catch up
with the intruder!

After months of military inactivity in Europe, aptly
referred to as 'The Phoney War', German armies are
reported to have invaded Denmark today, and are also
on their way to Norway. Rumours are already rife, of
course, amongst them one that 602 Squadron is about to
be involved in the Scandinavian theatre of operations,
although I doubt its authenticity, particularly as it did not
emanate from the Royal Hotel! Nevertheless one senses
a new feeling of awareness, tinged with a certain amount
of relief that something seems to be happening at last. In
contrast, Margaret, Claire and I went for a stroll over the
golf course this evening when everything was so still and
clear that it was hard to believe thousands are fighting for
their lives a few hundred miles away.

April 13th   Heavy fighting is reported in several parts of
Norway, with news that Allied forces have retaken the
ports of Bergen and Trondheim. The Royal Navy is much
involved and must be in the thick of it as HMS *Hunter* is
reported sunk in the Skaggerak and HMS *Hardy* beached
in the Narvik Fjord. All this action, albeit some distance
away, has made us take stock of our own position, and
the station shooting range has suddenly become a popular
venue, with everyone trying to get in much-needed firing
practice, especially with our Smith and Wessons, the only
side arms issued for our personal protection. Earlier

rumours have been partially realized by news that 602 Squadron is moving north tomorrow, one flight to Dyce and the other to Montrose.

George Pinkerton, not yet properly into the driving seat, has decided to accompany B Flight to Dyce, along with the squadron's orderly room staff, leaving Marcus and his boys to fend for themselves at Montrose. So George and I made a recce of both places in the Magister this afternoon to find out what was what. Whilst the A flight billet is passable, we are going to be better off at Dyce, as we will be able to operate from the more comfortable premises of the Aberdeen Flying Club.

April 14th   A flight left for Montrose at eight A.M. and we set off for Dyce three hours later, having stayed on at Drem to hold the fort pending the arrival of 603 Squadron which is apparently being given a spell at Drem to mug up their night flying training. They say that neither Dyce nor Montrose is suitable for night operations which may or may not be a boon when we get there. However, not for us the luxury of an Imperial Airways liner: our ground crews have had to find their own ways in buses, trains or private cars and, give them their due, they have all fetched up at the correct destinations. We are now taking stock of our new surroundings.

Dyce is another grass airfield, but exceptionally soft and muddy after a winter of heavy rain and snow; in fact the only areas fit to land Spitfires are along the camouflage strips where the tar-based paint has knit the soils sufficiently to bear their weight. Surprisingly the resident squadron of Coastal Ansons appears to be making light of the problem and continues to squelch through the mud as if their aircraft were taxiing on a marble floor!

We are also lacking many of the aids we are used to at

Drem. For instance, the RDF chain doesn't stretch this far and, for news of aircraft movements, we will have to rely on information passed from the coastguard stations, and even this has to be transmitted on normal GPO telephone lines. To make matters worse, the only telephone we have is installed in the CO's office. We are told that a new Operations Centre is in an advanced stage of planning!

The Flying Club is situated on the side of the airfield opposite to the main RAF station buildings, thus requiring those on duty to be self-supporting to a certain extent as it is too far to nip over to the Mess for meals, etc, as we did at Drem. However we now have a station commander who is on our wavelength; Wing Commander Finlay Crerar is an Auxiliary who is also a past CO of No 612 (County of Aberdeen) Squadron.

The wing commander was at the Flying Club to greet us and straightaway made us feel at home. However he sounded a note of warning about the proprietor of the Flying Club who apparently retains an office in the building. Mr Grandar Dower is one of Scotland's true pioneer aviators who has a reputation for taking officialdom to task whenever it looks like standing in his way, and Finlay says he was none too pleased that his latest plan to inaugurate an air service from Aberdeen to Norway has been nipped in the bud. So we are counselled to be diplomatic in our dealings with this gentleman, particularly as he is also a Member of Parliament.

Heavy snow is falling again, so B Flight is stood down until tomorrow.

April 18th The weather has been appalling since our arrival, with continuing squalls of sleet and snow turning the airfield into one vast quagmire, so much so that even

the Ansons have had to stop operating. Consequently no
practice flying has been possible and we have been going
around with our fingers crossed that the enemy doesn't
discover our predicament, as we would have enough
bother getting off the field, let alone trying to land back
on it. So we were not too happy when a Coastguard
station reported seeing a Ju88 in the vicinity of Lossiemouth and we were ordered to investigate.

After much slithering and sliding, Findlay Boyd and I
succeeded in getting airborne without couping our aircraft
and sped northwards, where it appeared some form of
aerial carnival was in progress. Five Oxford trainers, two
Whitley bombers and a couple of Coastal Ansons were
cavorting in the area, but we could find nothing which
looked like a Ju88.

Being out of range of Turnhouse's R/T we had no
option but to use our own initiative concerning the validity
of the sighting and I was on the point of calling off the
search when Findlay spotted a stranger at sea level some
way out to sea. This one looked more like a Ju88, so we
gave chase, getting ready to fire as we went along, and
were almost within firing range when it suddenly swooped
up and gave us a plain view of two enormous RAF
roundels. But the type was unknown to us and, suspicious
that it might even be a Ju88 masquerading as a Royal Air
Force aircraft, we continued stalking it as it jinked ahead,
obviously trying to shake us off. Findlay and I were still
wondering what to do when our target settled the problem
by hot-footing it towards the coast and landing at Kinloss
without further ado. We returned to Dyce.

When I telephoned Kinloss to speak to the ops officer,
he told me he had two irate pilots with him, wanting to
know what the blankety blank we thought we had been
up to. Did we not recognize a long-nosed Blenheim when

we saw one? Obviously not, so I am arranging for Intelligence to lay on a few recognition lectures as a matter of urgency! I also arranged for George and me to call on the coastguards this afternoon to find out how reliable was their aircraft sighting procedure.

We went by road and called on some of the stations dotted along the Morayshire coast – Kinnaird's Head, Muchalls, Girdle Ness and The Bullers of Buchan – fine-sounding names and manned by equally fine fellows, all alert and keen as mustard to help. 603 had already arranged with them to display a large white T in front of the station, with the head of the letter pointing in the direction in which the unidentified aircraft was last seen travelling, and claimed that the Heinkel they clobbered off Wick was triggered off by this system. So we would carry it on, particularly as the GPO has promised to give us direct links with our coastguard friends. It remains to be seen whether we will be equally successful.

April 25th   The state of the airfield continues to restrict our practice flying although Harry Moody and I managed to stagger into the air three days ago to investigate a report of ships being attacked off Stonehaven. However they turned out to be naval units carrying out gunnery training, news of which we would probably have learned in advance if we had had the services of a sophisticated operations room.

Marcus Robinson flew up from Montrose yesterday to tell us he has been posted to command No 616 Squadron at Leconfield and that Dunlop Urie will be taking over A Flight. Fortunately he had had the foresight to bring with him enough champagne to float a battleship so we were able to celebrate his coming promotion in proper style. That now makes me the senior flight commander!

There was a devil of a flap on this morning when Turnhouse reported that they had picked up plots of an intruder heading in our direction, although the RDF plots had gone off their table long before nearing our part of the coast. Paul Webb and I took off to have a look, more in hope than in anger, but saw nothing in the misty conditions, which was fortunate in the circumstances for, although the intruder eventually turned out to be a Luftwaffe Arado seaplane, it was being flown by three adventurous Norwegians who had nipped it from under the Germans' noses and coaxed it across the North Sea with nothing more than an old school atlas to help. They had touched down in the sea some four miles off the coast and taxied the rest of the way into Peterhead harbour.

As soon as we heard about this Ian Ferguson rushed off to Peterhead by car to bring them back to Dyce, telling us later he was surprised the old seaplane got as far as it did, for it was just about on its last legs. He brought the three intrepid Norwegians straight to dispersal where they greeted us in great humour. 'Johannsen!' announced a massive man wearing a lumberman's jacket and ski-boots, and offering a hand the size of a small tree trunk. 'Ve are happy to be here!' 'Johnstone,' I replied, taking the proferred hand. 'Ve most be brodders den,' was his rejoinder, nearly felling me with a friendly clap on the back. His companions, although of slightly less formidable stature, are equally exuberant and it seems the name Johnstone is enough to cast me in the role of mentor from now on. But I have handed them on to Finlay Crerar for the time being, and I hear the intelligence officer is having a hard time getting a coherent story from our welcome guests. Apparently whisky has been in short supply in Norway recently!

* * *

April 27th   Things haven't been going too well in Norway recently and Bomber Command has been putting a lot of effort into supporting our beleaguered troops. Consequently many returning bombers have been landing back at airfields along the Moray Firth rather than facing the long night haul back to their bases in Lincolnshire and Yorkshire. However the extra traffic is creating havoc with the coastguard reporting system for every movement is being processed by each station in turn as the bombers creep along the coast in search of a suitable landing ground. Now, therefore, we are kept up all night, jotting down the relevant information: John MacLean from The Bullers of Buchan has just been on – 'Ah've got an aeroplane here,' he announced, after ensuring we had logged his name correctly. 'Ah canna see it but ah can hear it; it's gaein bizz bizz bizz; Guid nicht!' And so it goes on as each coastguard station in turn passes its particular version of the same movement.

Our Norwegian colleagues are still weatherbound at Dyce and Finlay Crerar has asked the padre to put in an extra prayer for the weather to improve as his stocks of malt whisky are diminishing at an alarming rate. The Norwegians have been cleared by our security people and are now waiting for conditions to improve sufficiently to let them fly the seaplane to Helensburgh, and we are bidden to make sure they get there. I have not previously had the pleasure of escorting an enemy aircraft but hope all ack-ack units en route will be properly briefed before we set out. But the Norwegians are not the only victims of the bad weather; Bing Cross, an old friend and CO of 46 Squadron, was forced to land at Kintore the other day whilst on his way to Norway to recce the possibility of taking his Hurricanes across. However we sent a car to pick him up and drive him on to Invergordon where he was able to scrounge a lift in a Sunderland flying boat.

April 30th   A load of timber and a number of joiners turned up at the clubhouse this morning, apparently forerunners of the contractors to build a proper operations room. They were joined two hours later by a couple of Post Office engineers, and between them created such a din with their hammering and sawing that I was glad of the excuse to get out and visit Aberdeen where I gave a lecture to the gunners bedded down in the Beach Pavilion. I talked to them about fighter operations rooms.

Bing looked in on his way back from Norway and reports that our lads have their backs to the wall. Apparently the Germans are in control of most of the country and the only British fighters still flying are being operated from a frozen lake. Bing hopes to take some of his Hurricanes to join Baldy Donaldson's Gladiators, as they lost many aircraft when their frozen airfield was bombed and they fell through the shattered ice.

1940
May

May 2nd The Germans have started operating from captured airfields in Norway and there is a noticeable stepping up of enemy activity in the North of Scotland, particularly against the Navy at Scapa Flow. We are spending many frustrating hours trying to make contact with these raiders, many of them mine layers, but a lack of RDF cover and the continuing dicey weather is making our task extremely difficult. Nevertheless we press on as hard as ever and I managed to carry out a couple of night sorties recently, although still most unhappy about the state of the airfield.

The high ground all around is hidden in rain clouds and this, too, is taking its toll. Only last night a Whitley, fully bombed up and part of a force on its way to lend support in Norway, crashed into a nearby hillside and blew up on impact, killing five of the eight on board. The others, who miraculously escaped death, are nevertheless gravely injured and are in hospital in Aberdeen. A Henley also piled up near Huntly this morning, killing both occupants. We felt particularly sad about this incident as the pilot's wife was with us at dispersal, waiting to pick up her husband, when news of his crash came through and, even worse, we had actually seen the Henley when it fleetingly broke cloud overhead in its unsuccessful search for the airfield. Once again Finlay Crerar came to the rescue and took charge of the poor girl, who is utterly bowled over by the tragedy.

The news from Norway is also grim, with a full-scale

evacuation now in train. Naturally Bomber Command is stepping up its effort and the local air space is full of Hampdens and Whitleys day and night, which is giving us a feeling of impotence that we are unable to do more to help. We tried marking out a strip on the airfield corresponding to the dimensions of an aircraft carrier's landing deck and proved we could, at a pinch, operate at sea without the use of arrester gear. But Stuffy Dowding won't hear of it; he says Fighter Command is already seriously under strength because of its commitments in France and cannot be jeopardized further.

We are having new markings on our aircraft: yellow rings are to be painted outside the fuselage roundels and vertical red, white and blue flashes emblazoned on the tail fins. Furthermore the entire undersides of our machines are henceforth to be pale blue instead of the present pattern of half black and half white. As Q was already overdue for a major inspection, I flew her to Drem this afternoon to have all the jobs done together and brought back S, already resplendent in its new livery.

As the war is clearly entering a more active and ugly phase, George and I have invited our wives to join us in Aberdeen while the going is still good. Fortunately we've been able to get them booked into the Woodside House Hotel, which is only a few minutes' drive from dispersal.

May 7th   The girls were quick to react and turned up on Saturday afternoon, obviously keen to see us as neither has yet asked for a refund on her train fare. Happily, too, there has been a quiet spell recently and we've been able to spend some time with our wives, even managing to introduce them to the coastguard stations, at one of which they pulled up their skirts and went for a paddle on a nearby beach. When we later took the ladies back to dispersal, the boys rose to the occasion and produced a first-class afternoon tea.

Jackie Hoyle runs the station flight at Dyce, consisting of four Tiger Moths, and has been using the aircraft to mount his own version of a dusk patrol. He gets his chaps to cruise up and down the coast looking for anything suspicious but, as these little trainers carry neither wireless nor armament, I am unclear what they are meant to do if they come up against a U-boat or a Heinkel reconnaissance plane. Yet it shows the right spirit and I offered to lend a hand when not otherwise engaged, having in mind another means of taking the ground crews for a flight. However I soon found out my mistake for, on the only occasion I ventured into the air, I nearly froze to death in the open cockpit at 4,000 feet. Corporal Burnett didn't think much of it either.

The new operations room is beginning to take shape but, in the absence of a proper telephone switchboard, we now have twenty-three separate instruments to give direct communication with all manner of interested parties. But it has its drawbacks for, whenever a telephone rings, whoever is on duty has to run up and down the row of instruments to track it down, often replacing the wrong receiver in his panic to catch the caller before he rings off. Archie McKellar got into a frightful fankle with it last night when he thought he was speaking to the sergeants' mess, only to find he was delivering a rocket to the AOC.

May 10th The station commander has gone to a lot of trouble to draw up orders outlining what everyone is supposed to do in the event of an air attack. As far as we are concerned the instructions are simple; pilots will sit in their cockpits, wearing tin hats, whilst the ground crews will take shelter in the nearest trench. Crerar decided to try it out yesterday and unexpectedly sounded the hooters without telling anyone it was only a practice alert. The outcome would have been quite funny if it hadn't been so uncomfortable for, while we pilots did as told and took to our cockpits weighed down with metal headgear, the duty crews obediently leaped into their trenches, only to find them half full of water left over from the recent rains. They swear they will shelter behind a hedge in future.

Harry Moody and I chased a Bogey this morning, but Ops could only tell us it was last seen flying at 2,000 feet somewhere between Bell Rock and Fraserburgh. Because of the low height we thought it unlikely to be hostile and were not surprised to catch up with an Oxford trainer near Stonehaven, whereupon control told us to make it land at Dyce to account for its unannounced presence. So Harry took station on one side of the trainer whilst I did likewise on the other and did our best with hand signals to get the message across. All we got in response, however, was a cheery wave from the pilot whilst the Oxford continued on its merry way. The Controller didn't seem unduly worried by this and told us to let it go and return to base, leaving us thoroughly chastened that our aggressive intentions had been so contemptuously brushed aside!

Signals have been pouring into the office all day and our twenty-three telephones ringing incessantly. Germany has now invaded Belgium and Holland whilst other targets in Northern France have come under heavy air attack, which has resulted in our leave being stopped and anyone already away recalled forthwith.

The war is certainly hotting up with a vengeance!

May 14th   The Ops room is almost completed and additional personnel are being drafted in, although I don't know where they are going to find the space to work, as most of it is already taken up with our bedding and other pieces of domestic equipment. A brand new teleprinter arrived yesterday along with a pretty little WAAF to operate it, but she is a shy creature, clearly uncomfortable in such a masculine environment. The poor soul was most put out when some who had been sleeping at dispersal overnight unexpectedly appeared in pyjamas, although she unbent slightly once they had shaved and got into their uniforms.

Mary, for that is her name, sat at her machine throughout the day with nothing better to do than twiddle her thumbs and it was not until a Post Office engineer came in this evening and asked her what she was doing, that it transpired the machine was not connected at the other end. However about an hour after she had left in a high dudgeon, the machine suddenly stuttered into life and a higgledy-piggledy jumble of letters started appearing on the paper scroll. Archie was nearby at the time and waited until it stopped, whereupon he laboriously tapped out a message to the unseen operator enquiring whether she was blonde or brunette. The machine replied with indignant haste that it was being manned by an airman!

Another batch of Norwegians arrived today, having been brought off in one of our destroyers, and all bore tales of the heroic resistance being put up by their compatriots. While they were at dispersal an elderly lady rang from Aberdeen and told us in an agitated voice that she had just seen a party of German paratroopers landing on the sea front. However our visitors, well used to seeing the real thing, reckoned such an occurrence was unlikely without some sort of previous warning, although it shows how jumpy some people are becoming. Also, according to our pilots' reports, funny things are happening on the

R/T, so I took off in S to hear for myself. Right enough, many operational instructions are being subjected to jamming, but all I could do was to report it to Group Headquarters and hope they can sort it out.

Heavy fighting is now reported throughout Belgium, Holland and Luxembourg and the Government has cancelled the Whitsun holiday in view of the worsening situation. However things have been unnaturally quiet in this neck of the woods, the only excitement being caused by Ian Ferguson landing on a marker board and knocking the tail wheel off his Spitfire.

May 19th The wireless has been reporting a ding-dong struggle taking place near the River Meuse, which may be why the Luftwaffe is leaving us so much alone these days. We are able to take full advanage of the lull, too, for the sun has put in a welcome appearance and someone has found a few deckchairs and erected them on the verandah. A few of us even ventured into town the other evening and saw a film featuring Marlene Dietrich and James Stewart, when we came away with the feeling that it was somehow improper to be watching a German actress, however talented, performing in a British picture house.

A Highland battalion has turned up to protect vital installations on the station, although it appears 602 Squadron is not sufficiently important to be included, as none are to be deployed on our side of the airfield. On the other hand they may consider we are well able to look after ourselves, although I'd have thought the new Ops set-up would have merited consideration even though the GPO has forgotten to install the Ops B line, the most important connection of all!

I have just been on the line to Montrose and Dunlop

Urie tells me Hector MacLean had a narrow escape this morning when he was run into by a Master trainer whilst taxiing out for take-off. Apparently the trainer was fitted with practice bombs which exploded on impact and I hate to think what would have happened had they been the real things. Apart from anything else the squadron would have been on the lookout for another pilot!

The Spitfire's guns are spaced out along the leading edges, four on each wing, and must be adjusted every so often to ensure their fire power can be concentrated at a predetermined distance in front of the aircraft. Periodic alignments are carried out by the armourers who first raise the machine into a flying position before using geometrical calculations to sight each gun in turn on pre-positioned markings on the door of the hangar. A couple of armourers were doing just that this afternoon when the bloke in the cockpit accidentally pressed the firing button, causing all eight Brownings to spew straight through the hangar door and blowing the cap off an airman working on an aircraft inside. But the fusillade didn't stop there; bullets continued into the clubhouse itself, passing through both walls of the kitchen and into the offices beyond, where a piece of molten lead, spent but still very hot, plopped on to the desk in front of Gandar Gower who was about to put his signature on a letter of complaint to the station commander. That missive was immediately torn up and superseded by another considerably more forceful, which led to the incident being raised in the House.

The incident has done little to enhance our standing with the Honourable Member although all is not yet lost, for the AOC has just been on the phone to tell us we will be returning to Drem very soon.

*   *   *

May 27th Eight days have passed since the AOC's call and we are still at Dyce. Furthermore the rains have returned. However, uncomfortable things have been happening in France where the Germans have now taken Amiens and Arras, forcing our troops to retreat towards the Channel ports and placing a heavy burden on Fighter Command, which has been called in to help. We hear there have been serious losses, which is giving rise to a belief that we may be destined for a base in the south instead of the expected return to Drem. So we are giving priority to getting all our aircraft on the top line.

Three Ansons lobbed in yesterday but two came to grief when landing in the mud. Fortunately a new tail unit for Ferguson's aircraft was in the third, so Sergeant Connor's lads were able to have it fitted and bring the flight back to full strength. Shortly afterwards four Tiger Moths landed unscathed, all flown by girls of the Air Transport Auxiliary, who were taking them to Lossiemouth to go into storage. I discovered I was acquainted with two of the girls, Margaret Cunnison and Mona Friedlander, the former having slogged through training for a Commercial Pilot's Licence with me. However my previous meeting with Mona had been under more erotic circumstances when helping to extricate her from the remains of a greenhouse into which she had crashed during a forced landing in the summer of 1938. On that occasion Mona was wearing a pair of abbreviated shorts and I was among those privileged to assist in removing splinters of glass from her shapely legs.

Having delivered their Moths to Lossiemouth the girls came back to Dyce in an Anson flown by yet another aviatrix and we persuaded all five to stop overnight. The success of the ensuing party didn't come to light until we realized two of the girls had flown off next morning without their parachutes. Fortunately we were able to send them on in another aircraft which was going their way.

Boulogne has now fallen, which means the BEF really has its back to the wall, and we were in the course of discussing our prospects of becoming involved when the AOC arrived unannounced to confirm the original intention to move us back to Drem. Soon after Saul's arrival I was scrambled to investigate a sound plot off Findhorn, but it turned out to be nothing more aggressive than a small motor boat with a blown gasket.

I was able to borrow one of Hoyle's Tiger Moths this evening and take our WAAF teleprinter expert for a spin as a sort of parting present. Although it was her first flight, Mary said she enjoyed it, which shows how much she has blossomed under the squadron's experienced tutelage!

May 28th   I kept myself off the flying programme yesterday to help with the packing up. However Paul, Harry and Glyn all carried out patrols over the Moray Firth, although the plots turned out to be friendly. A signal also came in from Group Headquarters about our move stressing, among other things, that it was important for us to maintain an operational posture throughout. So I left at dawn with Yellow Section and reached Drem in time for breakfast. Dunlop arrived from Montrose with Red Section soon after.

Drem was looking strangely deserted, as 603 had already gone and one flight of 264 Squadron had also pushed off, with the other following as soon as we touched down. So, breakfasting and making myself presentable, I called on the station commander to let him know he hadn't been left entirely defenceless. The group captain

seemed taken aback to see me, for I don't think he had
realized it was 602 Squadron that was returning to torment
him. However he put a brave face on it and wished us
well, whereupon I brought Yellow Section to readiness to
wait for Donald Jack and Blue Section, with Archie
bringing up the rear with Green. In fact Archie didn't
arrive until after midnight, thus clocking up the squadron's first operational move in full darkness.

The BBC news is bad. King Leopold of Belgium has
now thrown in the towel, thus giving the Germans a clear
route to Dunkirk, where the BEF is concentrating. Our
summons surely cannot be delayed much longer.

May 31st   We are delighted to be back at Drem, for it is
a happy station and we can all be together again. The
squadron has been split in three for the past six weeks, as
our Second Line Servicing section remained at Drem
whilst the other two flights divided themselves between
Montrose and Dyce. I am particularly glad to have the
maintenance chaps nearby again as Q has been surging on
take-off recently and I can now put her into the hangar
and have the problem dealt with by the experts. Hopefully
they will be fitting armour plating behind the pilot's seat
at the same time.

I found Douglas Farquhar at Hillview Cottage when I
called in to let Claire know we were back. He had flown
north to collect some papers and tells me he is thoroughly
enjoying life at Martlesham Heath, although being kept
very busy. He certainly looks well and hopes to pay us
another visit in the near future. Claire was also pleased to
have us back and suggested Margaret should pack up her
job in Glasgow and join forces with her in Gullane for the
time being. Margaret didn't take much persuading and
has taken up residence in the cottage this evening.

No 605 Squadron arrived yesterday to fill the slot left vacant by 264. However they are in a sorry state, having been involved in the fighting south, losing nine aircraft and four pilots in a space of six days. But the Warwick-shire lads are made of stern stuff and I feel sure Walter Churchill will have them knocked them into shape again in next to no time. At all events we are delighted to have them alongside.

1940
June

June 4th Too many fighters are being destroyed on the ground in France these days, often because dispersal orders are being blatantly ignored, and we have no intention of being accused of similar neglect. So George and I flew to Macmerry in the Magister to have another look at the place and found work on the strip was completed. However the grass has not been cut and, after touchdown, we assumed the role of threshing machine as our prop mowed through the undergrowth when we taxied towards the clubhouse. Apart from that, Macmerry will make a suitable dispersal area so, having arranged with the resident engineer for the grass to be cut, George and I returned to Drem to work out a roster.

In the meantime our Spitfires are becoming ever more sophisticated, with rear-view mirrors fitted above their windscreens which should cut down the chance of a cricked neck every time one is embroiled in a dogfight. I can't think why no one has thought of them before. So, resplendent in new liveries, with the added protection from a strip of solid armour-plating behind the seats and the promise of constant speed airscrews to come, we will soon be ready to take on anything. I wonder if anyone will suggest fitting traffic indicators!

The enemy has left us severely alone for the past two days, probably because most of the fighting was centering on Dunkirk, where the BEF had been holed up awaiting evacuation. So, having sat at readiness throughout the weekend without being called on, I considered it safe to sneak off to the cottage for a spell and possibly scrounge lunch from the girls. To my surprise, however, the AOC was already there and immediately sent me back with news that 602 Squadron was moving to Northolt this very afternoon to provide much-needed protection for the big evacuation.

George had already got the message when I reached the airfield to find a hell of a flap going on, with essential stores being urgently packed and loaded into two Bombay transports which had turned up to take us South. The job was done in record time after which we could do no more than sit around at dispersal, biting fingernails and wondering what we were being let in for. So the afternoon wore on with no orders to get moving. 'Just stay where you are,' they said whenever anyone rang Control for information. 'We'll tell you when to go!' And thus it went on – three o'clock, four o'clock, half past four until, shortly before five, word came through that our move had been cancelled. At that point I wish I had kept count of the number of visits I'd made to the loo during the afternoon!

Birdie Saul was still at the cottage when I got back, just in time to catch the BBC news bulletin, with the Prime Minister announcing a successful conclusion to the evacuation from Dunkirk. But it leaves a large question mark. What next?

June 7th   The weather is playing ducks and drakes again; one minute bitterly cold, the next warm and sunny. However we are settling into our old routine after the excitement of the past few days and have been using the time trying out a number of new battle formations. I led the whole squadron the other day during an exercise in which 602 Squadron was acting as targets for Defiants of

141 Squadron and a few Hurricanes from 605, during which we were able to put into practice some of our new tactics. Some are good, but not all, and we'll have to put more work into them to be fully effective.

To break the monotony of night duty I took advantage of the clear weather and got airborne around midnight to do a spot of local flying. Climbing to 32,000 feet over Drem I was treated to a marvellous view, with visibility only limited by the curvature of the horizon, and able to see well beyond the lights of Glasgow. However it is all too easy to wander afield in such circumstances and it was not until Paul Webb suddenly popped up alongside, flashing the challenge of the day, that I realized how far I had strayed. It seems I had become an unidentified plot on the controller's table and Paul had been sent up to investigate. Although cursing myself for my carelessness, it is comforting to know the system is working so effectively!

In a further bid to extend mobility, we decided to investigate the disused airfield at Tranent as a possible alternative landing ground. So the CO laid on an exercise last Thursday to test how long it would take a refueller and a fire engine to get there in the event of us having to land. I took off with Green Section and circled over Tranent, only three miles east of Drem, and waited for the vehicles to arrive, not being permitted to land until at least the fire services were in position. In spite of the short distance, however, they got completely lost en route and it was over an hour before the vehicles turned up and we we were able to land. By then, of course, we were sorely in need of refuelling! But worse was to come, for the field was so badly rutted that our aircraft nearly rattled to pieces while taxiing in and I have recommended to George we don't use Tranent unless as a last resort.

A haar started rolling in this evening and we know from experience that this sort of dense mist can last for days. I have therefore cancelled the air firing practice at Acklington laid on for tomorrow and suggested we might take up Group's offer of allowing up to ten percent to take a few days off. George, as commanding officer and therefore first in the queue, has pushed off to inspect his rhubarb farm in Renfrewshire, so leaving me in charge.

June 10th The haar persisted for the next thirty-six hours, but lifted sufficiently last night for Dunlop and Hector to fly cover over an inbound convoy. They were no sooner in position than the mist returned and, although Red Section was recalled immediately, they had a difficult time trying to get down. Dunlop scraped in unscathed but Hector had a much more difficult time and finally thumped down like a drunken hen after several abortive attempts, breaking off a wing tip and buckling the undercarriage in the process. However the maintenance boys rose to the occasion as usual and repaired the machine overnight. So we are still up to full strength.

A warm sun soon burnt off the remains of the mist and, by the time I took off on a patrol in the early afternoon, it was so warm that I dispensed with normal flying gear and stooged around Bell Rock in shirt sleeves and with the cockpit canopy open. Later, taxiing back to dispersal and looking more like a beachcomber than a fighter pilot, I was embarrassed to find Lord Trenchard talking with the lads. However the Great Man made no comment about my unorthodox garb; indeed he was in terrific form and had us rolling in the aisles in next to no time and it is not hard to appreciate why he has been such a marvellous leader of men all these years. On closer inspection I became less concerned about my own appearance when I saw that Boom's rigout wasn't entirely regular either, for he still favours the old pattern slacks and tunic and continues to carry a white walking stick of the sort which went out of service in the early thirties. It was like a breath of fresh air to be in his company, even for such a short time, and we all hope he will pay us another visit soon.

The AOC had been escorting the noble lord and, as soon as we had seen him off in his Dominie, Birdie and I returned to the cottage and persuaded the girls to come for a swim. He has also given me permission to stop the night instead of doing my stint at Macmerry.

The news came through that the aircraft carrier *Glorious* has been sunk by a pocket battleship in the North Sea in the course of evacuating troops and aircraft from Norway and that Baldy Donaldson and his squadron have gone down with the ship. Bing Cross was also on board but, thankfully, news has just come in that he has been picked up from a raft, suffering from severe frostbite.

June 14th All manner of things are happening on the Continent, not least being the entry of Italy into the war on the side of Germany. I suppose Mussolini is hoping for a share of the spoils, particularly in the Mediterranean, where his navy should be of considerable help to our enemies. News has also come in that the French forces are crumbling, the German armies fast approaching Paris and the French Government has done a bunk to somewhere less vulnerable than the capital city. Winston Churchill is doing his best to keep their hopes alive by offering joint citizenship with Britain, but I fear it may be too late. Whatever the outcome, however, our prospects are now mighty grim and it looks as if we are going to be on our own.

Again we have been left in a vacuum, with the Luftwaffe leaving us in disdainful isolation. But we are not idle and are packing in as much training as possible while the going is good. Furthermore, we tried out Macmerry two nights ago and found it a very pleasant spot in which to spend the night. Our equipment officer has rustled up a number of beds and bedding to go with them, and we were given rations to prepare in the kitchen. Harry Moody was appointed chef for the occasion and manfully stripped to his underpants (the spell of hot weather is still with us) whilst he set about producing a fry-up of bacon and eggs. All went well until a link of sausages was added, when boiling fat spurted in every direction, much of it catching the cook on his tenderest parts, after which he resigned his post in considerable discomfort. However the emergency was salved to a certain extent when Alastair Grant unexpectedly turned up with a bottle of champagne with which to celebrate his engagement, and Harry was allowed a double ration.

Returning to Drem next morning after carrying out a convoy patrol on the way, a signal was waiting for Harry saying that both he and Pat Lyall have been awarded their commissions. Fortunately the Mess stocks are holding out as a suitable celebration followed in the evening at which our newly-formed station dance orchestra put in an appearance. This outfit has been knocked together from within the station's resources after someone discovered that three airmen had once been professional muscians, two having been members of Geraldo's band in the Mayfair and the other with Jack Jackson. At any rate they made a jolly good noise and added considerably to the success of the evening.

I also heard I am next in line for leave.

*   *   *

June 18th Having spent a night with my parents in Glasgow, Margaret and I have come on to Prestwick and are astounded at the changes which have taken place since our last visit. A large part of the north end is presently in the hands of contractors busily re-erecting the Palace of Engineering from the 1938 Glasgow Empire Exhibition, which Scottish Aviation Limited has purchased from the authorities. A hangar of equally imposing dimensions is also going up here and David McIntyre tells me he hopes his company will one day be able to produce its own aircraft. It sounds an ambitious programme but, knowing Mac, I won't be surprised if it succeeds.

But the four-engined Fokker is no longer with the Navigation School. Apparently it came to grief on take-off a few months ago when its two pilots disagreed whether they could get airborne when one engine began to cough. One said 'yes' and pushed open the throttles whilst the other said 'no' and closed them again, after which the pantomine was repeated until they ran out of airfield and the massive aeroplane ploughed straight into a hen run alongside the Old Mill and split itself in two. Happily no one was seriously injured and the forty occupants managed to scramble clear through a large gash in the wreckage. They say the hens were the only things to get airborne that morning.

Having spent a happy evening at the Orangefield Hotel with many old friends we went on to spend a few days with my uncle and aunt who live in Uplawmoor, a small village not far from Barrhead. Archie is a retired banker with a distinguished Army career during the Great War, and is now a leading light in the local ARP. Not to be outdone, Auntie Jean has followed suit and both are most conscientious about their duties and never go anywhere without their tin hats and gas masks. However, when an alert sounded while we were there, I was surprised to see Jean dashing off to her post, fully togged up with rubber boots, stirrup and gas mask, but sporting an enormous tea cosy on her head instead of the prescribed tin hat. She complains that the latter gives her a headache.

France is seeking an Armistice with Germany, which really puts us on the spot. I wonder whether the United States will now pitch in and lend a hand?

June 21st Arrived back at Gullane to find Claire in a state of jitters as the place is buzzing with rumours about more German parachutists, this time purporting to have landed in Aberlady Bay, not far from the cottage. Although this is nothing more than a rumour, the district is nevertheless swarming with Royal Engineers and civilian contractors busily putting up concrete pillboxes along the shoreline, and erecting jagged poles on the beaches themselves. The latter are being put there to prevent gliders from landing but, unfortunately, they will also prevent us from indulging in any more midnight bathing.

Things have been happening on the airfield too. A system of passwords has been put into operation in our absence and I had difficulty getting on to the station. Indeed I had to ring dispersal from the guardroom to fetch someone to vouch for me. Once there I found that five new pilots have turned up – Pilot Officer Nigel Rose and Sergeants Sprague, Proctor, Elcome and Whipps – but none with any operational experience. I also find that Archie McKellar has been promoted and posted as a flight commander to 605 Squadron, which will be a considerable loss to 602. So we have another hefty training job ahead although Birdie Saul is going to have Micky Mount posted to the squadron after he is given a proper Spitfire Conversion course. Muspratt-Williams will then become Birdie's ADC.

Business suddenly became brisk today, possibly an extension of the prevailing jitters, and the squadron was sent on no less than eleven patrols throughout the period. But we had no joy on any.

June 24th   The haar rolled in again a couple of days ago, clamping us firmly to the ground. It was unfortunate, as something hostile came over yesterday, but disappeared again when the gunners fired off a few rounds in its general direction. I suppose Jerry was just as frustrated as we are at not being able to see anything under the blanket of fog. But the weather cleared this morning, when I took the opportunity to fly to Turnhouse to arrange with George Denholm, CO of 603 Squadron, for our two squadrons to co-ordinate the readiness states in order that we may concentrate on training our new pilots. As expected, George has been most helpful and I arrived back at Drem to find the training programme well under way and the circuit full of Spitfires doing circuits and bumps. Whoopsie take-offs were much in evidence as the tyros struggled to master the intricacies of the under-carriage lever.

The news is bleak from across the Channel. The French have signed an Armistice with Germany and Italy, under the terms of which they will be allowed to set up a puppet government in Vichy and continue to run the southern half of the country from there. Alas, everything else, including the northern and western coastlines, will be under the Nazi jackboot, which will give them a conveni-ent springboard from which to launch an invasion.

*   *   *

June 25th I took a day off yesterday and spent it at the cottage. Birdie arrived later with news that Charles Keary's departure is imminent and that he will be replaced by Dick Atcherley, one of the legendary twins whose exploits are well known throughout the Royal Air Force. I can think of no greater contrast in personalties between the old and the new bosses, for Charles has always been a strict disciplinarian, inclined to be pedantic and aloof, whereas Dick is the exact opposite, being very much one of the boys and unorthodox in the extreme. He was also a member of the Schneider Trophy team which won the cup outright for Britain in 1932, to say nothing of having a reputation for knocking off policemen's helmets. It will be an interesting change.

Nearer home however, and with the safety of our nearest and dearest in mind, Birdie and I started to rig up an air raid shelter for our wives, making use of an old pigsty as the foundation. So when Micky and Spratt made a friendly call on the AOC they were immediately dragooned into helping, the four of us then spending the afternoon reinforcing the erection with sheets of corrugated iron surrounded by sandbags, before equipping it with camp beds, a supply of tinned goods, drinking water and a hurricane lamp. Stepping back to admire the finished product, Birdie told the girls they are to go to the shelter whenever the hooters sound, under dire threat to cut off their supply of gin should they fail to comply.

Bad news came down from the other side of the airfield. Barry Goodwin of 605 Squadron has just spun in near Dunbar and been killed instantly. It is a shame to go like that after surviving the hardships of Dunkirk.

June 26th After the exertions of putting up the shelter, I was weary and hoping for a quiet night in the cottage. But it was not to be and I was recalled to the flight shortly after ten o'clock as a number of X-raids were reported in the area, with reports of bombing near Lanark and Grangemouth.

Was ordered off around midnight and vectored towards Edinburgh where the beams of several searchlights were probing the night sky. I was climbing through 7,000 feet when I saw three beams suddenly converging ahead of me and, to my astonishment, clearly outlining the unmistakable silhouette of a Heinkel 111. 'Tally-ho!' I shouted into the R/T, switching on the reflector sight and turning the safety catch to the 'fire' position, the adrenalin now pumping madly in my veins. I was hardly aware of the ack-ack bursting round the Bandit as I opened wide the throttle and raced towards the target. The bomber was now brilliantly lit by the powerful beams and I suddenly found it growing uncomfortably fast as I sped in for the attack; so fast that I almost collided with it and had to pull away sharply before firing a single round. Fortunately the searchlight boys were on the ball and held the Heinkel in their beams while I took a deep breath and came back for a second bite at the cherry. This time I was more circumspect and approached slowly from dead astern before letting fly with all eight Brownings, when my victim disappeared from view. At first I thought I'd blown it out of the sky until noticing my windscreen was covered in oil thrown back from the bomber. So I had at least hit the wretched thing.

Flying to one side I could see flames and black smoke pouring from the Heinkel's port engine and a quick glance at my altimeter showed he was on the way down, so I stayed there and monitored his descent, helped greatly by the searchlights which continued holding the target firmly in their beams, and it was not until the Heinkel was down to a few hundred feet that they lost him. I too became temporarily disorientated at this point and it took a few moments to readjust and establish my position as being over the coastline near Dunbar. However I picked up my victim again by the flames from his burning engine and followed him towards the sea and watched, fascinated, as its landing light was switched on just before it crashed into the sea with a great splash, the beam from the landing light growing ever greener as the aircraft disappeared below the waves. Strangely I felt no sense of elation; only a sudden feeling of loneliness.

I circled the spot where I had last seen the light and pulled off the colours of the day, a red-red Very cartridge, to alert the rescue services before returning to Drem, where I discovered that I had delivered the coup de grâce directly overhead and in full view of the lads at dispersal. LAC Campbell was first to jump on the wing as I taxied in, pressing a mug of steaming cocoa into my hand, and he was closely followed by Flight Sergeant Connors who immediately pulled the airman away with a shouted oath to 'fetch the bleedin' pot and paint a flippin' swastika on the cockpit combing!' It now crossed my mind that Margaret and Claire must also have witnessed my triumph, but it was ages before I could shrug off the Intelligence Officer and get to the phone. 'What did you think of that?' I shouted down the instrument when Margaret answered. There was a pregnant silence. 'What did I think of what?' she replied eventually. Rather than risk their supply of gin, the girls had gone to the shelter and missed it all!

It transpires that three of the four crew have been brought ashore at Dunbar and are now under Army guard. According to the police superintendent who rang through, one is a proper little Nazi who spat in a nurse's face when she tried to dress a cut eye, so I am particularly glad my first blood has put the little so-and-so out of action for the time being.

June 28th Was trying to catch up on lost sleep this morning when summoned to the station commander's office to find our new master doing his best to humour a couple of disgruntled Army officers who were complaining loudly that their entire battalion had been stood-to as a result of the signal I pulled off over the crashed Heinkel. Through a lack of adequate communication neither had thought to advise the other about their respective codes of practice, and it is only now we hear that a two-star red signal to the Army means the country is being invaded from the sea. However Batchy quickly settled the matter over a few drinks in the Officers' Mess.

Encouraged by last night's success I put myself on the state again and was scrambled shortly before midnight to intercept another Bandit reported over Edinburgh. The controller assured me the target was dead ahead but failed to add it was coming towards me so, just as I was climbing through 18,000 feet at full throttle, I caught a fleeting glimpse of a He111 streaking past my starboard wing tip, but going in the opposite direction. Although I pulled hard on the stick and gave chase, he high-tailed it for home and I never managed to make contact, in spite of flying eastwards to the limit of my endurance.

Drem had been put under a Red Alert when I rejoined the circuit and the landing path had been extinguished, so I was forced to fly round the circuit while Ian Ferguson and Paul Webb dashed out and lit the first three flares. Even so it was a difficult landing as I kept losing sight of the abbreviated flarepath behind the exhaust flames every time I closed the throttle. I finally arrived off a violent sideslip, managing to yank the Spit straight just before hitting the deck. However Batchy was at dispersal when I walked in and promised to apply his inventive mind to the problem.

June 29th It appears Batchy has more important things on his mind than how best to spoon-feed his pilots, for I was summoned to his office for the second morning running, to find Walter Churchill already there and wearing a rueful smile. Clearly something was amiss. 'Useless! Utterly useless!' was the greeting on entering the office when it took a second or two to realize the CO was referring to our efforts to spread out our aircraft. 'Let's go and find a better way of doing it – now!'

So we piled into Keary's pride and joy, now liberally bedaubed with camouflage paint, and were whisked off with Batchy at the wheel on a whirlwind tour of East Lothian, in search of alternative dispersal sites. But none was forthcoming and even Atcherley admitted that Tranent, in its present state, is too risky, although it won't surprise me if he commandeers half the Council's work force to level it off. He is that sort of chap.

I have sneaked off to the cottage this evening, hoping to avoid a third summons to the station commander's office tomorrow morning. As I write, however, I hear Jerry keeping up the pressure and two Spitfires being scrambled to deal with it. However A Flight is on duty tonight and Dunlop and Donald are more than capable of keeping the enemy at bay.

June 30th The month is ending more peacefully than it began and I managed to take Sergeant Sprague on his first operational patrol, when he acquitted himself well. I later took Moody on another convoy patrol and made him take the lead to give him experience at the front end. Finding nothing further on the board after coming back from this effort, I nipped off early and joined the AOC for a game of golf on the links at Gullane. Alas, we had to abandon the game after seven holes as we had both lost all our balls.

1940
July

July 1st June may have ended on a peaceful note, but July is already making up for it. I led two sorties today, one of which might have reaped a reward but for our incompetence.

On the first occasion Control put us on to a firm plot, but it turned out to be a stern chase and Jerry was able to show a clean pair of heels. We chased him for over seventy miles out to sea but eventually had to turn back when weather in the area became atrocious, with a solid wall of rain clouds stretching from sea level to goodness knows what height, as we were still in it at 25,000 feet. We were not long back on the ground when lunch was interrupted and Paul and I were again scrambled, this time to Dunbar where the cloud, although still wide-spread, was broken in places.

Approaching from inland at 5,000 feet, we caught sight of a Ju88 nipping from cloud to cloud and heading straight for Dunbar. But our target must have seen us first for, before we got anywhere near firing range, he jettisoned his bombs and swung for home, after which a real cat and mouse chase developed, with the Junkers dodging from one bit of cover to the next and Paul and I jockeying for position on either side. Unfortunately the breaks grew fewer the farther east we went and, although we both managed to get in a few long-range shots at the target, he was still steaming along merrily when last spotted, boring into the really thick stuff, well out to sea. Alas, Intelligence is not prepared to credit us with any success, in spite of Paul's assertion that black smoke was pouring from both engines. This, they reason, is more likely to have been caused by the Ju88 pilot bending his throttles in an effort to escape! Nevertheless we must have given him a hell of a fright, which makes one wonder whether an additional category of 'Scared Fartless' might not be an appropriate addition to the list!

July 3rd   The Inspector General, Air Chief Marshal Sir Edward Ludlow-Hewitt, visited Drem yesterday and spent some time discussing our abortive brush with the Ju88. He was short of time, however, so rather than cutting me off in mid stream, suggested I flew to Turnhouse with him and continue the saga en route. This I did, but we had no sooner entered the Operations Room at Turnhouse when a flap began as a Dornier 17 sneaked in under the RDF cover, strafing Drem as it flew over at low level and apparently just missing Yellow Section when it was scrambling to deal with the belated plot. Unfortunately the flight failed to catch up with it. Although no damage was done in this instance, it nevertheless underlines how important it is to disperse aircraft widely when not in use.

I borrowed a Tiger Moth from Turnhouse to get home quickly and saw a number of large bomb craters between Dalkeith and North Berwick, fortunately all in open fields where they've done no more harm than rouse the curiosity of a herd of cows grouped round one of the craters, where I saw them ruminating over the loss of their pasture. As expected, I found Batchy in a towering rage and hopping mad that the Dornier got away.

It was B Flight's turn to bed down at Macmerry last night, but we are no longer permitted the comforts of the clubhouse. No indeed; the Atcherley dispersal bug has spread here also and we are now dotted round the perimeter, sleeping under canvas. As ill-luck would have it, there was a downpour in the night and our tents leaked; otherwise all was peaceful.

This afternoon I was scrambled to patrol Arbroath at Angels 20 and, whilst climbing through 14,000 feet, unexpectedly ran into a Do17 travelling in a southerly direction. I turned on him immediately and managed to get in a short burst before he took refuge in the clouds, but that was the last I saw of him. The Jerry rear gunner had the impertinence to fire back on this occasion but, as we both apparently missed, honours can be considered even! However I should have made more of the encounter if I hadn't got into such a tizz when he suddenly sprang into view. I must learn to take a firmer grip on myself in future.

Ops later told me the Bandit must have stuffed his nose down, for the plot disappeared off their table soon after the engagement. I would like to think it was because he had been shot down, but I know it isn't so.

July 7th Intelligence tells us the Luftwaffe is stepping up its efforts against our coastal shipping and, as there are a number of important convoys passing through the area, we are maintaining a section at stand-by during daylight hours. Consequently we are confined to camp for the time being which, although aggravating from a domestic point of view, relieves one of the necessity of having to remember the password! However Jerry must have got wind of our preparations for he hasn't shown up and, although we held the posture non-stop for seventy-two hours, I had to do only one patrol, and that over North Berwick where I saw nothing more aggressive than a small boy flying his kite from the harbour wall.

We are now being allowed out this evening so I took

Claire and Margaret to a picture house in Haddington
where we saw *When Tomorrow Comes*, starring Charles
Boyer and Irene Dunne. It was a very mushy film and the
girls wept copiously throughout. However Findlay and
Hector were busy in our absence. They shot a Ju88 into
the sea of May Island.

July 9th We were again interrupted during the lunch
break to scramble after an unidentified plot approaching
the Fife coast, when Paul and I did the honours. While
we were climbing at full throttle through unbroken cloud,
Control kept telling us we were getting close to our target,
but it was not until breaking into the clear at 20,000 feet
that we came upon a Heinkel 111 nipping in and out of
the cloud tops not far off, but on his way home and not
making for Scotland, as we had been led to believe.

We had to stalk our quarry for a considerable time as
he kept disappearing into the clouds and we never quite
knew where he was going to appear next. However we
eventually got it right and let him have a co-ordinated
burst from opposite quarters, when the Heinkel's starboard engine burst into flames before it dived smartly into
the nearest cloud. During the engagement both Paul and
I came under considerable return fire but happily neither
of us was hit. Drem was still under a Red Alert when we
got back but Intelligence are being more generous this
time and allowing us to claim a 'probable'.

Other items of interest regarding this raid are (a) a
number of bombs fell near Crail, causing no damage, and
(b) the girls remembered to take to their shelter.

George Pinkerton's rhubarb must be playing him up,
for he has gone off again, leaving yours truly in command.
However I hardly distinguished myself in the role by
being caught at the cottage this evening while A Flight

went off and shot down another Ju88, Dunlop and Donald being the victors. It's hardly the done thing for the acting CO to be washing the dog whilst his colleagues are overhead performing feats of derring do!

July 11th Apart from a small wood just off the southern boundary, there is not much natural cover anywhere around Drem. However these trees were enough to excite Batchy's interest and Walter and I were sent for to hear about his latest ploy for dispersing aircraft. 'Let's go and see if we could park some there,' he enthused. 'We'll go now!' Thus, in spite of muttered excuses about being rather busy at the flights, Walter and I, accompanied by a couple of airmen carrying pots of paint, found ourselves striding through the rain in the direction of the trees. Batchy was soon crashing through the undergrowth, selecting those trees to be marked for later removal. The job took most of yesterday afternoon and the whole of this morning with the result that Walter and I were utterly pooped by the time we finally escaped to the relative sanity of our offices. However a message was waiting for me that the AOC wanted to see me urgently at the cottage.

Birdie was even more affable than usual and introduced me to his brother, who has apparently just arrived from Canada. I thought it strange he should send for me merely to perform such a domestic gesture, when he surprisingly enquired after the health of the CO. I told him that George was on leave and that, as far as I knew, the CO was in the best of health. 'On leave, is he?' was the AOC's rejoinder. 'Then he is absent without my permission!' I was taken aback and assured him George's pass seemed to be in order as I had seen it myself. The AOC was grinning. 'Don't be an ass – Pinkerton is posted to Turnhouse and *you* are CO of 602 as from now!'

All feelings of fatigue vanished miraculously and, as today is also Claire and Birdie's wedding anniversary, the AOC took us to the De Guise for a celebratory dinner, although I was very conscious of the white paint showing under my fingernails.

July 13th In spite of a thick head, excusable in the circumstances, I approached the wood next morning with new-found enthusiasm. After all, I was now labouring for the wellbeing of *my* aeroplanes! But Batchy was on the job before me, accompanied by a group of construction engineers, working out a requirement for bulldozers, how much back-filling would be needed and so on. Certainly no one could accuse him of letting the grass grow under his feet. Indeed his enthusiasm is infectious and both Walter and I already find it rubbing off on ourselves.

Things are happening at the sharp end too, for Paul took Rose, Sprague and Phillips to Carlisle yesterday by train to collect four new aircraft from the MU, thus bringing our strength up to scratch. It is a particularly satisfactory way to begin my stewardship, especially as our latest intake of pilots has all been passed out fully operational by day.

The first project now safely launched, Batchy has turned his attention to finding a quiet haven for operational crews to bed down in when off duty, and commandeered our wives to help find him a suitable house, reckoning feminine intuition is needed for viewing desirable residences. So Claire and Margaret were whisked off in the staff car on a lightning tour of the district, again with Batchy at the wheel. It seemed a bright idea at the time until later both girls returned in a state of jitters as a result of his somewhat eccentric driving technique. Regretfully Batchy only knows two speeds – flat out and stop, and his method of negotiating a crossroads is to do so as fast as possible in the belief that the shorter the time it takes to cross, the less chance there is of hitting anything coming the other way. It is certainly the first time I've seen the girls drinking doubles!

After a busy night, when the squadron was involved in several patrols, I was back in the wood first thing this morning, along with Flight Sergeant Connors and a few of his men. It is good to see the troops showing interest in the project and many have volunteered to lend a hand. Connors, I fear, emerged with as much paint on himself as he had applied to the trees.

July 17th Two large bulldozers turned up on Tuesday and immediately set about clearing the undergrowth and, within two hours, had progressed more than 200 yards. While this was going on Walter and I were not idle and, clad in macs and wellies against a steady downpour, marked out areas to be used for fuel and equipment dumps. Now Batchy wants us to fly to Macmerry to do the same over there, once we've finished the job here.

It seems a CO's work is never done for, no sooner had I got back to the office to deal with routine paper work, when Batchy dragged us off to look over Hope House, which the girls had short-listed as a possible haven of peace for off-duty crews. We thought it fitted the bill admirably, having plenty of rooms, is safely tucked among the Lammermuir Hills and far removed from the hurly-burly of a fighter station. Indeed we gave it our instant approval, hoping to dispose of Project Number Two without further ado. George Pinkerton was in the office when I got back, waiting to do our handover, and it was late evening before all the formalities were completed. I feel sorry for George. He has not had long in the chair.

The air war is hotting up in the south, with many attacks on Channel convoys and RDF Stations reported. The latter are particularly worrying, for radiolocation is fundamental to fighter operations and must be kept functioning at all costs. However it seems our squadrons are giving a good account of themselves and exacting a steady toll of enemy raiders, so well in fact the Germans have now wheeled heavy artillery on to the French coast and are using it to bombard the shipping instead of exposing the Luftwaffe.

RAF Montrose was attacked yesterday evening when a Master trainer was hit and burnt out, but fortunately no one was in it at the time. Green Section was ordered off to deal with this attack but failed to make contact on account of the weather. Even the bulldozers are bogged down at present.

July 19th A Flight has gone to Dyce for the next few days as insurance against further attacks in the north-east, but I sent Dunlop to run the show as there is much to be done down here. However, now that our resources are so spread out, the AOC is allowing us to bring two Command reserve aircraft into the front line and I propose to operate them as Black Section. While in the course of arranging this, Jeffrey Quill turned up with Supermarine's latest toy to try out. I flew this Spitfire for an hour yesterday afternoon and found its variable pitch, constant speed airscrew a big improvement over the old push and pull device we've been used to so far. It gives much more flexibility, besides a much smoother ride.

In the meantime work proceeds apace in the wooded

dispersal. Batchy, however, thinks it should be accelerated even more and visited Fettes College in Edinburgh yesterday when he managed to talk the headmaster into sending his boys to Drem for a day, arguing that a spell in the fresh air would do them more good than sitting in classrooms conjugating Latin verbs. So a couple of double-decker buses rolled on to the station this morning and decanted a hundred fresh-faced youths, who were immediately led off to the wood to help clear the debris. They too must be affected by the Batchy bug, for they seem perfectly happy to toil away with nothing more to look forward to than a couple of square meals in the airmen's dining hall. However Batchy decided they should be taken for a trip before returning to school, whereupon every multi-seater aircraft at Drem was mobilized to form a sort of aerial circus. The Tiger Moths and Harvard trainers plus a gash Fairey Battle were pressed into service and the force augmented by a visiting Blenheim in which Batchy took the boys up four at a time. On one occasion I spotted this bomber flying inverted across the airfield at nought feet with four unfortunates on board who, incidentally, later assured us they had thoroughly enjoyed the experience. Diplomacy must take a high place in the curriculum of Fettes College!

July 25th   We have been flying an exceptionally large number of convoy patrols recently although I'm not convinced they are all necessary. A batch of fresh controllers has arrived recently at Turnhouse and it may be that they are still trying to find their feet and tending to err on the side of safety. Hopefully they will settle down soon, otherwise we will run out of aircraft hours.

   Douglas Farquhar is spending a few days' leave in Gullane and I flew him over the new dispersal to show him the camouflage. He is impressed with Batchy's effort but reckons there aren't sufficient trees around Martlesham to copy the scheme there. Later this evening, not long after Harry Moody had taken off on his first night sortie, a Ju88 unexpectedly streaked low across the airfield and disappeared in the direction of Edinburgh. I scrambled Ian Ferguson to give chase, at the same time ringing Turnhouse to let them know what I had done, but was surprised to discover Control knew nothing about the intruder. We have been caught out again through the lack of suitable low-reading radiolocation.

I heard later that Control never did get a plot on the Ju 88 which, in any case, did nothing more than drop a few bombs around Leith, one of which desecrated the graves of the German crews buried there after the Firth of Forth raid last October. Regretfully Ian never caught up with it.

July 27th Luftflotte Five, based in Norway, has been paying us a lot of attention recently and hardly a night now goes by without at least two patrols being called for. We have regular daylight visitors too, although they seem wary of venturing over land and more often than not turn tail as soon as they know we've been alerted. At any rate we are presently concentrating on night training, which has caused Batchy to remember his earlier promise to find some way of making it easier. He has also had a Q Site lit on a stretch of moorland to the east of Drem, hoping to delude the enemy into thinking it is the airfield proper.

McDowall and I were up on separate patrols last night, when Mac had a crack at a Heinkel momentarily caught in a searchlight beam near Dunbar. He claims to have hit it with a long burst, although unable to confirm any result as it hastily took refuge in a cloud. I also latched on to another raider off the Fife coast about the same time, but this one jettisoned his bombs and scarpered before I could get within firing range, and I lost it in the darkness. I was flying Q with its new VP airscrew for the first time and am very pleased with it.

July 28th   The Jerries are dropping a lot of mines along the convoy routes, mostly during the hours of darkness and, as they come in below RDF cover, are devilish hard to find. Unfortunately some mines are taking their toll and, only yesterday, I watched *Royal Archer* run into one off St Abb's Head whilst on escort duty over the convoy in which she was sailing. This upset me a lot, for I sailed to London in *Royal Archer* in the late twenties and felt I was losing an old friend. Happily her crew got away in the lifeboat before she went down.

Our searchlight friends have come up with another good wheeze by displaying different coloured searchlight beams from known positions. Now we will be able to fly along predetermined patrol lines from say, Haddington, marked by a green beam, to Dunbar, marked with a red, thus leaving one's attention free to concentrate on all-round searching instead of worrying where one is. Furthermore the searchlights will henceforth lay a horizontal beam pointing towards the airfield to assist anyone not sure of his course. We are most grateful for the help as it will greatly speed up our night training programme.

Had no sooner got down to the cottage last night than a message followed to say Nigel Rose had clobbered a marker board while landing at Macmerry and that a fire had resulted. I drove across later to find that his parachute flare had been triggered off, burning a large hole in the underside of the Spitfire so, instead of spending a peaceful evening in the bosom of the family, I had to spend the next few hours dealing with the inevitable paper work.

But today is Sunday – the day of rest. Or so it might have been if Batchy hadn't decided to give the padres a crack of the whip. So he had us on parade on the tarmac, flanked on each side by a Spitfire from 602 Squadron and a Hurricane from 605, during which he invited the men of God to bestow a blessing on the two aircraft. Thus Spitfire N, gleaming like a new pin, was duly consecrated before an invited audience which included, amongst others, Sir Harry Lauder and his niece, Greta. All was forgiven later when Sir Harry gave an impromptu concert in one of the hangars, a gesture much appreciated by all privileged to watch. I joined a great comedian while he tucked into a high tea of bacon and eggs beforehand, without which he said he wouldn't perform.

July 31st The AOC and his Senior Air Staff Officer flew up on Monday to put 602 Squadron through its paces, as a result of which Walter and his boys have been made fully operational again. As this should take some of the load off our shoulders in the immediate future, Margaret and I took the opportunity to drive to Glasgow to see our parents. But we had not been long in my parents' flat before an over-zealous special constable was at the door, threatening to run me in because I had not removed the rotor arm from my car parked outside. I told him that enemy parachutists were welcome to the old heap, as they wouldn't have got very far in it anyway. And I was not far off the mark, because we blew a gasket on the return journey and ran out of patrol half a mile short of our destination.

Indeed yesterday was not one of my better days for, no sooner had we trudged back to the cottage and reported in when Dunlop telephoned to say he had been caught out by the haar and broken his undercarriage in the course of a night landing. What makes it more annoying is that he was flying our only Spitfire modified with the new automatic undercarriage selector.

Fettes is back again and it won't be long before we can use the new dispersal. I have therefore put in a bid for Scylla's abandoned fuselage, for it will make a first-class dispersal – with loo and all! Naturally the flying circus was back in business this evening, Batchy this time managing to squeeze six passengers into his borrowed Blenheim.

1940
August

August 3rd Batchy is taking a few days off to visit his parents in Yorkshire and has left me in charge of the station. I wish he hadn't.

He had not been long gone before the Jerries started piling on the pressure, resulting in Findlay Boyd and Harry Moody being scrambled after two separate intruders in the middle of the night. While they were airborne, the haar rolled in and, by the time they had scoured the dark skies to no avail, were faced with a mist-enshrouded airfield when they rejoined the circuit. Findlay was first to have a crack at getting down but, after three abortive attempts to line up, gave up and diverted to Leuchars, which was still in the clear. But Harry had no such luck for, returning with insufficient fuel to risk crossing the Firth, he was left with no alternative but to get down at Drem, willy nilly. Sadly N is now a heap in a faraway hedgerow although I'm glad to say that Harry himself has got off with a few scratches, mostly acquired whilst disentangling himself from the briars.

Woke this morning to find the haar still with us and 602 Squadron scattered far and wide, Yellow Section being fogbound at Macmerry, Green Section marooned at Acklington, whence they had gone yesterday to fire on the ranges, and Findlay still grounded at Leuchars. I was tempted to ring Batchy to find out if he approved of our dispersal! But we are not alone, for 605 has just run one of its Hurricanes into the same hedgerow as Harry and left it with its tail sticking in the air. Thus both the aircraft blessed by our padres last Sunday have suffered the same fate. I am sending for Padre Sutherland to find out what kind of invocation he called down upon these two innocent machines!

Fortunately we now have a strong ally at Turnhouse, for the Duke of Hamilton, a past 602 squadron commander, has recently assumed the mantle of sector commander and has become our overall operational boss. As fog was again forecast for tonight, I rang for his advice. 'Black everything out and keep your aircraft on the ground,' was the practical answer. And how right it has been, for a Hun has just flown overhead, done an about turn, and headed back for base without doing any harm.

August 8th Our bombers returning from raids into enemy-occupied territory report widespread fog over large parts of Northern Europe, which probably accounts for the significant drop in enemy activity over here during the past few days, not that we are complaining, for we can do with the breathing space.

Batchy returned last Saturday, when I was glad to hand back his station; I don't think I'm yet cut out for so much responsibility! Hearing he was back, Douglo Hamilton called on Batchy, during which we became committed to help in some special exercise the former is cooking up for the benefit of the gunners and searchlight units. In the event the haar, for once, became our ally and the affair has been shelved for the time being. So we were instead able to devote some time to flight safety matters, especially those concerning night flying.

Our two main problems are still those of exhaust flames and frosting windscreens. As to the former, Batchy is working on a system of lighting which will guide pilots on to the approach path by following a series of glim lamps laid in a circle around the circuit whilst, at the same time, I have been trying to design a sort of baffle to fit above the exhaust stubs and so shield the pilot from the glare of the flames without completely obscuring their forward vision. We are making good progress on both. But, not to be outdone, our engineers have also come up with a gadget for squirting glycol on to the windscreens to clear the frost, and I was able to try it out last night. It worked well enough at speeds below 180 knots, after which a vacuum seems to set in which throws the spray clean over the windscreen. I have suggested that a spoiler might cure this.

Before getting down to these chores, however, I had gone across to Turnhouse last Wednesday to discuss the details of Douglo's projected exercise and had been caught there by the mist, not that I minded, for I was loaned a pair of the ducal pyjamas and spent a comfortable night with him in the Mess. Whilst transiting back to Drem next morning I overhead control vectoring Green Section on to a Bogey reported near Arbroath, and broke in to say I would join the chase. As it was, I reached the area just as Paul and his number two were having a go at a 111 which, however, was not prepared to stay and fight it out and stuck its nose down before high-tailing it for the nearest cloud with a couple of Spitfires hard on its heels. Aware that the cloud base over the sea was 2,000 feet, I immediately dived below the layer, hoping to cut off the Heinkel if it should break cover in its eagerness to escape. Alas, it never came through and, after probing about for another twenty minutes without making contact, we were ordered back to Drem.

Micky Mount joined us this afternoon, fresh from his conversion course. However one of our real old stalwarts, Alastair Grant, is about to leave having been posted as an instructor in Flying Training Command. I invited them both for a meal at the cottage this evening but we were not long there before the unmistakable sound of un-synchronized Daimler-Benz engines was rumbling over-head. When I rang Ops to ask if they wanted us back, they told me 605 Squadron was dealing with it, although one of their pilots was complaining of a strong smell of glycol fumes in his cockpit. I heard later that he did not return from the patrol.

August 11th   It appears the 605 Hurricane was seen to crash into the sea off North Berwick, but the pilot was found to be dead when the rescue launch reached the scene soon after. The poor chap must have been over-come by fumes and tried to get down, only to suffer a broken neck when he hit the water.

There are reports of increased activity along the south coast, with RDF stations being singled out for special attention. The BBC bulletins are full of stories of attacks on shipping in the Straits of Dover and we were even treated to a live outside broadcast while such an attack was actually happening. It sounded exciting. But our squadrons continue to give a good account of themselves, although I fear a number are suffering casualties in the fighting.

There has been activity here too, but of a different sort. Batchy thinks he has found the answer to our night landing problem and invited me to try it out for him. After studying the average flight path of fighters in the circuit, he has positioned a ring of glim lamps just inboard of it, so giving pilots a semi-circle of lights to follow by looking over the cockpit combing and these will eventu-ally lead them on to the approach path. Having first fitted an R/T set into the boot of the station commander's car, I flew round the pattern, all the while advising Batchy on R/T of any adjustments required, and found it worked a treat. The chaps should be delighted and Batchy has decided to christen his baby 'Drem Lighting' and proposes to have it wired up to the Watch Office so that the entire system can be switched on and off at will. Earlier I had tested the defrosting device, modified with a small deflector plate at the bottom of the screen, and found that it, too, worked admirably throughout a wide range of speeds and heights.

Being on state tonight, I was about to settle down with the latest detective novel when the door burst open to admit Harry Moody and Pay Lyall, both bubbling over with excitement. I knew they had intended to dine at the Royal Hotel, but hadn't expected them to overdo it. 'Boss,' they explained in unison, 'we've heard that 602 is moving south!', but much as I have learned to respect their source of information, I rang Turnhouse to check its validity. 'Yes,' I was told. 'Tangmere on the thirteenth. A signal is already on its way!'

August 12th The message, when it came, was more explicit. It appears our move is only temporary, for ten days at most, and we are to take only the first-line element with us. The squadron headquarters and second line are to remain at Drem. Nevertheless it entails looking out a lot of stuff – log books, servicing manuals, starter batteries, spares and all manner of other bits and pieces – which have to be crated and loaded on to the two Harrow transport planes already here to take this and our essential personnel to the new destination. I have decided to include our intelligence officer, Henry Grazebrook, in the party, for I think it likely his services will be needed.

Having first checked, and re-checked, the lists, I gave

Q a final whirl round the sky to test its defroster pump before dashing down to the cottage to collect a few items of personal gear for loading on to the Harrows and, while there, another signal arrived to say we are to go to Tangmere's satellite airfield, Westhampnett, and not to the sector station itself. I now find Westhampnett is a brand new field which doesn't even appear on the maps!

August 13th I awoke early to the sound of heavy rain battering on the window and, looking outside, was presented with a bleak scene of muddy puddles and dark rain clouds driving overhead. It was hardly an auspicious start to our great adventure. However the ground crews had been toiling throughout the night and I arrived on the aerodrome to find all sixteen Spitfires on the line – the twelve front-line machines plus the four reserves. The loading was also completed and the Harrows all set to depart. Right on schedule, therefore, the Harrows took off on the dot of ten o'clock and we followed two hours later.

Having taxied to the far end of the field and lined up the squadron in four flights of four, I was about to open the throttle when I happened to glance over the side and saw Batchy's staff car tucked beside my starboard wing tip with Padre Sutherland, bagpipes at the ready, hanging out of the rear window. The car kept station on us as the formation slowly gathered speed, bouncing and rocking over the uneven surface, when my last impression of Drem was of a burly red-faced person hanging on for all he was worth with one hand, whilst brandishing a set of bagpipes in the other. From then on I had to concentrate on instruments as we straightaway rose into a wall of dirty black clouds.

We broke clear at 15,000 feet only to find one Spitfire

missing. However a quick call on the R/T established McDowall's engine was playing up and he was returning to Drem. The remaining fourteen closed up as we headed southwards, the cloud cover stretching unbroken for as far as the eye could see. Having worked out that we would require refuelling en route, I had drawn a line which would take us close to Church Fenton, where at least we had some chums. However there was still no sign of a break in the clouds after half an hour's flying and I confess to offering up a silent prayer as I called the formation together, prior to letting down. The lads responded magnificently and stuck to me like leeches while we thumped and bumped downhill until, around 2,000 feet, we broke through the wispy tails of rain clouds to find ourselves over open countryside, which was unrecognizable in the murky gloom. So, rather than straying too far south at this stage, I started to swing the formation in a wide circle, hoping to pinpoint our position on the way round, when, without warning, an airfield with Spitfires on it appeared ahead. It seems my prayers were being answered, for it was Church Fenton.

Our erstwhile colleagues from 72 Squadron gave us a warm welcome and, besides arranging for our aircraft to be refuelled, fixed up a spanking good lunch in their Mess. But the rain persisted and the best the Met people could offer by way of a forecast was a possible clearance beginning in the south about the time we would be due there. Hardly an encouraging prospect, and prudence dictated we should stop at Church Fenton, at least until a proper clearance was assured. But HQ 11 Group insisted we must press on as their war was hotting up and our help was badly needed. So, taking a deep breath and offering up another silent prayer, I led them off again into the prevailing clag, but this time breaking clear at 10,000 feet.

We flew on above the vast sea of unbroken cloud for the best part of another hour, seeing nothing until a veritable forest of barrage balloons hove into sight. Only London could be that well defended, I reasoned, and promptly altered course in the direction of Southampton when shortly afterwards a break appeared and we could make out the features on the ground. The Met man's crystal ball had done him proud! As we approached the coastline, now clearly visible ahead, we could see a dog-fight going on away to our left but, as our sets were not fitted with the correct frequency crystals, there was little we could do to help. As it was, our fuel states were again low and I still hadn't been able to locate Westhampnett. When I finally did so and got the boys down, I began to wonder what we had let ourselves in for.

On the centre of the field a Hurricane lay on its back whilst, from behind one of the boundary hedges, a thick pall of black smoke was rising lazily into the air. However the Harrows were there, parked in front of a number of nissen huts, the only buildings I could see. A small group of airmen ran out to greet us and my spirits rose when I recognized the cheery faces of Burnett and Campbell among them. At least we were not alone. Then an officer, his right arm in a sling, came forward and introduced himself as Johnny Peel, CO of 145 Squadron, whose outfit we'd come south to relieve. Johnny greeted me affably and straightaway put me in the picture.

He told me 145 had taken a lot of stick and was now down to four aircraft and the same number of pilots. 'That,' he said, pointing to the Hurricane inverted on the field, 'is what's left of mine. I got badly shot up and had to land without ailerons. I stopped a bullet in the arm too; hence the sling. However, on a cheerier note, the smoke is coming from a downed Nazi.' He added that his four aircraft had already left, but that he had stayed on to see us in. If I had no objection, he too would like to push off. So saying he climbed into his little sports car and, with a final wave from his servicable limb, drove away to join his lads at Drem. The Harrows, now laden with 145's gear, followed soon after. The handover was presumably completed!

Shortly after, having got wind of our arrival, Tommy Thomson, who turns out to be the station adjutant at Tangmere, drove in and showed us round the amenities: Five nissen huts, three of them conveniently tucked under the trees, comprise the only working premises on the airfield itself, whilst two substantial farmhouses are to serve as the Officers' and Sergeants' Messes. As for the airmen's billets, Tommy apologized, they would have to put up with the Duke of Richmond's dog kennels a little way up the hill but, hopefully, something better would be found for them soon. 'Westhampnett has only been going for a few weeks, you see,' he added by way of explanation. So here we are, Westhampnett: Let's see what we can make of you!

August 15th   Jack Boret, the Station Commander Tangemere and therefore our new sector commander, called this morning to make his number and promised to give what assistance he could. But my spirits fell when he warned that Tangmere carried no spare parts for Spitfires, all previous squadrons operating from his sector being equipped with Hurricanes. We would probably scrape by, he added, as our stay was to be limited to ten days so, with that cheery introduction over, Jack got back into his car and drove off at high speed.

Nevertheless, having now had time for a closer inspection, I think Westhampnett will suit us well. The two

Messes, whilst devoid of furnishings, are pleasant little properties, each with its own patch of garden. A small copse along the eastern boundary will provide cover for some of our aircraft and I'm told we might be allowed to make use of the facilities on the racecourse, should we need them. That however will depend on how much transport Tangmere is willing to spare us. In fact the thing I'm most unhappy about is the airmen's sleeping quarters, for the kennels are still redolent of their previous occupants. As for the airfield itself, it is simple in the extreme. Three fields have been knocked into one, the dividing hedgerows having been ripped out and camouflage paint put down in their place, so successfully, in fact, that it is hard to spot that the area no longer consists of three separate fields. I have allocated the more exposed area on the northern perimeter to B flight and put the remainder under the trees towards the eastern edge, retaining the smallest nissen for my office.

It was not long before our new masters remembered we are here and our flights were scrambled on no less than seven occasions throughout the day. I only took part in one sortie, during which we intercepted a friendly Blenheim which gave the correct response when challenged. However Findlay had a brush with a He111 off the Isle of Wight yesterday afternoon and was able to claim a 'damaged'. Then the weather closed in and we were left in comparative peace, apart from my having to take A Flight to Tangmere to cover the night state. There are no night flying facilities at Westhampnett.

We were not called on during the night, so had plenty of time to acclimatize to the new surroundings. It seems strange, and not a little discomfiting, to be no longer under the familiar umbrella of Turnhouse and the paternal interest of Birdie Saul. Now we are among strangers,

The day war broke out. A Flight at dispersal, Abbotsinch. Seated left to right. Muspratt-Williams: Grant: Urie: Robinson: Boyd: Stone. MacLean standing front right with Padre Sutherland left back row

B Flight at dispersal 3rd September 1939. Standing left to right (centre) Webb: Johnstone: Doc Allen: Farquhar: Rintoul: Graeme and Bell. Pinkerton seated on prop boss

Ian Ferguson

LEFT: Ferguson tries out his .38 at dispersal. Abbotsinch September 1939
BELOW: Hodge solo on Spitfires at last! Left to right – Webb, Bell, Hodge, Johnstone, Ferguson, Jack, Robinson, Hodder and Grant. Abbotsinch September 1939

JIMMY HODGE SOLO ON SPITS!

Drem. November
1939

McDowall

Strong

Maclean

ll   Proudman

Babbage

Fred
Wheeler

Marcus Robinson

Sell-

'. . . Everyone looked unfamiliarly tidy when the King visited
Drem . . .' Including Farquhar, Robinson and Johnstone.
February 1940

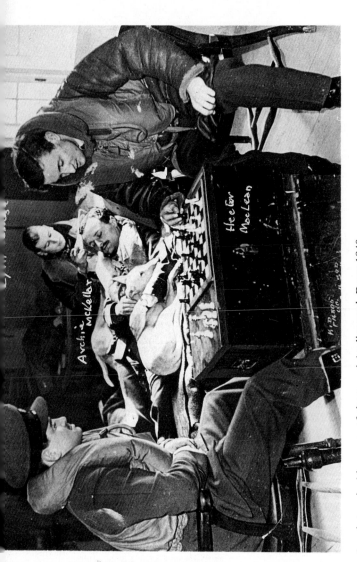

'. . . interminable games of chess . . .' At dispersal, Drem 1940

ABOVE: '. . . I found the place a shambles, with smoke still rising from smouldering buildings . . .' Tangmere after attack on 16 August 1940

RIGHT: With Ian Forsyth at Upton. September 1940

Pedro Hanbury and Nigel Rose at Westhampnett. October 1940

ABOVE: Prestwick 1941
BELOW: John Willie Hopkin with the two Sergeants Brown.
Prestwick March 1941

ABOVE: Wreckage of Rudolf Hess's Messerschmitt 110 at Eaglesham. May 1941 *(Inset)* Rudolf Hess

McDowall and the author with Sir Archibald Sinclair, Glasgow 1941

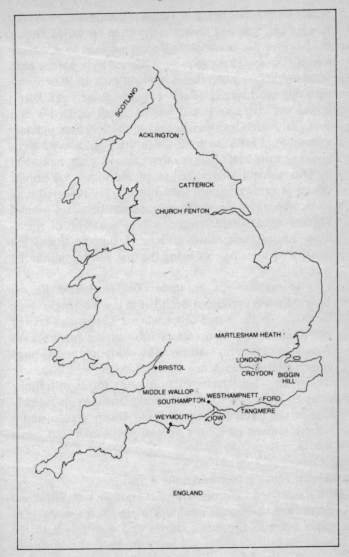

Sector Operations being at Tangmere and our new AOC, Keith Park, wielding his authority from far-off 11 Group in Uxbridge. No doubt we will soon get used to it. At any rate it's obviously going to be a darned sight harder here for, even before I had taken A Flight back to Westhampnett this morning, B Flight was scrambled over Portsmouth and battling it out with a batch of Do17s and Ju88s, although bad weather made the outcome indeterminate. Paul failed to return with the flight and we were about to write him off as our first casualty when he turned up fifteen minutes later, red-faced and somewhat embarrassed at getting himself lost! But Findlay reported they had come under fire from the ack-ack batteries around Portsmouth and later menaced by a squadron of Hurricanes during their return to base. I suppose this is the penalty we must pay for being the first Spitfire unit in the sector.

Q is overdue for an inspection, so I flew her to Tangmere this evening and left her in the big hangar. Jack Boret was in the watch office when I landed and invited me to dine with him, afterwards driving me back to Westhampnett in his staff car. The old farmhouse seemed empty after the opulence of the Tangmere Mess which, incidentally, I remembered from 602's fortnight training camp in 1936. It is hardly surprising, for the sole furnishings in the farmhouse are one old Dutch dresser and a rickety kitchen table. It's as well we brought our camp kits.

August 16th It has been quite a day!

Granted the morning was quiet enough, with 602 stood down from operations until lunchtime when I was able to catch up with the office chores and pay a visit to the airmen's billets, which still smell strongly of dog. It was while we were in the middle of our meal the alarm was raised.

We realized something out of the ordinary was up when scrambled from 'released' with no previous warning, but the cause was immediately clear when we scampered outside in time to catch sight of a string of Ju87 dive bombers screaming vertically down on Tangmere and releasing their bombs at the nadir of their dives. The noise rose to a crescendo as explosions from bursting bombs mingled with the din of Bofors guns firing from positions all around us and, even while we were hurriedly clambering into our flying gear and dashing out to the waiting Spitfires, large chunks of shrapnel and spent bullet cases were cascading down on us. The ground crews were already on the job, some on the wings, waiting to strap us in, and others poised beside the starter batteries, but all looking strangely unfamiliar in tin hats.

There was no time for an orderly departure; we roared off as soon as ready, A Flight aircraft streaking across from the east and B Flight from the north, the whole airfield becoming a cauldron of Spitfires fighting to get into the air through hell or high water. I shall never know how none collided. I got airborne in the middle of the mêlée and called the boys to form up over base at Angels 2. A Flight was already with me but B Flight was nowhere to be seen. But there was no time to wait for them as the air around us had become a kaleidoscope of whirling dervishes with dozens of aircraft swooping and diving in all directions. I felt like pulling the blankets over my head and pretending I wasn't there! I never imagined anything could be so chaotic. Without thinking, I selected a gaggle of Me110s and dived to attack. Out of the corner of my eye I had a fleeting impression of a Spitfire having a go at another 110 and blowing the canopy clean off it. A

Hurricane on fire flashed past and I was momentarily taken aback when someone in the aircraft in front of me baled out, until realizing he had come from the 110 I was firing at. Then suddenly the sky emptied and it was all over.

I wasted no time getting back, when the ground crews were so eager to get on with their job of turning round the aircraft that an armourer was on to one wing and unscrewing the gun panels before I had even completed my run in. Some had landed ahead of me whilst others drifted back singly, or in pairs, until a quick count revealed we were all down with the exception of Micky who, it later transpired, had collected some bullets in his coolant tank and had had to lob down at Odiham.

Henry Grazebrook was in his element and straightaway got down to collating the combat reports. We seem to have done well. Findlay, Dunlop, McDowell, Rose and myself have all claimed victories, with others collecting many minor successes. Findlay's 'confirmed' must take pride of place, for he encountered a Stuka pulling out of its dive just as he was taking off and blasted it from the sky before he was properly airborne. Findlay was so taken aback that he merely completed a tight circuit and landed again, without even retracting his undercarriage. I don't think he was airborne for more than a couple of minutes.

I drove to Tangmere later in the evening and found the place a shambles, with smoke still rising from smouldering buildings. Small groups of airmen milled around, many dazed and still deeply affected by the pounding they'd taken. The station commander was on the lawn in front of the Officers' Mess, a parrot perched precariously on his shoulder. Jack Boret was covered in grime and the wretched bird screeching its head off, trying to sound like a Stuka at the height of its dive. The once immaculate

lawns were littered with personal belongings blasted from
the wing destroyed by a direct hit; shirts, towels, socks
and a portable gramophone – a little private world for all
to see. Fortunately the bar had escaped and was doing an
unusually brisk trade.

Tommy Thomson took me to see the damage on the
airfield. Heaps of rubble were everywhere and all three
hangars had been badly damaged, the big one now
reduced to a mass of fallen bricks and twisted girders. I
crawled under this and discovered Q looking very much
the worse for wear, a girder having fallen on her and
severed one of the mainplanes. She wasn't going to be
much use to me now and I was already feeling the loss
when I rejoined Tommy, standing beside a massive
hangar door lying flat on the ground. 'My Dolomite's
under that.' He was almost in tears. 'I only bought it last
week!' What more was there to say?

Four of our aircraft have been damaged in the hangars,
thus accounting for the whole squadron reserve in one fell
swoop. But we are not alone, for 601 and 43 have also
suffered severely; indeed the remains of Billy Fiske's
Hurricane still smoulders on the airfield and I gather Billy
himself is gravely injured in the station hospital. But
stories are already going around of how the men reacted
during the onslaught. Some were numbed by the enormity
of it whilst others, often those least likely to become
heroes, seemed spurred to greater action and came
through with flying colours. Such a man is our MO, Doc
Willey, who never left his post throughout the raid and
was instrumental in saving many lives.

I now hear that Biggin Hill, Kenley, Manston and
North Weald were also on the Germans' calling list today.

* * *

August 18th   Sitting in the garden, basking in the warm sunshine, I cannot help thinking how mutable our lives have become: one minute up to our necks in a holocaust of gigantic proportions, the next enjoying the sanctuary of an old English garden. By courtesy of our enemies, we have been left severely alone for the past twenty-four hours and I am taking advantage of the lull while it lasts.

When I called to see Boret yesterday I found him on the airfield, busily dragooning a squad of surly German prisoners into clearing up some of the mess they'd created on his station. I am not quite sure how this accords with the Geneva Convention, but I would be the last to interfere. At all events he was rubbing their noses in it good and proper, and greeted me warmly. 'By the way, a signal's just arrived to say your move here has been made permanent and that the rest of your lads are on their way. I hope they're bringing plenty of Spitfire spares.' They have, for the two Harrows were already at Westhampnett when I returned, although more personnel are yet to follow by rail.

Was on the state last night, during which I was sent on one patrol over the Isle of Wight without making a contact. Transiting back to base this morning, however, I was diverted to destroy a drifting barrage balloon which was menacing power cables with its trailing mooring lines. This is not so easy as it sounds for, to be effective, it is either necessary to puncture the envelope from above or set it alight with incendiaries, neither of which are permitted for fear of causing casualties on the ground. So, after dodging around the flailing tethering cables and emptying my ammunition tanks into the monstrous envelope, I had to leave it still floating lazily across Portsmouth, although looking considerably more flabby than it was before I began working on it.

After coping with the influx of additional personnel all morning, I was feeling all in and handed over to Dunlop for the afternoon. I had no sooner turned in when a hell of a shindig started up and the squadron despatched to tackle another large gaggle of Stukas, this time making for the neighbouring airfield at Ford. The boys were set on by a large number of escorting fighters as soon as they approached and, before they were able to get among the bombers, found themselves embroiled in a real old free-for-all with 109s and Stukas all mixed up together. And they gave a good account of themselves, accounting for twelve in all, but not without cost to themselves. Dunlop, Micky, Ian Ferguson, Harry Moody and Sergeant Whall all took a knock and, although Micky and Whall managed to land their damaged machines at Tangmere, the others were not so fortunate. Ian ran into high-tension cables when trying to force land at Merston and Dunlop, although managing to coax his badly damaged Spitfire back to Westhampnett, now finds his aircraft is a complete write-off. Harry, it appears, took to his parachute, but has landed safely in the middle of a girls' school near Lewis. But Ian and Dunlop are in hospital, the former with a damaged back and Dunlop with his legs full of shrapnel.

August 19th   As a result of recent activities, we are rapidly running short of our few remaining spares and it seems we cannot expect fresh supplies for a few days yet. So I telephoned the CO at Middle Wallop, our nearest neighbour operating Spitfires, requesting a temporary loan. 'Certainly! Send a lorry and we'll do our best.'

Connors put a young corporal in charge of the detail, not expecting it to bring back more than a few bits and pieces. But he was pleasantly surprised when the party returned with enough spare parts almost to build a complete new aeroplane. We were naturally curious to know how they did it.

Apparently they were only a few miles short of their destination when Middle Wallop came under a heavy attack, whereupon Corporal Parker halted his vehicle while the lads climbed out to watch the fun. When he thought it safe to go on, the lads were piled back into the lorry and were about to move off when they spotted a German airman parachuting towards them and tumbling into a nearby field. They gave chase and found the Jerry in a cornfield, nursing a damaged ankle so, rather than leaving him to be claimed by someone else, they bound his arms together with his parachute cords and bundled him into the back of the lorry with themselves. When they arrived at Middle Wallop, everyone seemed fully occupied in putting out fires so, having first handed their captive to the duty guard, they found their way to the station stores and helped themselves, leaving the station without further ado. When I later rang Roberts to thank him for his genorosity he was unaware our chaps had been there but said we were not to worry about replacing the items as he would write them off as having been destroyed in the raid.

I led A flight on two patrols today. On the first we ran into a large formation of Ju88s over Thorney Island and managed to knock down three before the escorting 109s appeared on the scene, after which it became a free-for-all with lead flying in all directions. I felt the thud of something striking my aircraft but, as it wasn't affecting its airworthiness, I ignored it and gave chase to a couple of 109s, firing repeatedly at them, but with no visible effect! This was one of these days when I must be firing rubber bullets! However we all got back safely with the exception of Harry, who had to bale out for the second day running, but with a less erotic outcome. He has just been on the phone to say he came down in a field well-used by cows. Later, checking J (which I have taken over after losing Q) I found we had picked up nothing more serious than a couple of bullet holes in the tail fin.

The second sortie took place in the early afternoon, when we intercepted a low-flying Ju88 going hell for leather back to base. We think he was probably a follow-up recce after this morning's raid on Portsmouth but, be that as it may, he never got his pictures back, for we downed him easily. He dived into the English Channel nose first and immediately disappeared from view.

Was delighted to find our Adjutant, Crackers Douglas, in my office when I landed. He had just brought the last of our troops down by train, so we are complete at last. After I had briefed him on what we had accomplished so far, Crackers pushed off to take the admin into his capable hands. In the meantime a number of friendly neighbours have been calling at the Mess and are offering to loan us items of furniture, having seen our austere conditions. 'Just send along a lorry!' they say. I wish we had a spare one to send!

In the meantime our wounded heroes are on the mend, but slowly. When I drove Dunlop to hospital in Chichester the medicos said his wounds would take some time to heal. And it was a similar tale when I enquired about Ian Ferguson; he too will be off flying for many weeks to come. But Crackers has not been letting the grass grow under his feet, for he has already arranged for the airmen to be moved from the kennels and into the clubhouse at Goodwood Golf Club.

* * *

August 21st Harry accompanied me to Tangmere this morning to fetch a new parachute, when he showed me a letter he had received from the head girl of the school he landed in. It is couched in affectionate terms, begging him to become their very own pen pal in return for which the girls will knit him pullovers, and what were his favourite colours? I told him it was his own fault for being so darned handsome!

Bing Cross paid a welcome visit this morning. He is now on sick leave after his terrible experience in the North Sea. He told me he had never heard a noise like it when shells from *Scharnhorst* started exploding on *Glorious*. By the grace of God he and Jamie Jameson were picked up from a raft but everyone else, including Baldy Donaldson and his squadron, were lost. Bing almost lost both legs because of frostbite, but the medicos did a good job on them and he is already making fair progress on a couple of sticks.

It was only while helping to site two Bofors guns this morning that I saw how woefully inadequate were our defences generally, for the only deterrent between us and the general public is a broken-down wooden fence running the length of the northern perimeter. I have passed this one on to Crackers to deal with. Later the Duke of Richmond looked in for a lunchtime drink and has told us to make use of the buildings on the racecourse if they are of any use. He added that the Goodwood Racing Calendar is in abeyance for the duration! As a matter of fact I hope to take up the offer, for the spaces beneath the main grandstand would make an excellent Stores section.

August 23rd B flight had a brush with a Ju88 over Portsmouth this morning, when Findlay only managed one long-range shot before it scampered into the clouds.

However he was forced to break off the engagement when the ack-ack from Portsmouth locked on to B Flight instead of concentrating on the raider. Also Control omitted to warn him there was a Hurricane squadron in the area and the first he knew of it was when Glyn Ritchie collided with one as it emerged from a nearby cloud. Unfortunately the Hurricane pilot had to bale out, although Glyn managed to nurse his Spitfire back to base with a badly bent prop.

Things have been happening on the domestic front too. Jack Boret turned up unexpectedly with the Duke of Kent in tow and found us looking like a lot of tramps. However HRH didn't seem to mind and I drove him round our domestic sites, during which he made copious notes in a little book. He told me he was making an official visit in his capacity as chief welfare officer, and hoped he could do something to make our lives more comfortable. In the event he has instructed Jack to increase our allocation of transport forthwith, which is a beginning. At the same time, our friendly neighbours have been coming up trumps, for the Mess now boasts three easy chairs, a dining room suite and a coal shuttle, whilst Crackers tells me he has been offered the loan of a vi-spring mattress, and would I like it? Indeed we are doing so well that it is about time we dismantled the room on the left as you come in. We have been keeping this room sparsely furnished with odd pieces of camp kit in the hope that new visitors will take pity and offer to loan better things. And the ploy has worked, for most react with an 'Oh my dear fellows, we can surely find you something better than this. Just send along a lorry . . .!'

Friendly neighbours have been calling at the airfield too. Mrs Euan Wallace and Virginia Gilliat turned up this morning in a YWCA mobile canteen and have offered to make it a regular call. The Euan Wallaces live at Lavington Park and have invited me to dine there tonight. Needless to say, the troops are delighted at the prospect of regular visits by such charming ladies and their canteen is assured enthusiastic custom.

Before we left for Lavington, however, a low-flying Ju88 suddenly appeared from nowhere and streaked across the airfield before disappearing in the direction of Tangmere. I drove immediately to the nearest Bofors site to enquire why it had not been fired on, only to find its crew huddled round a portable wireless listening to the evening news. Not only had they failed to see the intruder, but swore they never even heard it! I must discuss our ground defences with Jack at the earliest opportunity.

Lavington stands proudly amidst many acres of well-kept parkland and is a beautiful home. Captain Euan Wallace, once Minister of Transport in Chamberlain's government and now Commissioner for London, was a generous host and made me most welcome. I sincerely hope to be asked back in spite of putting up a monumental black at the end of dinner for, when offered a bowl of saccharine tablets as a substitute for sugar, I put a generous spoonful in my coffee instead of picking out one single tablet.

August 24th I wonder if AC2 Wyer knows what he's letting himself in for by volunteering to be my batman. At all events I am delighted to have him. Small in stature and wearing a pair of horn-rimmed spectacles, he bears a striking resemblance to Peter Lorre, the film actor, and has been immediately nicknamed 'Mr Moto'. He tells me he is a silver merchant when not fighting a war and, although eager to be involved at the sharp end, his eyesight prevents this and he has settled for something less glamorous. At all events I have left him to settle in while I discussed the gun incident with Jack, who was paying us a visit. As a matter of fact we discussed our lack of adequate defences in general and, as a result, we are to be given our own Ground Defence Adviser.

We should have been stood down today, but things hotted up to such an extent that we were pressed into service and sent after a raid approaching Portsmouth from the south. It was a large raid too, and very high – possibly 27,000 feet or more – and we saw the vapour trails soon after becoming airborne. As we continued climbing at full throttle, the trails began to twist and spiral, which indicated that the Tangmere Hurricanes were already among them, but we were still too far off to be of assistance. The Portsmouth guns were also putting up a solid barrage, but the shells were exploding far below the targets; indeed they were rapidly becoming more of a menace to us than to the enemy.

Palls of dense black smoke started to rise from Portsmouth and Southampton, thus indicating that some bombers had managed to get through, and the thought of what these towns must be suffering spurred us to even greater efforts. But we saw the bombers turning for home before we even reached 25,000 feet and they were well out over the Channel, hotly pursued by the Hurricanes, before we got to our operational height. We were too late and, apart from a couple of lone Me 109s which sniffed at us briefly as they sped after their companions, we took no part in the fray and were ordered to pancake as quickly as possible. The sector had been left unguarded in our absence.

This was the precursor of more raids on towns and factories and there are signs that the Luftwaffe is stepping up its efforts in these directions besides continuing to

keep the pressure on our fighter and RDF stations, often
with serious results. It seems Reichsmarschall Goering is
throwing in everything to deliver a knock-out blow.
Certainly the strain is beginning to show, for many are
noticeably more short-tempered and twitchy and one
wonders for how much longer the lads can go on taking
it. The news from Southampton hasn't helped either; a
large section of the city centre is destroyed and a picture
house full of children received a direct hit.

There now seems little doubt that Hitler means to
launch an invasion soon. Bomber crews speak of large
concentrations of landing craft in the Channel ports and a
massive build-up of transport and troops in the immediate
hinterland. But, so that no one will be taken unawares,
the Government has forbidden the ringing of church bells
throughout the country until such time as an invasion is
actually taking place. Then, God knows what will happen.
We just hope they won't resort to poison gas.

August 25th I led the squadron twice this morning but
on both occasions the blighters turned tail before we got
within range. So we were not very optimistic when
scrambled in the middle of lunch and ordered to Angels
15 over Weymouth. However this turned out to be a
different kettle of fish, for the Bandits turned up as soon
as we were in position – a sizeable force of Ju88s and
Do17s with the usual gaggle of escorting fighters – grind-
ing inexorably towards our shores. But we had the advantage of the sun at our backs.

Having ordered B Flight to tackle the fighters, I led A
Flight down on the bombers which scattered immediately
we were spotted. Nevertheless all six of us got in an
attack, although we had no time to assess the results
before the fighters were among us, after which the sky

became a maelstrom of bombers, fighters and escorts swooping and swerving all over the shop. The air waves reverberated with shouts of 'Look out behind you,' 'I've got one!' or just simply 'Jeezis Christ!' as planes were locked in individual battles. I could only leave the boys to get on with it as best they could; in any case I already had my sights on a 110 and managed to nail it from below, when its entire tail unit exploded and the crew baled out.

I had dived below the mêlée to take stock of the position and had just started to climb again when a burst of tracer whizzed past my port wing tip. I had a quick flashback of Harry Broadhurst warning us that if we saw tracer being used, it was odds on it was being fired as a sighter so, praying he was right, I immediately sideslipped towards it, whereupon another tell-tale streak passed up my starboard side. A quick glance in the mirror showed a 109 glued to my tail, when I pulled hard back on the stick, expecting it to pass underneath. But he was a wily character and clung on, while I continued to urge every last ounce of power out of the trusty Merlin. But it was too much for it. I suddenly flicked over in a violent stall turn.

The manoeuvre must have taken Jerry by surprise, for he hesitated momentarily and, before he could get out of the way, I was almost on top of him as he presented a broadside target, which even I could not miss. I can still see the look of agonized surprise on the German's face when his canopy shattered around him and the Messerschmitt went into an uncontrollable flat spin, from which it never recovered. I followed him down until he crashed into a spinney on the outskirts of Dorchester and burst into flames. When I looked about me, everyone had disappeared, so I called the boys and told them to find their own way home.

Some of the lads got back before me and Westhampnett was bubbling with excitement by the time I landed. Refuellers and armourers were already hard at work turning the aircraft round, whilst Henry buzzed about like a bee on heat, frantically trying to piece together what had taken place. And the final tally is impressive too – fourteen confirmed, four probables and two damaged, for a loss of two of our own. Sprague baled out over the sea, but was speedily rescued by an amphibian Walrus, and Roger Coverley had to abandon his blazing Spitfire over Gloucestershire, but has already telephoned to say that, apart from an urgent need for fresh underwear, he is unscathed. As for myself, I can hardly credit it; two confirmed on one sortie! Maybe my bullets aren't made of rubber after all!

August 26th   A florid-faced flight lieutenant with a chestful of World War One medals reported this morning and informed me his name was Macintosh and that he was my new Ground Defence Adviser. I explained what I wanted:

Firstly he was to secure the perimeter and, having done that, make arrangements for a guard to be placed at the main gate. 'Verra guid, surr!' acknowledged the old Scot and toddled off to do my bidding, after which I had to spend the rest of the morning writing up our so-called 'Incident Reports'. These wretched things must be filled in whenever anything, however trivial, befalls any of our aeroplanes, although I confess those emanating from this office are brief in the extreme! Fortunately I managed to clear the decks in time to entertain Jack Broome and his wife to lunch in the Mess.

Until recently, whenever one of our aircraft was shot up in action, it has had to be dismantled and taken by road to the Supermarine factory beyond Southampton.

However, thanks to Broome, a long-time member of the Vickers team, we now fly the damaged aeroplane straight to the factory, where its pilot (always assuming he is fit to do so) picks up a refurbished replacement and brings it back here. So the least we could do by way of thanks was to invite Jackie and his wife for lunch.

True to form, however, Jerry intervened and had us abandoning our guests in mid-spoonful and racing off to intercept a large raid approaching the Isle of Wight. The Controller made a first-class job of the interception and positioned us 1,000 feet above the target and with the sun behind us. We spotted them a long way off, Ju88s and Do17s roaring northwards immediately above an unbroken layer of cloud. It was a classic interception. And, joy of joys, there were no escorting fighters. Then a strange thing happened.

I was about to give a ticking off to our chaps for misusing the R/T when I realized it was German I was hearing in my headphones. By coincidence we were both using the same frequency and, although I don't speak the language, it appeared from the monotonous flow of conversation that they were still unaware of our presence. But not for long though for, as soon as we started the dive, we were assailed by an agonized scream of '*Achtung Schpitfeuren, Schpitfeuren!*' as our bullets started to take their toll.

Having allocated targets during the dive, I had chosen to go for the Dornier leading the first vic of three. Down and down I went, firing like billyo at my target when, to my surprise, the Dornier in the centre of the second vic blew to pieces and disappeared earthwards in a series of separate flaming balls. It appears my deflection shooting is not all it might be. But never mind, it counts as a 'Destroyed' just the same!

In spite of having taken Jerry by surprise our bag was only six, with others reported as being damaged, before the remainder dived for cover and turned for home. Indeed we saw no more of them and returned to Westhampnett to find two of our aircraft missing, although we were able to account for their drivers soon after. Cyril Babbage had taken to his parachute after stopping a couple of cannon shells in his engine, but was picked up by a lifeboat and landed at Bognor, where he has been taken to the local hospital. Hector, on the other hand, has not got off so lightly. He, like Babbage, stopped a number of cannon shells, one of which struck his ankle and blew off his foot. Although aware his aircraft was also damaged, Hector realized it would be curtains for him to bale out while losing so much blood so, after doing his best to apply a tourniquet and turning the oxygen full on, he gingerly nursed the damaged Spitfire back overland, and managed to make a wheels-up landing at Tangmere. The emergency services were quickly on the spot and found Hector lying by the side of his aircraft, with his damaged leg propped against the wing and cursing loudly at his rescuers for taking so long to come to his aid. As the ambulance was about to drive him off to hospital, Hector told a medical orderly to fetch his shoe from the cockpit but, when that worthy looked at the missing footwear and saw what was still inside, he promptly flaked out and was carried off in the ambulance alongside Hector.

I have just spent fruitless hours touring Selsea Bill with McDowall in search of a Heinkel he claims to have shot down. He swears he saw it land near the shoreline.

August 28th   The Huns took a breather today and left us severely alone, so I took the opportunity to catch up with the paper work. Jack looked in about ten o'clock and we were having a chat in my office when he happened to glance out of the window. He called me over. 'I don't believe it!' he cried, pointing to a family group settling themselves down besides one of our Spits, 'I thought you told me Macintosh had seen to your fence!' We jumped in his car and drove on to the airfield to where Mum and Dad were spreading out their picnic whilst their two children disported themselves around a Spitfire. Then, having discovered how they gained entry and seen them off the premises, we went to inspect Mac's handiwork.

He had indeed carried out his instructions to the letter and laid a roll of barbed wire the whole length of the fence, but he had secured it to the inside of the fence itself, thus making it easy for an intruder to climb on to the wooden posts and step over the wire. The old Scot resented our criticism and insisted, 'The field is verra weel defended, Sirr!' but, having had the error of his ways further explained, amended the assertion to 'Weel, at least the main gate is verra weel defended!' Jack took him back to Tangmere, promising to send over a replacement.

When Doc Willey and I visited Hector in the Royal West Sussex, we found him sitting up in bed, sporting a real shiner. He hit his head on the reflector sight when he crashed, he told us. But he has had to have his leg amputated below the knee, although swears he can still feel his missing foot itching. In spite of his grave injuries Hector is as chirpy as a sparrow, seems highly pleased with the calibre of the nurses looking after him and suggests losing a leg is as good a way as any to get a spot of leave! He has the heart of a lion and will be much missed at the flights.

Having satisfied ourselves about Hector's wellbeing, the Doc and I went on to Bognor to check up on the other

casualty. We found the gallant sergeant fit to be discharged and undertook to take him back with us. However his clothing was still damp after its immersion in the
Channel and we had to borrow an overcoat from a
hospital porter before bundling him into the back of the
car. Then, having dropped Babbage off at the Sergeants'
Mess, Willey and I joined some of the 43 Squadron chaps
for a meal at the Dolphin, in Chichester. It must have
been a good meal, too, for no one heard the sirens
sounding.

August 30th I don't know whether the party at The Dolphin had anything to do with it, but my tummy has been
playing me up for the past two days and Doc has grounded
me pro tem. As he aptly put it, 'You don't want to be caught
with the trots at 30,000 feet!' Nevertheless I risked going as
far as Chichester and found Hector making a steady recovery, although suffering a lot of pain. As Dunlop was due
back off sick leave, I also picked him up at the station and
was able to catch up on news from the North.

According to Dunlop, the squadron is being well written up in the local papers and the Lord Provost of
Glasgow is keen to take us under the Civic wing. As a
matter of fact the L.P. wrote me the other day, suggesting
he should sponsor our so-called benevolent fund, an offer
I am keen to take up. When sent a cheque for £100 on
taking over 602, I wrote to the donor, Jose McIndoe, for
her permission to open a deposit account with her gift,
rather than blow it on woolly comforts and the like. We
were already well supplied with such items. At the time
of writing, therefore, the 602 Squadron Benevolent Fund
accounts stands at £312/4/10 and a further boost would
not go amiss.

Bombs fell this evening, close enough to rattle our

windows but, as the Tangmere Hurricanes are on state tonight, we have otherwise been left in peace. In fact we may soon be relieved of much of the night chores as the Fighter Interceptor Unit at Ford has just been declared operational. The FIU Blenheims are fitted with airborne RDF sets.

August 31st   We found a number of unexploded incendiaries lying on the airfield this morning, presumably dropped during last night's raid, and I've told our lads to leave them alone. In the meantime I have used my enforced idleness to complete the officers' confidential reports and, as no one could be blessed with a better bunch of rascals to command, there is no need to perjure myself!

Findlay led the squadron on a patrol over Biggin Hill and Gravesend this afternoon and tangled with a bunch of Ju88s and Me109s all mixed together. This was unusual, for the escorts normally fly well above their charges. However it didn't stop the boys from claiming three 109s and a Ju88, although Sergeant Elcome got shot up and had to make an emergency landing at Ford.

More bombs are falling tonight, but I've had no reports of any damage.

1940
September

September 2nd   It seems no time since we were grumbling incessantly about the bad weather, and now we are complaining because it is too good. What a perverse lot we are! But our present discontent is for an entirely new reason, namely that the Luftwaffe is able to attack in greater strength when the weather is clear and has less difficulty finding its targets. Our attrition rate goes up, too, for the heftier the opposition the greater is our chance of losing aircraft although, in fairness, Jerry is being similarly penalized. At all events we are losing too many aircraft for comfort, although Supermarines are pulling out all the stops to make good our losses. Regretfully their factory cannot turn out pilots to match. We are beginning to suffer from a dearth of trained drivers, so it is as well I am again fit to take my place in the line.

The enemy is concentrating more on targets in the south-east these days and I led the squadron over Kent yesterday, hoping to cash in on Biggin Hill's preserves. But the fun was over by the time we got there and the Huns had departed to lick their wounds. Things were comparatively quiet when I returned to Westhampnett so I took the opportunity to make my number with Ralph Hubbard, the Duke's factor, to thank him for his help and to regularize a number of outstanding requisitions. At the same time our Mess continues to flourish, and when Henry Grazebrook recently invited a WAAF officer for tea, it was served on real china! Indeed, during the past ten days we have been inundated with loans from nearby homes and now boast several carpets, sofas, easy chairs and pictures, to say nothing of a number of spitoons purloined from local pubs. Mr Moto clearly disapproves, for he tackled me about them the other day. '. . . There is yet *another* cuspidor, Sir . . .' he announced, disdaining to refer to them otherwise, '. . . I trust you will do something about them, for they detract from the dignity of our establishment!'

Facilities on the airfield are also looking up, for a Bessoneau hangar has been erected in the field across the road, thus providing some cover for airmen working on the aircraft. We have had to pull down a portion of Macintosh's defences to wheel the planes over the road.

Glen Niven turned up today but, as he has been trained on Hurricanes, we will have to convert him ourselves. When asked why he insisted on coming to a Spitfire squadron, he asserted there was only one squadron worth coming to, namely 602! We've told him he is nuts.

September 4th   Keen to become operational as quickly as possible, Niven wasted no time getting started, but he is finding a Spitfire more difficult to manage than he had anticipated. As a result I have just spent an agonizing half hour watching his antics in the circuit although, to give him his due, both he and the Spitfire are down in one piece. Two more pilots, Payne and Hanbury, have also put in an appearance, but they have come straight from a Lysander squadron with no experience whatsoever on fighter aircraft. It seems we are meant to convert them ourselves, which will put a severe strain on the flying hours.

We had a disappointing sortie in the Dover-Eastchurch area yesterday and only intercepted two Hurricanes followed by a squadron of Blenheims on its way to drop bombs on the Channel ports. In spite of Bomber Command's sterling efforts, the threat of invasion is no less imminent and Jack has ordered our allocation of small arms to be broken out and distributed to the appropriate airmen. Officially we are allowed only fifty rifles for the squadron yet when I later called a muster, no fewer than eighty-five armed airmen turned up for the parade, but I didn't enquire whence the extras had been scrounged. It is sufficiently gratifying to know that Glaswegians are capable of looking after themselves when the chips are down!

I said nothing of our windfall to Jack when he called this afternoon, for he obviously has much on his mind. Nevertheless I reminded him of the Duke of Kent's instruction about allocating more transport, whereupon he immediately despatched one of our MT corporals to Tangmere with instructions to report to the Senior Admin Officer. However there was nothing to spare at Tangmere but, nothing daunted, the SAdO marched up to the main road and stopped the first Southdown double-decker which came along, commandeering it on the spot. The unfortunate passengers were made to disembark at the roadside to await the next bus and the bemused driver was issued with a receipt for his vehicle, whereupon our corporal turned up 'Special' on the destination board and drove it straight back to Westhampnett. Even Jack was taken aback; indeed he was probably sorry he came to visit us, for he too was subjected to a spell of Niven aerial juggling in a Spitfire, which only helped to raise his blood pressure. As a result he suggested our latest recruit would be more profitably employed in 601 Squadron, which is also very short of trained crews. So Nuts has gone to Tangmere.

The Tangmere Wing is being called on more often to

operate over Kent on which occasions 602 Squadron, being the sector's only Spitfire unit, invariably flies top cover for 601 and 43 Squadrons. Our primary role then is to take on the fighter escorts whilst the Hurricanes wade into the bombers. However when we turned up at Beachy Head this morning in response to an SOS from the Biggin Sector, the whole area was covered by a blanket of heavy cloud stretching to 15,000 feet, thus adding to our difficulty in making an early sighting. Not only that, but a prolonged climb through ice-laden clouds has been known to freeze one's guns and, whenever such a possibility arises, I have acquired the habit of test-firing them to make sure they are free, particularly if there is a combat in the offing. I can think of nothing more embarrassing than to find one's weapon inoperative at *le moment critique*.

On this occasion we broke clear just above 15,000 feet, when the Hurricanes made straight for a formation of Dorniers whilst we sped on to tackle a gaggle of 110s circling several thousand feet above. I had already fired a precautionary burst long before reaching attacking range, when one of the escorts unexpectedly broke away from the circle and dived seawards with a lot of smoke belching from its port engine. We were soon in the thick of it, with aircraft flying in all directions, but it seemed I was having another of my rubber bullet days. The Hurricanes did better. They downed six Do17s whilst our lot claimed three 110s, yours truly being a non-contributor. 'But what about the one that went down at the beginning?' they queried. 'None of us test-fired our guns, so it must be yours!' It seems a jammy way to notch up a victory, but I don't propose to argue!

A Flight claims to have encountered a batch of 113s this evening, but they turned tail as soon as the Spitfires

approached. If the identification is correct, it is the first
we've seen of this type. At any rate I left the lads arguing
amongst themselves while I went off for another dinner at
Lavington, where I was relieved to find the bowl of
saccharine tablets had been replenished.

September 5th   Had a session with the Senior Controller
this morning to ask about better communications between
the Ops Room and ourselves. Until now we have made
do with a single field telephone line operating on a
'number of rings' arrangement, whereby one ring alerts A
Flight, two B Flight, and three when the entire squadron
is on demand. Four rings puts one through to the Officers'
Mess. The sequence was playing hell with our nerves, as
A Flight would leap for the phone on ring One, then
mentally relax on Two, only to leap for it again on the
third, whilst all the time it was only the Controller calling
the Mess steward to enquire what was on the luncheon
menu. It was some time before Findlay had the nous to
suggest allocating the single ring to the Mess, since when
our nerves have been spared a lot of jangle.

Only did one sortie today, leading the squadron over
Biggin Hill at Angels 20. As there was no trade for us I
returned to Westhampnett to find Mr and Mrs MacLean
in the Mess, having travelled south to visit Hector. I drove
them to the hospital and later joined them for dinner at
the Dolphin, during which there was a heavy raid on
Portsmouth.

September 6th   Those working at the A Flight end of the
airfield are sufficiently close to the Messes to make use of
their facilities when nature calls. But B Flight is not so
well placed and has to make do with a wooden sentry
box-cum-Elsan affair sited near the dispersal. Not surpris-

ingly this convenience is in considerable demand, especially in the mornings, but a certain B Flight member, who shall remain anonymous, has not yet managed to wean himself from his peacetime habit of esconcing himself on the throne for an extended session. It was not until the culprit was spotted sneaking into the box with a daily newspaper under his arm that Findlay decided to act so, waiting until Flying Officer X was comfortably settled, he taxied his Spitfire in front of the erection, turned it tail-on and opened wide the throttle. The result was spectacular. The loo came to rest in the field across the road, but the victim was not so fortunate. He got caught up in Macintosh's barbed wire in considerable embarrassment and not a little discomfort.

Led three sorties today, the first coming to nothing after patrolling over Horsham at 20,000 feet. But the second was more interesting when we were ordered over Mayfield to intercept an outgoing raid reported turning over the Thames estuary. We caught sight of it a long distance away and gave chase but, before we could get within firing range, I awoke to the fact that we were crossing the French coast and that a horde of angry 109s was on its way up to meet us. They wasted no time about it either, and before long we were embroiled in good old free-for-all during which Glyn Ritchie's instrument panel was shot to smithereens. Fortunately Sergeant Proctor came to his aid and shot down the attacker whilst Pat Lyall had an inconclusive brush with another. I decided it was time we went and called the lads together to escort Glyn back to base, where he was able to make a reasonable landing with help from a lead aircraft. However he has collected some shrapnel in his legs and will be off flying for some time. Our third patrol had us flying in the Biggin Hill area where the air seemed full of bursting ack-

ack shells. The gunners must have been firing at us however, for there was no sign of enemy aircraft. A message was waiting for Findlay to say he has won a DFC, so am about to join him for a celebratory drink in the Mess.

September 7th Am coming to the conclusion the Germans must be late risers, for we had another morning free from strife and I was able to call at the hospital to see how Hector and Glyn were progressing. I also came across our double decker bus parked outside Woolworth's with 'Chichester' run up on the destination board, so presumably Flight Sergeant Connors has been organizing a shopping expedition for his lads.

Had not been on the afternoon shift long when Jack arrived accompanied by the Chief of the Air Staff, Sir Cyril Newall, but we were no sooner introduced to him than the entire Tangmere Wing was scrambled to patrol Hawkinge at Angels 15. It has been very warm today and a heat haze has been covering the south coast to a height of 17,000 feet. We caught up with the Hurricanes as they were climbing out of Tangmere and the wing was soon in full cry, reaching the patrol area in double quick time. Units based in the Tangmere Sector have an advantage over the Kent-based squadrons in this respect for, taking off that much further west, they are able to climb directly to the zone, whereas squadrons taking off from such bases as Biggin Hill and Kenley are forced to spiral uphill. At all events we got there first and, being in our usual role as top cover, 602 was naturally first to break through the haze although, when we did, I nearly jumped clean out of my cockpit. Ahead and above, a veritable armada of German aircraft was heading for London, staffel after staffel for as far as the eye could see, with an untold number of escorting fighters in attendance. I have never seen so many aircraft in the air all at one time. It was awe-inspiring.

They spotted us at once and, before we had time to turn and face them, a batch of 109s swooped down and made us scatter, whereupon the sky exploded into a seething cauldron of aeroplanes, swerving, dodging, diving in and out of vapour trails and the smoke of battle. A Hurricane on fire pulled up in front of me and spun out of control whilst, to the right, a 110 flashed across my line of sight, only to disappear before I could draw a bead on it. Earphones were filled with a cacophony of meaningless sounds. A mass of whirling impressions – a Do17 spinning wildly with a large section of mainplane missing; pulling sharply to one side to avoid hitting a portly German as he parachuted past me with his hands raised in an attitude of surrender; streaks of tracer suddenly appearing ahead when I instinctively threw up an arm to protect my face; diving back into the haze every so often to take a breather and hoping to find another Villa aircraft, only to be pounced on again whenever I poked my nose above the protective cover of the haze. And so it went on in a series of quick, darting probes at passing Heinkels and Dorniers, then back into the mist to dodge the escorts, all the while conscious of the seemingly endless waves of approaching bombers.

Once I tried flying further to the east, hoping to outflank the enemy, but as soon as I poked my nose up again, they were there, bombers and fighters as numerous as ever. I was being carried along with the tide of battle for now, directly below, were the docks at Tilbury with smoke and flames belching from the warehouses scattered nearby. A glance at the gauge showed I was running short of fuel but, just as I was about to head for base to rearm and refuel, three 109s loomed out of the mist and offered a point blank target. I let fly at the nearest, whose canopy shattered into a thousand pieces as he pulled away in an inverted dive, whereupon I banked steeply to meet the others head on, only to find I was out of ammunition when I pressed the button. I don't know whether they were aware of my predicament, but they were certainly incensed at my impertinence and locked on to me as I high-tailed it earthwards.

I doubt if any Spitfire ever travelled so quickly when I dived near-vertically, foot on the throttle, weaving madly from left to right in a desperate attempt to shake off my pursuers. But no matter how hard I dodged and jinked, they followed my every move and it was not until I began to haul out of the dive around 2,000 feet that a quick glance in the mirror showed me they'd gone. When I looked ahead again the reason was all too clear; I was making straight for the balloon barrage flying around the town of Slough.

Thank God the old brainbox continued to work for, recognizing I was flying over the main road out of London I reasoned there would be no balloons actually flying from the A4 itself. So, by throttling right back and following every twist and turn of that magical highway, I emerged through the other end safe, sound, but shaking like a ruddy leaf! God bless Slough's balloon barrage! Only six gallons of petrol remained when I landed at Westhampnett.

CAS was still at dispersal and listened while I told him what was happening. 'London?' he repeated, incredulously. 'Oh my God!' whereupon he bade us a hasty farewell and set off for the Air Ministry. CAS must be a worried man, and with reason, for we hear the raids are still going on and it is now eleven o'clock at night.

It is impossible to assess results accurately after such a schemozzle, as no one was able to follow their victims down. Furthermore, when so many aeroplanes are involved, it is always on the cards that a crippled enemy could be attacked by more than one fighter during its descent. Although we are claiming several 'probables' and others damaged, I am much more concerned that neither Harry Moody nor Roger Coverley has come back. Hanbury and Aries have also been clobbered but I'm told they are both down in fields somewhere in Kent. But what of the man in the street in the capital city? I for one would not like to have been there when that raid was taking place.

The threat of invasion hangs heavily over us.

September 9th Although yesterday was a Sunday, I cannot believe the Luftwaffe left us alone because of religious scruples. Rather I like to think they are pausing to lick their wounds after Saturday's big effort, as we have been doing. This action has had a profound effect on the lads, not so much because of the staggering strength of the attacks, but because we seem to have suffered our first fatal casualties in action. There is still no news of Harry and Roger and we are beginning to fear the worst. But the show must go on and, as if to remind us of the fact, three replacement pilots are already with us. Pilot Officers Barthropp, Eady and Fisher reported in while we were battling over London. Furthermore Paul Webb has become a flight lieutenant.

The lull continued this morning and, although we undertook a couple of non-productive patrols during the period, the real fun didn't start until after lunch, when I led the squadron. We were ordered over Mayfield and got there just as a sizeable force of Do17s was being ripped asunder by some Hurricanes diving from above. It was a well-executed attack and thrilling to watch; one moment a threatening armada thundering towards London, the next a confusion of German aeroplanes trying to dodge the murderous attacks. We turned immediately and went after the strays.

Soon had my sights on a Dornier whose crews didn't wait to argue for, as soon as I opened fire, they baled out and left the stricken bomber to its own devices. I caught sight of three parachutes opening as I pulled away, feeling very pleased with myself; too pleased at it turned out, for I never saw the 109 coming up my tail. Fortunately Pat Lyall was on the spot and sent it packing. I reckon I owe Pat a double for that! I then swung after a Do17 and was busily firing at it from long range when a Spitfire, trailing smoke, passed me going in the opposite direction, although I didn't see who it was. It was not until I landed that I discovered it had been Paul Webb.

I have just been to see what is left of Paul's aircraft, the remains of which are scattered over a wide area near Walburton. I reckon he was lucky to escape with his life. Having been hit in the course of the action, he was on his way back to base when I passed him, unaware that three 109s were hard on his heels. The Jerries gave him a good going over and, in spite of weaving and jinking for all he was worth, Paul was forced almost to ground level, his rudder shot away, with no aileron controls and much too low to bale out, leaving him no option but to fly on until he hit the ground. As it was he flew straight into a small wood.

A swathe has been cut through the copse, and walking along its length I first came upon the port mainplane caught in the top branches, followed a short distance further on by the starboard wing which suffered a similar

fate, but had dropped to the ground. Then a section of
rear fuselage with a tangle of broken control wires sticking
from it lay in the undergrowth, not far from the engine
with the prop still attached. But I couldn't see the cockpit
section. Indeed it was not until I had cleared the wood
that I came on it jammed against a hedge. This is where
Paul had been discovered, semi-conscious and swearing
like a trooper. It is remarkable that he has got away with
nothing worse than a broken wrist, four inoperative
fingers and a bad gash in his nut. Nevertheless it is enough
to keep him off flying for a while.

Sergeant Whall was also shot up and came down near
Arundel and is complaining of a stiff neck.

September 10th   Never thought I'd see the day when we
would welcome a spell of bad weather. Woke to a cold,
wet and blustery day which will not only reduce the level
of enemy attacks, but should make Hitler think twice
about launching his invasion. As a matter of fact the bells
in our local church did ring last night, but it turned out to
be a false alarm. Nevertheless it made us jump and has
done nothing to lessen the tension. Indeed we are taking
no chances and have decided to sleep at dispersal for the
time being. However the weather is bad enough to reduce
patrols to section strength and, after taking Red Section
on one in the Southampton area, which was abandoned
soon after starting, I handed over to Micky and drove to
Chichester to visit the wounded.

St Richard's Hospital was buzzing with activity and the
forecourt jammed with ambulances when I got there, so
had to park my car in the roadway outside and walk the
rest. Then, having battled my way through a constant
stream of porters bearing stretchers to the waiting ambulances, I discovered the hospital was being evacuated to a

safer place and that Hector, Glyn and Paul were already
on their way to be entrained. As ill luck would have it, I
arrived at the station just in time to see the hospital train
pulling out of the platform.

Micky has been promoted to flight lieutenant and
Sergeant Whall awarded a DFM. I am delighted about
the latter for Whall is a fellow who says very little and
gets on with his job without fuss or bother. I am also
delighted about the former, for Micky will now take over
A Flight from Dunlop, who is not yet fully recovered
from his injuries and is being given a rest from operations.

A Flight caught up with a batch of Do17s this afternoon
but the weather was atrocious and they lost them in the
clouds without launching an attack. Later, as dusk was
falling, Micky, Hanbury and Elcome were scrambled in
spite of my warning the controller that none was fully
night trained. Nevertheless they were kept on patrol to
the limit of their endurance and came to grief when
landing in the dark at Tangmere. Micky and Hanbury ran
off the runway whilst Elcome hit a tree near Felpham.

September 12th Although the weather is slightly
improved, trade continues to be slack and only appears in
penny packets, sometimes only a pair of fighters on their
own, and it makes us wonder what the Germans are up
to. Occasionally a larger force is plotted over the Channel
and A Flight ran into a spot of bother when they intercepted such a raid this afternoon. Granted they accounted
for four 109s, but Rose was shot up and Sergeant Sprague
shot down. It would seem Sprague crashed into the sea
and is now posted as 'missing'. I am very sorry about this,
particularly as the poor fellow only got back fom his
honeymoon four days ago.

The sector as a whole is desperately short of aircraft.

Although 602 might find five serviceable aircraft at a pinch, the two Tangmere squadrons can only raise seven between them, and the shortage of qualified aircrews is even more acute. Indeed I have had to recall Findlay from leave and was expecting to see him yesterday, only to find he was caught up in the air raids on London where the entire transport system is in a state of near chaos. Waterloo and Victoria stations are out of action and many bus services have been suspended because of the difficulty of driving through the streets in the city. In fact Findlay said the only way he was able to get about was by Underground, but that, he pointed out, does not yet run as far as Chichester. In spite of everything, though, Londoners are getting on with the job and still manage to raise a cheery grin. But it is no laughing matter, and other cities are also coming under frequent attack, Southampton being one. The City Hall is now the only public building left standing.

A fresh supply of gongs must have come in for I have just been awarded a DFC and Doc Willey an MC. A Military Cross seems a strange decoration for a Royal Air Force Officer to receive, although no one is complaining. It is well won. But the customary celebrations will have to wait until tomorrow for I've just brought Blue Section to Tangmere to do the night state.

September 14th Had my first taste of leading the wing today, not that there was anything special about it, as we could only raise twelve aircraft from among the three squadrons. In fact I led it twice, on both occasions to the Biggin Hill area, but we had no joy on either patrol. On the first trip we were encouraged by seeing no less than five separate squadrons of Hurricanes over the south of England but less encouraged on the second when we saw a number of 109s flying far above us, possibly as high as 33,000 feet. We decided to leave them alone, as Spitfires and Hurricanes tend to run out of steam at that altitude.

Was meant to be dining in style tonight, but Fate and a German intruder decreed otherwise. The Duke and Duchess of Norfolk had invited me to dine at Arundel, but would I mind driving via Lavington to give Virginia a lift, as she was to be a fellow guest? This entailed a cross-country route over a network of narrow country roads.

Hadn't gone far before we heard the sound of bombing nearby so I doused the headlights and continued on sidelamps alone when, without warning, a sneak raider roared low overhead and dropped a bomb which nearly blew us off the road. At the same time an unlit cyclist, no doubt frightened by the same explosion, swerved in front of us, causing me to wrench the wheel over and sending the car rolling down an embankment to come to rest upside down in a neighbouring field. And the wretched fellow didn't have the decency to stop!

Having disentangled Gini's legs from around my neck and making sure she was not hurt, we walked to a nearby inn full of jolly farmers who immediately started plying Virginia with drinks while I telephoned the Duke to tell him what had happened. His Grace thought it a hell of a joke and remarked wryly that if I was able to get a girl on her back before dinner, what earthly chance would she have once it was over! I gather we are to be invited again.

Largely due to Virginia's charm there was an abundance of volunteers to manhandle the car back on the road, when we discovered the front wheels looking decidedly knock-kneed and a hole in the radiator. However I had no difficulty starting the engine so, after straightening the wheels with a wooden mallet and borrowing a pail of water from the landlord, we limped back to Westhampnett. I am relieved to know that our own chaps can repair the damage, as otherwise I will be faced with a few awkward questions to answer.

Sporadic raiding has taken place on several points along the coast and a few bombs dropped inland. It was one of the latter which almost did for us.

September 15th Joined up with 607 Squadron and patrolled between Beachy Head and Mayfield for almost an hour this morning without encountering anything worthwhile. Jack and the Under Secretary of State for Air were at dispersal when we got back and accepted our invitation to stay for lunch. Harold Balfour was a fighter pilot in the Great War, thus ensuring for himself a welcome not normally accorded to our political masters. He is also a friend of the Euan Wallaces and staying with them at Lavington, which gave me food for thought. Fortunately I was able to stop him from commenting about last night's misadventure as Jack doesn't know about it and might have been tempted to take the car away. I was very glad to get the Minister's conspiratorial wink from across the table.

Patrolled the Biggin Hill area this afternoon and ran into a gaggle of Do17s. We had no difficulty with them as they had left their escorts in France. We succeeded in downing five before the remainder took refuge in the clouds. Several other British squadrons were in the area, which is most encouraging for it is a long time since we've seen more roundels than black crosses.

Roger Coverley's body has been found hanging from the top branches of a tall tree near Tunbridge Wells, but there is still no sign of his Spitfire. From the nature of his injuries it would seem he baled out of his blazing aircraft. Still no news of Harry however.

*   *   *

September 17th   The long hot summer is over for the day
began with lots of low cloud and heavy rain and progressed through periods of squally showers. It is now
blowing a full gale, and long may it stay that way, for not
even the Germans are foolish enough to attempt a crossing in such conditions. But they are apparently not bad
enough to stop us from being sent off, for we were
scrambled after a plot near Winchester this afternoon.
Not surprisingly nothing came of it, as we never got clear
of the cloud and ended up doing an ogo-pogo. Padre
Sutherland was at dispersal when we returned and
announced he was staying with us for the next few days. I
have forbidden him to practise any more mumbo-jumbo
on our aircraft and hope he's left his bagpipes at Drem!

Findlay and I have arranged to take day about for the
time being, as most of our patrolling is now being done at
section strength. There is no point in both wearing
ourselves out. So, while Findlay got away with Red
Section this evening and shot down a Ju88, Micky and I
were being entertained at Lavington.

September 18th   Findlay took advantage of a bright moon
and flew the dawn patrol an hour earlier than usual, but I
made him wait until I'd finished breakfast before taking
over.

Ordered off to patrol Gravesend later in company with
607 and, while climbing through 21,000 feet, we were
jumped by some 109s coming out of the sun. Indeed the
first we knew of their presence was when Jimmy Vick's
two weavers keeled over with smoke belching from their
engines after which the 109s shot off at such a rate that
we had no earthly chance of catching up with them. We
wondered whether they had gone to join up with a
bomber force but, search as we could, there was no sign

of one. So we turned disconsolately for home, having lost two, with nothing to show in return when, out of the blue, we came upon a lone Dornier 17 and gave it the works. Three crew members leapt out but I never saw their parachutes opening. The Germans seem to be changing their tactics, but we'll leave it to Grazebrook to find out what they are.

This afternoon 607 joined us on another sortie when we were given London as our patrol position. We thought this odd for, besides being the first time we've been sent specifically to the capital, it is such an extensive area to cover and is also bristling with guns. It was even more strange when we got there, for absolutely nothing happened and we were sent home immediately. I called Vick on the R/T during our transit back to base and arranged to meet him this evening to fathom out what is going on. In the event, we met for dinner in the Dolphin, but left none the wiser.

September 19th   Things still peaceful this morning so was able to drive Padre Sutherland round our set-up, later calling at Goodwood House to visit Ian Ferguson, whose back is still playing him up. The Richmonds have made their ancestral seat available as a convalescent home for the duration, so we found him in pretty comfortable surroundings. The tea waggon was on the airfield when we returned, so was able to introduce the padre to the charming helpers, who today were Virginia and a girl I hadn't previously met, Pauline Wynn. Pauline is a guest at Lavington and Gini tells me that Eddie Ward, an ex-601 colleague and now a controller at Tangmere, is a frequent companion, so I invited all three to join me for dinner at the Ship Inn. David Niven was already there, dining by himself, and as Gini knew the famous star, he joined us at our table.

The threat of early invasion is receding; something to do with unfavourable tides, I'm told. At any rate we have reverted to Alert Two and can sleep in our beds again.

September 20th   Continuing high winds are posing problems for some of our new trainees, as the narrow undercarriage of the Spitfire makes it vulnerable to couping if landed cross wind. Nevertheless most are coping well and should be fit to come on state fairly soon.

Was made wing leader again when patrolling over Biggin Hill today, but apart from a number of 109s flying at a great height above us, we saw no enemy aircraft. These were possibly a batch of the new 109Es with modified engines, giving them an advantage over us at height, so we left them to their own devices. In any case they were not doing any harm up there. During the transit back to base we were ordered to spread out by flights to carry out a sweep, in the course of which we encountered a solitary Harrow transport, of whose presence Control was unaware. For reasons not divulged, we were told to make it land at Farnborough, which we did.

Two distressed ladies were at dispersal when we returned, the tea waggon having broken down, so we invited them to have lunch in the Mess. As one was the Duchess of Norfolk, Mr Moto borrowed a pair of white gloves to wear while serving the meal, which went down very well with our charming guests. Jack happened to look in while they were here and complimented the lads on their performance so, taking advantage of his expansive mood, I got his permission to take the weekend off.

* * *

September 22nd   Jimmy Wick has loaned me his Magister in exchange for the Humber estate car (now repaired!) so am presently enjoying a peaceful weekend far removed from the hurly burly of a fighter station. I flew to Harwell in the Magister and joined up with Ian Forsyth, and old school chum, who is a navigation instructor there. Ian and Muriel have rented an olde worlde cottage at nearby Upton, and it is most comfortable. Indeed the luxury of a real bed and clean sheets must have been too much for me, for I didn't surface until midday. It is also a relief to escape the telephones.

September 24th   Am back at Westhampnett, much refreshed after the flesh pots of Upton, although I had a job retrieving my car from Jimmy. He did not want to part with it. And I am glad to find that the lads have not been idle in my absence, Pat Lyall and Pedro Hanbury having downed a Ju88 near Bosham on Saturday. Not only that, but it appears this aircraft was carrying some interesting new equipment which is now being evaluated by the boffins. The AOC has also sent us a strawberry for delivering it into their hands. Maybe I should go away more often! As for the rest of the news: The padre has returned to Drem, McDowall has won a DFM and we are once again at Alert One.

The lull seems to have been short-lived for 602 Squadron flew no less than fifty-five hours today, mostly in sections of two, in the course of which Lyall again made the news by tangling with a modified Ju88, known as a Jaguar, which is reputed to be much faster than a Spitfire. Be that as it may, Pat managed to catch up with it and riddled it with bullets before it disappeared into a convenient cloud.

Jack threw a party at the Ship this evening to celebrate

his promotion to group captain. As the law now requires
all places of entertainment to be closed down by ten
o'clock it was, of necessity, a session of concentrated
severity!

September 25th The weather has turned noticeably
colder, so was agreeably surprised when sent at low level
to patrol over a convoy described by the Controller as
'Special'. However there didn't seem anything very
special about it when we got there; merely a rusty old
merchantman of some 2,000 tons, escorted by a couple of
destroyers. It must therefore have something to do with
the cargo which, as one wag suggests, is probably a fresh
supply of cigars for our Prime Minister! And while we
were circling this strange flotilla Pat Lyall was again in an
aggressive mood and tackled another Ju88 over the Isle
of Wight, leaving it with one engine on fire. He is being
allowed a 'probable' for this one.

We were scrambled as a squadron this afternoon to lie
in wait for a raid reported to be heading for The Needles,
but it veered off to the west in mid-Channel and was re-
allocated to 10 Group. It was probably making for Bristol.

The squadron clocked up another fifty hours today with
little to show for it. Strangely we find this more exhausting
than the more active sorties, when one has the stimulus
of battle to help keep the adrenalin flowing. At all events
the chaps are becoming noticeably more weary, often
falling asleep on hard-backed chairs, and even on the
floor.

Archie McKellar phoned me from Croydon with the
sad news of Walter Churchill's death in action. On the
brighter side, however, Archie has been awarded a bar to
his DFC and also been given command of 605 Squadron
in Walter's place.

                    *   *   *

September 27th   Yesterday Findlay led the squadron on a successful sortie over Southampton, shooting down four, although two of our aircraft came back with nasty-looking shell holes in their fuselages. I am concerned about the nature of the damage to our planes, for the Ju88s were unescorted, which means they must have been fired on by the bombers' front guns. I hope the lads are not becoming blasé and throwing caution to the winds.

It was my turn at the sharp end this morning and I was nicely settled over Dungeness with A Flight when six 109Es swooped from a great height. Fortunately we saw them coming and were able to side-step as they flew harmlessly past when Babbage, who was on the outside, drew a bead, but with no visible result. It appeared they had no intention of mixing it with us for they whizzed off at top speed and climbed away like bubbles in a bath.

As it was quiet in the afternoon I got down to a spot of stocktaking and find the squadron has accounted for seventy-one enemy aircraft destroyed, with another twenty-one in the list of 'probables'. On the debit side we have lost twenty-two aircraft in action, with three pilots killed or missing. Nonetheless it should be remembered that most of our chaps who baled out are back in the air, whereas the enemy have usually ended up in POW camps.

September 29th   Had a dicey experience with my under-carriage yesterday when it failed to lower properly on joining the circuit. Pedro, flying astern of me, reported I had one wheel down and the other in the up position, a configuration not confirmed by the warning lights, which showed two reds. So I cleared the circuit to try and shake it loose but after much diving, swooping, tugging and flying inverted, Pedro's report remained unaltered – one up and one down! It was now a case for the emergency

air bottle, but this only had the effect of giving me one
red and one green light on the dashboard – more attrac-
tive to look at but no less lethal in fact. However Pedro
thought both wheels looked OK so, heart in mouth and
with fingers crossed, I put her down gently and breathed
a big sigh of relief when I finally came to rest in an upright
position. They tell me it was only a small hydraulic leak.

September 30th   Had a pleasant surprise this morning
when George Pinkerton strode into the office. He is in
the middle of a Controller's Training Course at Stanmore
and took a day off to visit his old friends, although he
must think me a rotten host, as I was for ever having to
dash off and leave him.

In fact I did three sorties today. The first came to
nothing and we were pancaked after only ten minutes in
the air, whilst the second was hardly more fruitful and
only led us to a friendly Blenheim. However the third had
us tangling with twelve unescorted Ju88s over the Isle of
Wight when we quickly accounted for six before the rest
fled for cover in the clouds. I was firing sure-hit bullets
today and my victim went down minus its port main
plane, the engine having exploded dramatically. I saw one
Jerry jumping out just as the Junkers disappeared below
me in a series of flick rolls.

Was in the midst of dressing to go out when Jack called
to say the pilot of my Ju88 was in the guardroom at
Tangmere and had expressed a wish to meet the blighter
who shot him down. Could I spare a few minutes on my
way to Arundel? So, having first telephoned Gini to say
I'd be late, I found myself confronted by a fresh-faced
youth in Luftwaffe uniform who greeted me with considerable formality and a click of the heels. According to the
interpreter, who was present throughout, Helmut

Schweinhart thought it only right that it was to me, his vanquisher, he should formally surrender, so I am now the proud possessor of a German Luger automatic, a flying helmet, mae west and a bright orange-coloured ersatz velvet neck scarf which, Helmut was at pains to tell me, had been given to him by his mother as a good luck keepsake. It seems to have let him down sadly.

Our late arrival at Arundel Castle in no way lessened the warmth of our hosts' hospitality, and Gini and I returned to Lavington well fed, well wined and, in my case, well bruised, after being shown how to play billiards fives by Bernard. Indeed the pleasure of the day was completed when, on later getting back to Westhampnett, I found a message waiting from Eddie Ward to say he popped the question and Pauline had said 'yes'. Would I join them for drinks tomorrow?

1940

October

October 1st I had invited the Duke of Norfolk to meet
the lads this morning and was hoping the Luftwaffe would
leave us alone, particularly as Micky was feeling off colour
and I was taking his place. But the Luftwaffe is apparently
no respecter of the aristocracy for we were scrambled
soon after Bernard arrived. Fortunately Gini and her
waggon turned up at the psychological moment, so I was
able to leave the Duke in her capable hands whilst I
attended to matters aloft.

We were ordered to the Isle of Wight to meet a raid
approaching at Angels 15 and got there in double quick
time, only to find the area covered by thick broken cloud.
A sizeable force of 109s suddenly pounced on us from
behind a bank of cumulus and we would have been in
sore straits if Paddy Barthropp hadn't spotted it and
shouted a warning, so giving time to dodge the attack.
Nevertheless I was none too happy about the situation,
for we had four other newcomers in the formation, not
that I need have worried for one, John Willie Hopkins,
managed to get in a burst at a 109 as it went past, although
I don't think he hit it. At least he had broken his combat
virginity and doubtless it won't be too long before the
others follow suit. In fact he was the only one to fire, for
the 109s never reappeared in spite of the controller's
insistence that their plots were still in our vicinity. He
eventually sent us to The Needles where he said the sound
of firing was being reported, but it was not long before he
woke up to the fact it was nothing more than retrospective

information about out recent engagement, and sent us home. Bernard was still there, propped up against the waggon and in the middle of his third cup of coffee.

October 2nd Findlay had Barthorpp as his number two this morning when they were vectored on to a singleton Ju88 and clobbered it good and proper, but that was the only excitement all day and I sense that things are beginning to ease off. Apart from our brush with the 109s yesterday, most recent interceptions had been of single aircraft or 109s flying so high that there is little point in trying to reach them. It must be the same further east, for we are seldom called on by the Metropolitan sectors these days.

The lowering tension is also allowing the lads more leisure time and many are being invited to dine with neighbours, although we have to be careful not to overdo it in case old Hitler has something up his sleeve. Nonetheless we mean to make the most of it.

The upsurge of social activities is placing an extra demand on the bath. We have only one in the Mess, into which we put four at a time with legs dangling over the edge and, as a further measure to save time, have fitted a long board which traverses the bath from the tap end to the other, on which Mr Moto serves drinks in the course of our ablutions. Indeed Wyer does an excellent job in this respect and was once spotted using a stop-watch to ensure accuracy of delivery after I had asked him to '. . . bring the same again in three minutes!' So, following the popular trend, Jack and I became guests at Lavington this evening along with the Cowdrays and Davina Erne, although Euan had to excuse himself as he is none too well. Barbie is obviously very worried about her husband's health and has arranged for him to be admitted to a nursing home in London.

I called at the Operations Room after dropping off Jack and was pleasantly surprised to find the plotting table devoid of counters. However London is still coming in for a nightly dosage of bombs.

October 4th   The barometer has fallen ten points in the past two days and it has been raining continuously throughout. Findlay took off this morning to test conditions aloft, but wasted no time getting back on the ground on finding himself in cloud below 200 feet so I took the opportunity to call on the Chief Constable to seek his help in closing the road bordering the airfield. It is still very vulnerable in spite of the protective fencing, and we are forever having to shoo away the over-curious.

But one sightseer just won't budge. Mrs Sprague turned up two days ago with a friend, since when she has done nothing but sit in her car, gazing forlornly at the B Flight dispersal as if willing her husband to walk through the door. We too are being affected by her grief and doing all we can to console her, but the harsh fact is that we have had no word whatever about the sergeant's fate. Nor is there any news of Harry Moody, whose brother has already been in touch with me. It is at such times that the wider responsibilities of being a commander come home to roost and I find it particularly hard to choose the right words when writing to next of kin. But somebody has to do it.

Indeed it is a depressing morning all round for, having earned a hangover after another evening at Arundel, I overslept and missed breakfast. Now I'm told the tea waggon has broken down at Boxgrove.

* * *

October 5th The barometer is rising at last and it is quite a change to be airborne again, not that my two morning patrols yielded any profit. But Micky and Pedro were luckier in the afternoon when they intercepted a Ju88 as it was clearing the Isle of Wight. They gave chase and caught up with it near the French coast, leaving it heading for Boulogne with port engine on fire.

Lady Diana Duff-Cooper was Virginia's helper today and they were on the airfield when a dogfight started up somewhere in the region of Middle Wallop. The ladies dismounted from their van and joined us in a grandstand view of 609 Squadron taking on a gaggle of 109s in the distance, although it was clear from the number of Messerschmitts falling out of the sky that the Auxiliaries had the upper hand. This was my first experience of watching aerial combat from the ground and much enjoyed the spectacle. As far as we could make out, all our Spitfires were still flying when the action disappeared from view.

Westhampnett had another surprise visit from a low-flying Ju88 this evening but our gunners were awake on this occasion, when they filled the air with brightly coloured flaming balls swooshing over our heads from all points of the compass. Then the Tangmere guns joined in, after which it became a veritable Brock's benefit with fiery tracer streaks going everywhere except into the fuselage of the Ju88, which rapidly escaped into the nearest bank of cloud. The guns must have frightened him off, however, for there have been no reports of any bombs being dropped.

Sir Cyril Newall has been appointed Governor General of New Zealand, which is a signal honour for the Royal Air Force. We hear that Sir Charles Portal is taking over as Chief of the Air Staff.

* * *

October 7th   Findlay is taking a spot of well-earned leave and Donald Jack has returned from his. He reports that all is quiet in Glasgow and he also took time to call on Margaret and found her in good spirits.

The AOC arrived in his own Hurricane today. This is my first meeting with Keith Park, the tall New Zealander who carries the can for the way we operate, although he seems well enough pleased with the results so far and was full of praise for the manner in which the Tangmere Sector is acquitting itself. I was invited to lunch with him, in the course of which he disclosed that Jerry has fitted bombs to a number of 109s and warned us to be on the lookout for them. They must be very tiny bombs!

Had no sooner got back to Westhampnett when we were ordered off with 607 and 213 Squadrons towards the west but, before we were in position over Portland, Jimmy's two weavers collided and spun into the ground. I saw only one parachute opening. We nevertheless carried on and circled the Weymouth area for the best part of thirty minutes without meeting any opposition, before being sent back to Southampton, where again nothing turned up. Eventually a solitary plot was reported near Brighton and I sent Blue Section, comprising Donald and Sergeant Whall, to deal with it, whilst I took the rest back to base. Blue Section shot down a Do17 in the ensuing engagement but, during the transit back to Westhampnett, Whall suddenly dived away from his leader and hit the deck near Arundel. The cause of the accident is a mystery for Donald is certain they got no return fire from the Dornier and Whall gave no indication he was in trouble. We can only assume the poor fellow suffered a blackout.

I led the squadron on one more patrol this evening, but nothing came of it and we were pancaked shortly before darkness fell. However it made me late for Eddie's engagement party at the Ship.

October 9th I don't know what conditions are usually like here at this time of the year, but we have certainly had the lot during the past two days – low clouds, heavy rain and now a full-blown gale. I flew a weather test this morning to find a possible break coming up from the west, but eastwards it was real old Harry Clampers. Nevertheless it brought us a bonus in the shape of Archie McKellar who was unable to make it back to Croydon and chose to divert his squadron to Westhampnett instead. It is a tonic to see him again, although he looked very weary; not surprising when one considers the pressures under which the London-based squadrons are operating. They are not only called on more often than us, but seldom get a decent night's rest on account of the bombing. But it will take more than that to keep Archie down and he is full of enthusiasm as ever. He tells me he shot down five 109s on Monday.

Alas, the weather began to clear over the Home Counties and Archie took his squadron back to Croydon, thus depriving us of their company overnight. The weather began to clear here too and we were soon airborne over Southampton in response to reports of a raid approaching that area. But the low clouds made an interception impossible. I was not flying on this sortie and, while I waited at dispersal for the squadron's return, a low-flying Ju88 suddenly appeared over the far corner of the airfield, releasing a salvo of bombs. Everyone froze, as if mesmerized by the scene, until they woke to the fact that the Jerry gunners were also blazing away with their fore and aft guns and strafing the field as they flew over when, to a man, they dived for cover. Peeping

from behind a tree, I watched the intruder streaking off
in the direction of Tangmere, hotly chased by the tracer
from our Bofors, and waited for the explosions. Indeed
they went off with a hell of a noise, although nothing was
hit and we could breathe again. I was hoping our lads had
got wind of the 88 and would make short shrift of it, but
it was out of range before the message got to them.

I flew the next patrol myself when the squadron was
sent to Brighton to deal with some 109s making a nuisance
of themselves with their little bombs. However they had
disapeared into thin air by the time we reached the spot,
which is a pity, for I wanted to see what this new breed of
fighter looked like. A full gale had blown up by the time
we returned and I almost couped J on to her nose on
landing cross wind.

October 11th Have lost count of how often sections were
scrambled today, and all to no purpose. To a certain
extent we can blame weather conditions for our lack of
success although the enemy is not helping by appearing
only in penny packets instead of in large batches, which
are much easier to pin down. But London is still the main
target for the night raiders, so I took Donald and
McDowall on a barrier patrol off the south coast hoping
to intercept one of the early marauders, but the ploy
didn't work. Of course it was fully dark by the time we
returned, so I ordered the others to put down at Tangmere as we have no night facilities at Westhampnett. At
the same time I thought I would have a stab at getting
into our own base by the beam of my landing light so,
first identifying the main road from the amount of traffic
on it and using it as a datum, I turned left at Merston,
switched on the light and scraped into the field by the skin

of my teeth, missing the A Flight dispersal by a mere fraction. At least it alerted the ground crews!

The squadron collected more honours today. Findlay has a bar to his DFC and Cyril Babbage a DFM. But there is sad news too. Sergeant Sprague's body has been washed ashore near Brighton after being missing for the past three weeks.

October 13th The tempo of operations is clearly slowing down and even the controllers are complaining they don't have enough to do. When the enemy does put in an appearance, it is generally with small numbers of 109s carrying bombs and we have found no difficulty in dealing with them whenever contact is made. Nevertheless we are not getting off entirely scot free, for Babbage was shot down near Lewes yesterday and Hart returned with category two damage today. Micky later made up for it by shooting down a Ju88 in mid-Channel.

David Niven dined with Jack and me at the Ship this evening. He is cheesed off at being taken off ops to make a film for the Public Relations people.

October 14th Was at Tangmere with Crackers, making arrangements for Sprague's funeral, when told that B Flight had been scrambled from Westhampnett in spite of a previous order grounding all aircraft on account of bad weather. I left Crackers to deal with the funeral arrangements and dashed to the Operations Room to find a controller on duty whom I had not previously met. It transpired this was his first attempt at fighter controlling and, doubtless wishing to impress his new boss, he had ordered off B Flight, even against the advice of Ops B. By the time I had sized up the situation, B Flight was already at 25,000 feet and still in the clag, with Donald complaining bitterly that it was as dark as hell outside and that he was having trouble trying to keep the flight together, especially as he had a couple of tyros with him. I am afraid I lost my rag and grabbed the microphone from the controller, telling him I'd justify my action later. Fortunately the 602 plots were clearly identifiable on the table so I was able to direct Donald out to sea in a gentle let-down until they eventually broke cloud at 800 feet. Fortunately Bunny Hewitt, the senior controller, came in in the middle of the drama and exonerated me for my action. I won't be surprised to hear that the other bloke has joined Pinkerton at the Controllers' Training Unit at Stanmore!

Westhampnett is not the only satellite airfield in the sector. Merston, situation mid-way between Tangmere and Bognor Regis, is another, but as yet unused except for emergency landings. However Jack decided he would put 213 Squadron there and issued the necessary instructions to Stuart McDonald, the CO. I was still at Tangmere when 213 took off for Merston, so thought it would be a nice gesture if I drove over to welcome Stuart and his boys at their new home. To be honest, I was curious to see how they would make out, for one of our chaps happened to drive past the place a few days ago and reported it looked as soft as a sago pudding, and it has been raining ever since. So I was not unduly surprised on arrival to find Mac in a towering rage as he glared at seven Hurricanes scattered about the airfield, all up to their armpits in mud! I gather Jack has now decided to keep 213 Squadron at Tangmere, at least until the engineers instal some decent drainage at Merston.

Another surprise visitor today. The Duke of Hamilton has turned up unexpectedly and proposes to stay the night. Am due to dine at Arundel so have just spoken to

Lavinia who says to bring Douglo along. Strangely it will be the first time both premier dukes will have met.

October 15th Led the squadron on a patrol over Portsmouth this morning when our target was a mixed bag of 109s and FW190s flying very high. Normally this would have been a straightforward interception as we spotted their vapour trails soon after taking off from Westhampnett but, by the time we had struggled up to 34,000 feet, our quarry had gone. Probably as well, for we were virtually hanging on our props at that height and would have been at a considerable disadvantage if we had had to slug it out.

Jack called a meeting of his squadron commanders and the senior controller this evening to discuss this latest problem and we have agreed to limit operations to a maximum of 27,000 feet in future. Bomb-carrying 109s can't fly any higher and those without do not harm.

October 20th Have just got back from a weekend at Lavington which, as usual, was full of house guests, although Euan is still laid up. John de Bendern, better known as John de Forest, the amateur golfer (Shrubbery to his friends), was among those staying and Euan mentioned how thrilled his two younger sons would be if the two of us took them out from school for an afternoon. Fortunately Shrubbery knew his way around Eton and we eventually made contact with the boys at the Burning Bush and whisked them off to the Hind's Head at Bray for lunch. That was our first mistake, for the lads disdained our offer of a pre-prandial ginger pop and settled instead for a Pimms No 1, not that it did anything to diminish their appetites. The second mistake was to take them later to a picture house in Windsor, only to find it showing a most unsuitable film about sex. However we were not required to stay until the end because the Pimms unexpectedly caught up with Wallace Minor before the plot became too difficult to explain, when we just reached the toilets in the nick of time. Shrubbery and I were decidedly relieved to hand the boys over to their housemaster.

October 21st An official war artist, Turps Orde, has been commissioned by the Air Ministry to sketch pictures of a number of fighter pilots, yours truly among them. So I spent most of the morning having my mug drawn for posterity by this famous artist, although neither of us thought much of the finished product. Turps says he will do another one later. I became more active in the afternoon and led two of the five patrols undertaken by the squadron but, as they were both concerned with high-flying 109s, the results were blank. Indeed we see very little daylight bombing now, most of the damage being done at night. However the overall signs are encouraging, for Bomber Command has started to hit back and is now sending bombers as far afield as Berlin and Northern Italy.

Margaret telephoned last night to let me know she's expecting a baby next spring so I have arranged to take leave in ten days' time providing things stay as they are. However this good news is somewhat tempered by another message from the Lord Provost to say he will be arranging a special lunch in the City Chambers while I am in Glasgow at which he will expect me to speak.

October 23rd Am feeling unsettled at the thought of the forthcoming furlough but fortunately kept well occupied chasing the 109s which continue to come over in dribs and drabs. I cannot imagine what they think they are achieving by this futile waving of coat tails, unless they are hoping we will be daft enough to climb up after them. If so, they will have to go on hoping!

We are due to be fitted with new R/T sets, but the first batch has arrived minus their slings and I will have to wait until I get back off leave to try them out. They are crystallized on a very high frequency which is supposed to cut out interference.

Am spending the night at Lavington as Virginia is tomorrow giving me a lift as far as Birmingham to spare me the discomfort of the nightly bombings in London. I have left the squadron in the capable hands of Findlay Boyd.

October 24th   The Morris Eight behaved impeccably and Virginia dropped me at New Street Station around six o'clock. As my train was not due to leave for another two and a half hours, I decided to treat myself to a dinner at the Queen's Hotel.

Few were about when I entered the dining room, the only other occupants being an elderly couple seated at the far end of the room and a lieutenant-commander at the table next to mine. Notwithstanding the limited clientele a small string orchestra was already scraping out a selection from *Maid of the Mountains*. Indeed I was just thinking what a pleasant way this was to start my leave when the sirens sounded and the rumble of gunfire could be heard in the distance but, as no one else seemed to be paying much attention, I set about the plateful of smoked salmon the waiter had just placed before me. Then the bomb struck.

The noise of the explosion did not seem all that loud; it was more like a door being slammed. Then there was an instant when the world seemed to stand still; rather like freezing a frame of a motion picture. One minute a waiter was in full stride, tray held aloft, the next no longer there, although his tray remained in view as if suspended in animation. The music disappeared along with the members of the band who were now miraculously transposed beneath the grand piano. I found myself looking at my naval neighbour who was looking back at me, both arrested with fork poised twixt plate and mouth. Then the full impact was upon us.

Two large plate glass windows imploded on to the carpet, showering the room with particles of heavy glass. At the same time a fierce blast of dust-laden air forced open the service doors, propelling the head waiter onto a nearby table. He was covered in thick dust and shouting 'Help!' at the top of his voice, whereupon the Navy and I ran to the kitchens to be met with a shocking sight. The whole area was full of smoke and steam from overturned cooking vessels and the floor littered with pots, pans and heaps of broken crockery. Two white-coated chefs lay half buried beneath a pile of fallen rubble, whilst a third was screaming in agony, being trapped against one of the hotplates by a massive fallen beam. We managed to prise him free by putting our shoulders under the beam, by which time the poor fellow had fortunately lapsed into unconsciousness. Soon the place was swarming with the rescue services, and we were able to retire from the grisly scene. 'Woodroffe,' my companion announced by way of introduction, 'Tommy Woodroffe. BBC.' I couldn't have chosen a better man!

It was a long night. The station also took a direct hit and they tell me it will take several days to clear the tracks, so there was nothing I could do but stop where I am. In the event Woodroffe and I were soon pressed into service and found ourselves shovelling incendiaries off the roof or dowsing them with a stirrup pump, something I had always wanted to try my hand at. We were given a pat on the back by the fire chief for our efforts. Then the head waiter sought us out to thank us for our assistance in the kitchens which, he told us, are completely out of action. Nevertheless the excellent fellow wheeled up the remains of a side of smoked salmon and bade us help ourselves, but that only generated a man's size thirst which, fortunately, we were able to slake in an underground bar which was being kept open and doing a very brisk trade. Once we poked our heads outside to see what was going on but had to beat a hasty retreat when Marshall and Snelgrove's store across the street came crashing down and showered us with burning embers.

Have taken a bedroom for the rest of the night, but it is none too comfortable. The windows have all gone and the carpet is strewn with bits of glass. The bed too has a thick layer of dirt and pieces of broken plaster all over it. Nevertheless it will be somewhere to put my head down for a few hours, although I will be furious if I hear tomorrow that London has had a bomb-free night!

October 25th Woke with a throbbing head and was immediately conscious of a strong smell of smouldering timber. My ill-humour was further compounded when offered nothing more than a plateful of cornflakes and a cup of revolting coffee for breakfast and it reached boiling point when the management insisted on charging the full rate for my night's lodging. This was when I wished Woodroffe and I had left the ruddy place to burn down!

Most streets are cordoned off to let the rescue services grapple with their grim task of burrowing through the huge heaps of rubble in a desperate attempt to free the victims buried beneath. The silence seemed almost unreal, broken occasionally by a solitary shout or by a hollow-sounding 'clunk' as another chunk of masonry was pitched to one side. Of course, there was no transport to be had, which meant I had to hump my heavy suitcase through the shattered streets, as I tried to find my way to Monument Lane Station, where I was told a few trains were running.

After trudging for the best part of half an hour I came to a road on which the traffic was flowing and started to look around for a passing taxi. I was suddenly hailed by a cheerful 'Wotcha Chum!' to find Dunlop and Mary Urie alongside. I could hardly believe my eyes. It turned out they were on their way back to Glasgow after Dunlop's spell in a convalescent home at Torquay. At last things were beginning to look rosier. But not for long, for we had to stand in the corridor for the entire six-hour journey without heat, food or drink and Glasgow never looked so beautiful as it did when Central Station finally hove into sight. Nevertheless I'm home, and Margaret seems quite pleased to see me.

October 30th I can hardly believe it is five days since I started my leave, much of which I seem to have spent asleep. I have been encouraged in this by my wife who now uses the stock excuse of morning sickness to indulge in protracted lie-ins, not that her interesting condition has in any way dampened her appetite whenever we go out to dine.

The Lord Provost's special lunch is now a thing of the past and I'm told my speech went down well with the assembled company which, incidentally, included J. B. Priestley. After it was over the Lord Provost insisted on dragging me off to a charity football match at Shawfield Park where a team from the British Army was playing one from the Norwegian Army. I found myself seated next to Prince Olaf whose stentorian encouragement far outdid in volume anything Padre Sutherland could possibly achieve, even at full throttle. In spite of the princely exhortations, the Norwegians were beaten by two goals to nil.

Had a surprise visit from Paul Webb last night, for I thought he was still convalescing in the south. He had read of my presence in Glasgow in the local papers. Paul seems to be making a good recovery and can waggle his fingers again to say nothing of tilting his elbow. By a strange coincidence he was with me when a telegram arrived from Crackers to say the squadron had just shot down eight enemy aircraft without loss to themselves. If it happens again I shall know for certain they get on much better without me!

1940

November

November 2nd   I don't know what normally motivates a Civic Head, but the exploits of 602 Squadron seem to have fired the imagination of Paddy Dollan, the dynamic Lord Provost of our native city. He has taken me firmly under his wing and hardly a day goes past without the LP trying to get me involved in some worthy cause or another; not that I mind, for it has already reaped a substantial reward for the squadron benevolent fund which, thanks to the Lord Provost's intervention, now stands at over £15,000. In view of this, I suggested it is now too significant a sum to be handled by amateurs and, under the aegis of the Territorial Army and Air Forces Association, a permanent committee has been set up to handle the fund's affairs. The Lord Provost, ex-officio, is to be the chairman, with the squadron CO, the Dean of Guild and the Deacon Convenor of the Trades its other officers. Paddy Dollan and myself are, additionally, to be life trustees.

Now cast as the prize exhibit, Paddy had me on parade this morning when he was inaugurating another fund in aid of War Charities, the centrepiece of the show being a captured Ju88 on display in Blythswood Square. Not unexpectedly, Paddy made the most of this and assured the attentive audience that the Jerry bomber had been shot down by Glasgow's very own squadron although I was sorely tempted to interrupt and point out it would have had many more bullet holes in it if it had been! Nevertheless the venue was handy for the Royal Scottish

Automobile Club, of which I am a member, so was able
to repay a little of his hospitality by taking the LP to lunch
there after the ceremony. By good fortune Hector Mac-
Lean was at the club, sporting a tin leg, so I introduced
him to Paddy, thereby doubling the LP's sense of involvement with the squadron in one fell swoop.

My brief spell as a civic celebrity is over and I am now
on my way south in the night train. But the embarrassing
attention followed me to the end for, whilst talking to my
father before the train pulled out, an official party,
including the Lord Provost, the City Treasurer, the Chairman of Rangers Football Club and the City Officer,
arrived unexpectedly on the platform, the last-named
trundling a luggage trolley loaded with a number of large
parcels. These, the LP explained, were a present of bed
linen for the boys, 'to make their living conditions more
comfortable!' The surprise gift is apparently in response
to a facetious remark I had made two days ago when
asked if there was anything we are short of, and I had
said 'Only sheets!' No doubt they will be well received.

But the day has not been without its sadness. Crackers
telephoned while I was packing to tell me that Archie
McKellar has been killed in action. Apparently he was
involved with some 109s over Mayfield when he copped
it. I find it hard to take in, for Archie somehow seemed
indestructible, and he will be much missed. He is certainly
the bravest fellow I have ever met, a fact substantiated by
his outstanding record which has netted him a DSO and a
double DFC, all within a period of one month.

November 5th   Back in harness again and opted to lead
the early patrol, not only to get the feel of it but to test
one of the new VHF sets, which turns out to be every bit
as good as they said it would be. Free from interference

and more like talking on the telephone. However only one sortie was called for, to the Isle of Wight, but it was a false alarm.

Mr Moto has been busy in my absence, for I came back to find two large floor rugs in the bedroom and a thoughtful vase of autumn leaves on the dresser. Wyer has had leave at the same time and I was glad to hear that his home escaped the bombing in Birmingham, although houses round about were apparently not so lucky. He expressed satisfaction that no more cuspidors were collected during his absence and further considers the addition of bed linen does much to raise the tone of our accommodation.

The nights are drawing in, so we were released as early as six o'clock, when I drove to Tangmere to let Jack know I was back. Caught him just as he was setting off for a party at the WAAF Mess, when he insisted I went with him. We did not stay for long, however, as I almost fell asleep in the middle of it, the night in an LMS sleeper having caught up with me. I have yet to master the ventilation system in these carriages.

November 6th　　Was trying to catch up with outstanding bumff when the whole squadron was ordered to scramble, so I dropped everything to lead it, as it is some time since we've been sent off in toto. We intercepted a large force of bomb-carrying 109s approaching the Isle of Wight, but they jettisoned their load as soon as we turned up, and turned tail. That they made no attempt to fight seems a sure indication of how demoralized Jerry has become, although it didn't stop us from going after them. In the ensuing chase, McDowall got close enough to send one down in flames and Stuart MacDonald's boys, who turned up in the middle of the engagement, managed to cut off another before it could get away. The rest eluded us with their superior climbing speed.

Had to dash across to Tangmere as soon as we landed, for I was due for my B Licence medical. I feel it important to keep it valid in case I want to return to civil aviation once the war is over. I was surprised to pass quite easily after the ravages of two weeks in Scotland.

Was ordered up again during the lunch break, when Nigal Rose and I suddenly found ourselves face to face with a Ju88 swooping round a large cloud over the Channel. I think Jerry was even more taken aback than we were, for he pulled away sharply and presented a broadside view of his underbelly which we were not slow to exploit. I saw bullets ripping into the pale blue underside and, when the aircraft swung upright, the rear gun was pointing vertically upwards and the gunner slumped over his scarf ring. Unfortunately it then divided into a cloud and we lost him, although Intelligence is allowing us to claim a 'damaged'.

November 8th Jerry still likes to sneak in after dark and we were paid a visit last night by a low-flying Ju88 which scattered a stick of incendiaries on the airfield, one of which ignited close to a Spitfire. A duty guard was fortunately close enough to kick it away before it did any damage, but these things are a confounded nuisance, as the fragments have to be located and swept up before they damage the tyres of taxiing aircraft.

At Tangmere 145 Squadron, whom we relieved here last August, has taken over from 607 Squadron. Naturally we are sorry to lose our old colleague, Jimmy Vick, but also glad to welcome back Johnny Peel, happily recovered from his injury. Dunlop Urie also turned up unexpectedly and is having his leg pulled at timing his visit so well. He had arrived just in time to attend 'Jack's Mammoth Party'.

It is no secret that Jack dislikes Germans and, on the pretext that Hitler could still launch his invasion, he is insisting that the Mess funds are disposed of before the Nazis can get their hands on them. So he ordered the Mess Committee to organize a super function to ensure no money will be left for any would-be invaders. The party took place tonight.

Invitations had been sent far and wide and the Mess was bulging with guests from all walks of life, ranging from Ministers of the Crown to the youngest pilot officer ever connected with the station. The C-in-C even put in an appearance, as did the Crazy Gang and girls from the Windmill Theatre. The Humber was pressed into service and I drove to Lavington to fetch some guests from there, amongst whome were the Chief Whip, David Margesson, and Harold Balfour. By the time we got back to Tangmere the place was in a state of utter turmoil, a solid mass of humanity either struggling to get into the bar or struggling to get out of it, whilst the corridors were hard to negotiate because of the crowds thronging to and fro. The only way to communicate was by shouting at the top of one's voice.

But everyone was having a whale of a time and rumour has it that the first to pass out was a Mess waiter who was seen to keel over half an hour before the party was due to begin. Not surprisingly the Crazy Gang was unable to perform, but no one cared, nor even noticed. At some point during the evening I came upon Jimmy Nervo sitting in a corridor, flanked by two curvaceous Windmill girls plying him with champagne which, in turn, was being served by Teddy Knox and Bud Flanagan, both pressed into service as auxiliary barmen. They tell me it was a stupendous party. And I'm sure they must be right.

Certainly I was taken aback when Harold Balfour rang this morning, thanking me profusely for driving the Chief Whip and himself back to Lavington and seeing them safely into bed. I could have sworn someone else had driven *me* home!

November 10th Nuts Niven has also chosen his time well, for he has managed to wriggle free from 601's grasp and get posted back to 602. And who can blame him? If he feels sufficiently fit after last night's shenanigans, he will survive anything we can throw at him. At all events, welcome back Nuts! Indeed he joined us on this morning's patrol when we were all praying the Germans wouldn't show up, a sentiment no doubt shared by Jack when he came on the R/T to enquire after my health, his voice sounding like a load of gravel pouring into my eardrums. I gather he hadn't been to bed. Thankfully our prayers were answered and we were allowed home to wallow in our hangovers. God protect me from this social whirl which has now reached threatening proportions for, not only am I bidden to Gee Wallace's wedding in a couple of days time, but the Duke and Duchess of Richmond have decided to pay us a call tonight. But maybe the war is over and nobody had thought to tell me.

November 12th The Hun must have given us up as a bad job, for there has been no enemy activity whatsoever for the past two days and we have been able to use the break to push on with the training programme. I feel sorry for those posted in without previous experience on Spitfires and expected to go straight into action. I certainly would have had kittens if I'd been made to tangle with a Messerschmitt, knowing little about my aircraft, and one cannot help admiring the gutsy way these lads have been tackling it so far. It must be a relief for them to get into the air with the sole purpose of familiarizing themselves with the Spitfire.

Gee Wallace and Elizabeth Koch de Guyrend were married yesterday in Midhurst Registry Office and later held a reception at Lavington. Barbie's parents, Sir Edwin and Lady Lutyens, were there and I was particularly thrilled to meet the famous architect, whose eye for the perpendicular is only matched by his appreciation of a pretty face. When enjoying the company of this genial old gentleman it is hard to imagine he had been responsible for the creation of such remarkable buildings as the Cenotaph in Whitehall and the Government buildings in New Delhi, to say nothing of the many Royal Air Force stations which owe their distinctive design to the architectural genius of Sir Edwin.

Douglas Farquhar flew from Martlesham to spend the night with his old squadron and couldn't have chosen a better time to do so, for Micky Mount has just been awarded the DFC. No one is more admired and liked than Micky, as the subsequent celebrations proved, and I am pleased Douglas is here to share them.

November 13th Some have all the luck! Sat at readiness all morning with nothing to show for it, even after scouring the skies on two occasions, but had no sooner handed over to Findlay when B Flight was ordered off and shot down a Ju88. Dunlop was with Findlay on this trip, having his last ride with 602 Squadron before taking up his new post as an instructor at No 55 Operational Training Unit, Aston Down. Johnny Peel is complaining that his boys had seen the Junkers first, but were pipped at the post by B Flight. I could only remind him that all is fair in love and war!

Another war artist, this time a lady, is here to paint portraits of Micky and myself. So Mount has gone off to Dower House in Goodwood Park with Olive Snell, but only after assurances that she has no desire to portray him in the nude. I had to surrender the first sitting to Micky as the Duke of Kent came back for another visit and stayed for dinner. Ian Ferguson, whose back is still unserviceable, has just been appointed ADC to His Royal Highness, so we now have a friend at court!

November 15th　Yesterday was a quiet day, with nothing more exciting to report than a few routine patrols. Maybe it was as well, for a sudden outbreak of influenza has floored a number of chaps, thus making it necessary to recall those on leave. And I did so just in time, for Jerry has unexpectedly come alive again.

I led the squadron three times today when German fighters were reported active along the entire south coast. We saw nothing on the first occasion and only a few high fliers on the second. On the third, however, a gaggle of 109s put in an appearance around 27,000 feet and I determined to go for them. We got within 1,500 feet of them and were getting ready to launch our attack when a further batch of 109s bore down from out of the sun and soon had us in severe trouble. It was a miracle none of us was hit, for the sky seemed full of tracer as we scattered to avoid the fire and, by the time we'd sorted ourselves out, they had all gone. Vamoosed. We had been taken for a ride! There was nothing more we could do, other than swallow our pride, so I gathered together those who were still within sight and told the others to find their own way home. It was only then I discovered that McDowell had, in fact, taken a knock during the encounter and had made a wheels-up landing near Birdham with shrapnel wounds in his face. I fear the affray has done nothing to improve Mac's appearance, his temper or his language!

November 18th   It has been a short shooting season, for Jerry has gone back into hibernation, at least as far as we are concerned, and has left us alone for the past three days. No bad thing as it turns out, for Mac is hors de combat for a few weeks and Babbage has now succumbed to the flu bug. However three new lads have been posted to us but have still to turn up, and Jack has been on to say a second squadron is being moved into Westhampnett sometime soon.

If the Prime Minister's announcement in the House of Commons is anything to go by, it appears we have been taking part in a famous battle. He has been telling the people that they owe it to the pilots of Fighter Command for not being invaded in September. It's nice to know we have been of service although, to be honest, it has not seemed like a battle to me: rather an extension of what we have been doing since we first came up against the Hun a year ago last October – only more so!

November 19th   Spent this morning with Jack, determining how best to fit in another squadron. Seemingly 302 (Polish) Squadron is due to arrive on Saturday and it is going to be difficult to accommodate everyone. There is insufficient space in our buildings, that's for sure, and Jack is left with no alternative but to put the Poles under canvas. Rather them than us, for the far side of the airfield is very soft after all the rain that's fallen.

Jeffrey Quill has been here again, this time bringing a Spitfire fitted with metal ailerons. Findlay and I both tried it out and consider it a great improvement over the present fabric-covered models. Nonetheless I have suggested to Jeffrey that all our aircraft should be modified together, as the metal ailerons alter the flying characteristics – albeit for the better.

November 23rd Mr Churchill's Commons speech must have been heard by our enemies, for they seem to have taken it to heart and accepted defeat. Certainly they have stopped coming over here. But nothing is being taken for granted and Control sends us into the air to investigate everything which appears on their table even, as one wit observed, when a fly happens to settle on it. The Prime Minister's glowing tribute has also inspired nationwide interest in our aircraft and we are now much in demand to put in appearances at all manner of Spitfire Fund Appeals in aid of the war effort. Indeed I have not escaped, and Barbie Wallace had me drawing tickets for her local raffle which won for the lucky number a bottle of Haig whisky. But the raffle alone brought in over fifty pounds.

It has been raining on and off for the past week and a particularly heavy downpour last night has flooded the airfield and made it unserviceable. In fact, parts of it are so soft that I almost tipped J on its nose whilst taxiing to a drier spot. However the enforced grounding is allowing Micky full rein to meet his obligations as an artist's model and he tells me his portrait is nearly finished. He is well pleased with it, too, and relieved that he hasn't been requested to remove even his jacket.

Yesterday 302 Squadron should have flown in but was delayed on account of the flooding. But conditions improved this afternoon and the Poles were able to make it this evening, by which time Jack Boret was ready to explode as several tents had collapsed under the weight of water. Despite such dismal conditions Jack Satchell, the Poles' English commanding officer, seems reasonably happy with the arrangements and, while Boret and I were welcoming the new arrivals, John Willie Hopkins decided to stage his own welcoming ceremony by landing his aircraft on top of mine, which was parked outside my office, writing off both Spitfires. It is hardly the done thing to wreck the boss's aeroplane in front of his very eyes and I'm afraid young Hopkins has incurred the grave displeasure of his commanding officer and his sin is further compounded by the fact that J is one of the few aircraft fitted with metal ailerons. It is lucky for him I'm spending the weekend at Lavington.

November 25th   Have decided to transfer my flag to F, although I don't like it as much as J. However Connors says he will have the letter changed to J to avoid confusion when we get back into the air. The boys are now used to seeing their leader with his initial on the fuselage.

Barbie has just rung to let me know that Euan is going to a London clinic where he can be under the supervision of specialists. He certainly looked very poorly when I saw him at the weekend.

November 28th   The Germans have definitely lifted the pressure and we are now under no more strain than we were during our service in Scotland. What little action we see is against fleeting darts by high-flying fighters although there is still a considerable amount of bombing in the capital, but only during the hours of darkness, so we are not involved. It was therefore interesting to talk to Air Marshal Sir Sholto Douglas who today paid a visit in his capacity as our new Commander-in-Chief, Stuffy Dowding having handed over last week.

The C-in-C was out to pick our brains and quizzed us about many things, such as our feelings about going on the offensive and taking on the Luftwaffe over its own bases. He also wanted our opinion on the comparative merits of employing wings of fighters in a defensive role as against single squadrons, or even flights. Having had no time to consider the matter in detail we could only tell him we had done well enough the way we have been doing it. Although we were unaware of the fact, there has apparently been a school of thought in High Places which favours the former method, although I should think it would take too long to get a wing into position in time to achieve the aim of stopping bombers from reaching their targets. That, after all, is the principal purpose.

The squadron was scrambled in the middle of the C-in-C's visit and Micky led it to meet a number of high fliers approaching the coast. I don't know whether the controller was trying to impress our distinguished visitor or merely had a sudden rush of blood to the head, but he ordered the lads to 33,000 feet where, of course, they were no match for the 109Es, which set about them in no mean fashion. They were at a considerable disadvantage and, in the course of a short but sharp engagements, Pat Lyall's aircraft was hit, although he seemed to have it under control throughout the subsequent let-down. In fact everything was all right until Pat inexplicably dived over the side at around 1,000 feet and was seen to hit the deck before his parachute opened. The rest got back safely, although several aircraft required extensive patching.

November 30th Boret listened sympathetically when confronted by his three enraged squadron commanders demanding an explanation for yesterday's debacle. Apart from suggesting that Micky should have ignored the controller's instructions, he had none to offer, so the wretched controller was summoned before us and given such a bollocking by Jack that he was quickly reduced to tears. A case of crying over spilt milk, maybe, but we have lost a darned good friend as a result of his ineptitude.

But the show must go on, as they say, and go on it did in the matter of Eddie and Pauline's wedding, which took place today in a small church on the outskirts of Maidstone. Pauline looked lovely and Eddie looked apprehensive. Johnny Peel and Stuart MacDonald drove over with me in the Humber and, after the ceremony, we joined the other guests for the reception in Leeds Castle, the home of the bride's mother. It is a fine setting for such an occasion, although I couldn't help thinking back to my own wedding day as I was crossing the moat for, if I had been privileged to have had our reception at Leeds, it is not on to the roof of a taxi I would have been deposited! Later, making my way through the guests in search of refreshment, I became aware of much curtseying and bobbing going on all around, but it was not until the Group Captain walking ahead turned to greet me that I realized the cause. HRH was there to share the fun.

1940

December

December 2nd As an indication of how quiet things now are, we spend most of our time practising attack procedures in squadron strength, often against 65 Squadron which recently flew in to take over from 213. MacDonald has taken his lot to Leconfield. In fact I have only been called on to fly one operational patrol during the past three days, over Mayfield it was, when nothing showed up. However I have recently become embroiled in a rumpus of a different kind, this time on the ground.

Under the terms of its charter, the NAAFI has the monopoly for supplying canteen facilities to all service units, however remote the area. Westhampnett, however, seems to have escaped its notice, for its services have been conspicuous by their absence ever since we got here – until yesterday, that is, when a NAAFI individual presented himself in my office to inform me he was setting up canteen facilities in a small marquee behind the A Flight dispersal, at the same time demanding that the YWCA mobile canteen should henceforth be banned from entering the airfield. I managed somehow to keep my temper and saw our visitor off the premises with a promise to consider the matter, when immediately I consulted various experts who, regretfully, could only substantiate the NAAFI man's claim. Shortly after, Connors delivered a message from the airmen, who have sworn to boycott the NAAFI if the mobile canteen is banned, pointing out that the NAAFI has chosen to wait until the airfield is no longer under threat before deciding to set up business, whereas Virginia and helpers never failed to put in a daily appearance, even during the worst of the bombing. I am much encouraged by this, and have stuck my neck out and told Gini to carry on with her visits, at the same time writing to the Under Secretary of State seeking his help. Somehow I feel Harold Balfour will come up trumps.

McDowall has been awarded a bar to his DFM and Olive Snell is ready to begin painting my picture.

December 5th Low clouds, poor visibility and long periods of steady drizzle have effectively kept us grounded for much of the time, with the result that I've become a dab hand at Ludo, the only pastime remaining at dispersal since Hector took away his chess set. However I was able to test a replacement aircraft during a short clearance and have earmarked it to replace J, although it clearly wants something done to the undercarriage as we bounced a mile into the air on touch down; like jumping on a springboard. Something to do with too much fluid in the oleos, they tell me.

Olive Snell started the portrait this morning, although it amazed me she was able to hold her paint brushes steady, for the Dower House is one of the coldest houses I have ever been in. I imagine an igloo would provide more comfort. It is a strange building, too, being entirely circular, with rooms radiating from the centre like spokes of a wheel. Built by one of the present Duke of Richmond's ancestors to house one of his beloveds, everything is designed to accommodate two persons – small settees for two, double beds, foot warmers for two and even the loo is constructed as a two-seater. That really must be the ultimate token of affection! However Olive has found an ordinary kitchen chair for me to sit on, and the portrait is under way. I was, however, slightly alarmed to see her reach for a tube of ultramarine when about to paint my nose. I didn't think it was all *that* cold!

December 8th The squadron was stood down in toto today, the first time it's happened since we came south. Nor could it have happened at a better time, for it ensured a full turn-out at Pat Lyall's funeral which took place this afternoon in the Brighton Crematorium. Pat's mother had asked especially for the ceremony to be held in the south so that as many colleagues as possible could attend, and was naturally very pleased to see so many there. Before setting out for Brighton, however, I endured another sitting in the Dower House with Olive, who is making good progress. She has me wearing my black flying overalls and I've also put on Schweinhardt's orange scarf to add a touch of colour.

Three new pilots have turned up, but I have yet to meet them. Also news of Babbage's commission came through while we were at the funeral.

December 10th Thanks to the continuing lull, Jack suggested I fly to Glasgow to see Margaret so, needing no further bidding, I set out in my new Spit. The weathermen had assured me of good conditions along the route, but he was wide of the mark, and it took ages to reach Abbotsinch. Not only had I to land and refuel on the way because of headwinds, but had to fly right round the Ayrshire coast to dodge the Cu Nimbs over the Dumfriesshire hills. Abbotsinch has changed hands since we were there, the Royal Navy being the new occupiers. Indeed it has been renamed HMS 'Something or Other' and seems to be swarming with sailors and WRNS all saluting each other in little round hats. Margaret was surprised to see me, for I hadn't warned her I was coming in case something cropped up to kibosh the trip, but it didn't lessen the warmth of my reception. I too am glad to get home and out of my flying boots, for I forgot to pack my shoes in the rush to get away.

December 12th Had a more comfortable flight back, weather conditions being fine throughout. However the squadron was not at Westhampnett when I got there, having been scrambled to the Dover area half an hour earlier. They were in action, too, although they didn't exactly cover themselves with glory, having failed to score, and losing Jake Edy's aircraft into the bargain. Jake had a lucky escape, for a sizeable chunk of one of his mainplanes was shot away during the fight and the rest parted company with the fuselage when he then crashed into a flock of sheep grazing in the Kentish field.

Fred Nancarrow, air correspondent of *The Glasgow Herald* and *The Bulletin*, turned up at Westhampnett yesterday to write an article for his readers. Instead, he got something of a scoop for, before the poor chap had time even to sharpen his pencils, news came through that 602 Squadron will be moving to Prestwick on Saturday. Apparently 610 Squadron from Acklington is to relieve us.

The news has been received with mixed feelings as there are not many aircrew left who actually come from Scotland: A large proportion of the original Auxiliaries have been posted elsewhere or are wounded. But the ground crews are delighted at the prospect of getting home for Christmas, as am I, and we are grateful to Fighter Command for the thoughtful gesture. I hear 603 Squadron is also getting home in time for the festive season.

Suddenly there is much to do. All our gear to be packed up; next week's party to be cancelled; Olive's picture to be finished; borrowed furniture to be returned to its rightful owners, to which was added, at Mr Moto's insistence, cuspidors to be returned to their respective pubs.

December 14th   Our orders are to fly first to Acklington to swop aircraft with 610 Squadron, ours having all the latest modifications embodied. As a matter of fact the move should have been completed already, but thanks to another spell of dreadful weather we are stuck on the ground at Westhampnett.

By dint of working round the clock, we were packed up and ready to leave on time. The advanced party left yesterday afternoon by train, along with most of the heavy stores. The farmhouse was stripped of its furnishings, the Harrows loaded with the first-line equipment, Olive's portrait completed and our farewells said at Lavington. Fortunately the squadron had been released from operational duties, as most of the starter batteries have gone in the train. Then the weather closed in and the move was postponed.

As our camp beds have already gone, Micky and I are being put up for the night at Lavington.

December 16th   Two days have passed and we are still weatherbound at Westhampnett, disconsolately sitting it out at dispersal in case a break should appear. Sixteen Spitfires outside, dripping. Sixteen pilots inside, cursing! My suggestion to complete the changeover by rail was met with scant enthusiasm by Group on the grounds that the weather *might* improve. In fact it looked like doing so once, when we saw the tops of the trees for the first time, and decided to have a crack at it but, when I saw the first Harrow disappearing into the clouds as soon as it became airborne, I had serious misgivings about the venture. Nevertheless we did take off and managed to form up over the sea, but as soon as we flew back over the coast we were enveloped in cloud at 200 feet. I was not prepared to force a way through with so many inexperienced pilots in formation, so returned to Westhampnett to find one of the Harrows had also turned back.

Alas, the confusion did not end there. No sooner had everyone fixed their accommodation for the third night running when Group came on the line, ordering us to travel by rail after all. Three buses turned up to take us to London, whereupon the telephones went red hot as sleeping arrangements were apologetically cancelled. At last we were on our way, or so we thought until the convoy was stopped by the police outside Midhurst, when I was handed another message from Group, telling me we would be flying back tomorrow as the weather was definitely going to clear.

I hadn't the neck to ring Lavington again; Micky and I turned up unannounced to find Barbie not in the least surprised to see us. In fact our sheets were still on our beds.

December 17th As promised, conditions improved dramatically and we finally left Westhampnett with no bother at all. A stiff breeze was blowing from the south which, the Met people assured me, would persist throughout our route, thus making it possible to reach Acklington without having to refuel on the way. However it soon became clear they were wrong for, after flying for half an hour, we were not making the progress we should and it seemed the wind was now meeting us head on. We would have to land somewhere after all.

I decided to make for Catterick but, try as I would, was unable to raise them on the R/T. No station likes to be invaded unexpectedly by sixteen thirsty Spitfires, so I was pleasantly surprised when we were immediately mar-shalled to the refuelling point where a fleet of bowsers stood ready to pump in the petrol. Not only that, but the duty officer was on the tarmac to greet us with an aircrew bus to take us to the Officers' Mess where, he assured us, lunch awaited. It seemed too good to be true.

Lunch was almost over when the peace of the afternoon was shattered by the roar of another squadron of Spitfires joining the circuit, whereupon our host leaped from his seat and looked out of the window. 'You *are* 603 Squad-ron, I take it?' he asked, a perplexed look on his face. It was then we discovered that George Denholm was bring-ing his outfit back to Turnhouse and had taken the precaution of ordering the facilities in advance. I confess to a twinge of conscience when we later passed our Edinburgh colleagues trudging wearily towards the NAAFI canteen, the Mess having exhaused its daily quota of spare rations.

We are back at last; back in the land where the air smells so much fresher! No time was wasted swopping aircraft with 610 Squadron at Acklington and we arrived at Prestwick to find everything well organized, for Crack-ers and his merry men had had plenty of time in hand. One Harrow had managed to get through on Saturday and the other beat us to it by a couple of hours.

We have been given the Old Mill as our headquarters, the same the Fokker ran into nearly a year ago, and an operations telephone line has been installed. When I used it to let 13 Group know we had arrived, the duty controller suggested A Flight should come to immediate readiness, but I don't think he was willing to put into practice what I told him to do with his suggestion! Tomorrow will be time enough. Nevertheless it is nice to be back in Cloud Cuckoo Land.

December 19th It is taking time to become acclimatized to our new surroundings, for this is the first occasion when we've shared an airfield with units not primarily concerned with active operations. The circuit is full of ab initio trainers jockeying for positions with the Ansons of the Navigation School, but although we are supposed to have priority, it is not always possible to enforce with so many trainees at the controls. Nevertheless David McIntyre is delighted to have his old squadron on his airfield and does all in his power to safeguard our interests, even loaning me a small two-stoke DKW for my personal use. Our return to Scotland has also stirred up much local interest and, besides finding ourselves featuring in the Scottish press, I have been bidden to broadcast to the nation on the BBC, a propect which fills me with dread. Maybe my diary will come in handy at last.

I have been taking a number of the new boys on training sorties to familiarize them with our fresh area of operations and had just landed from one this morning when George Pinkerton turned up to see what we were up to. While we were chatting in my office, Findlay and Crackers burst in to say they've both been posted, Findlay to command 54 Squadron and Crackers to an Admin post in the Middle East. At least I was able to look after our guest this time and wasn't forever having to dash off and leave him. George must have appreicated the attention, for he stayed on to join in Findlay's promotion celebrations.

* * *

December 21st An atmosphere of 'winding down' is
noticeable these days, probably as we no longer have the
imminence of action to keep the adrenalin flowing. Also,
of course, many of the old guard have left, or are about
to, for, in addition to Boyd and Douglas, Donald Jack
had word he is being posted as a controller at Headquarters 13 Group. Indeed, after they have gone, only Paul
Webb, McDowall and I will remain of the pilots who
began the war with the unit and, to make matters worse,
none of our newcomers has any operational experience
behind him. It seems we will become a glorified Operational Training Unit for the next few months and the
sooner we can get on with it, the better.

In the meantime the task of manning the readiness
states inevitably falls on the few trained pilots remaining
and I was called to stand-by at 1.30 this morning, as a
bogey was reported to be heading for Glasgow. In the
event I was not required, as a night fighter was scrambled
from Drem and managed to drive it away. Then, having
breakfasted and shaved, I flew down to Newcastle to
attend a Squadron Commanders' Conference at Group
Headquarters when I met our new AOC, Jock Andrews.
Birdie Saul has moved south to become AOC 12 Group.
George Denholm was also at the meeting but I forbore to
ask him what sort of lunch 603 had had at Catterick!

We had a welcome visit from Hector MacLean this
evening, but his leg is giving him a lot of bother. He fears
it will require further amputation.

December 23rd Some wives have turned up to spend
Christmas with their nearest and dearest and the Orangefield Hotel is beginning to assume the role of a Married
Officers' Mess. Having first set the training programme in
motion, Findlay and I took our ladies into Ayr to do

Christmas shopping and stayed on to see a Laurel and
Hardy film. Amy Johnson was at the hotel when we got
back, having flown in to pick up an Oxford Trainer being
refurbished by Scottish Aviation Ltd, but it is not ready
for collection and we have invited her to join our party.
Whilst pleased to accept, Amy still hopes to get south in
time for her own Christmas celebrations, although her
prospects are none too good. The weather forecast is
hardly encouraging.

December 28th   Prestwick was blanketed in fog throughout Christmas Day, an unusual occurrence in this part of
Scotland. And the fog turned out to be widespread,
thereby scuppering Amy's hopes of getting away and
condemning her to a spell of Scottish rowdyism instead of
the hoped-for sophistication of an English Yuletide occasion. Nevertheless she seemed to enjoy herself amongst
strangers and certainly succeeded in enrapturing Dad
when he found himself sitting next to her at dinner. My
parents have joined us from Glasgow.

Weather conditions remained foul until late yesterday
evening and we have had to put off the training programme until this morning. However I had to take myself
off the schedule when Douglo Hamilton rang to say he
was bringing over plans for setting up an operations room
in the west. Instead of flying, therefore, I spent most of
the morning locked in conference with MacIntyre and the
Duke, when the procurement of suitable accommodation
proved to be the main problem. However Mac knows of
a nearby property which has just come on the market and
will follow it up and report back.

Later, imbued with the festive spirit, Micky and I called
on the ack-ack boys at Stevenston and arranged to set up

a number of training flights for them and arrived back at Prestwick in time to see Amy Johnson off in her Oxford.

December 31st   In my opinion, Rosemount, a large house standing in its own grounds a few miles up the Kilmarnock road, would make an ideal site for our operations room, so I spoke to Douglo who responded at once and flew across in his Hornet Moth, when one look at Rosemount was enough to confirm my opinion. He is to put the matter in hand forthwith. I had to leave Douglo with Mac, as I was invited to lunch with the Lord Provost who has come up with more bright ideas for raising funds, amongst them that of asking Fred Nancarrow to write a book about 602 Squadron and donating the proceeds to our Benevolent Fund. When approached, Fred agreed with alacrity.

Sir Archibald Sinclair, Secretary of State for Air, called to see us on his way north to bring in the New Year with his constituents, bringing with him news of Euan Wallace. It seems he is very ill indeed and unlikely to recover, which is an unhappy note on which to bring to a close my chronicle of 1940. Nevertheless, who knows what next year will bring? Whatever it is can hardly be more exciting than our lot this year and I, for one, look forward to it with pleasurable anticipation. But one thing is certain; I mean to bring in 1941 in the company of my colleagues and have no intention of repeating last year's performance. This time I will visit the loo with plenty of time to spare!

1941

January

January 3rd Saw in the New Year in more orthodox
fashion this time, starting it with nothing more painful
than a sore head gained from the high jinks going on in
the Orangefield Hotel. However the news of Amy Johnson's tragic death has put a damper on things to a certain
extent, for we got to know her fairly well during her few
days' enforced stop with us. Apparently she landed in
Yorkshire to refuel before running into appalling weather
in the south which prevented her from letting down over
her intended destination, Hatfield. Instead she was
tracked on CHL, heading out to sea to make another
unsuccessful attempt to break clear before turning inland
again, when she presumably ran out of petrol and decided
to bale out. Amy was seen to parachute into the Thames
Estuary and a Naval tug put out from Sheerness to go to
her aid but, in spite of a heroic attempt on the part of a
RN officer who dived in to help, both he and the
distinguished aviatrix lost their lives in the subsequent
rescue attempt.

True to form, the Scottish weather has turned
extremely cold – so cold that the radiator of my staff car
blew up soon after I started her up, thus giving me a built-
in excuse for missing the AOC's conference scheduled for
later in the day. In any case the first day of January is no
time to expect any self-respecting Scotsman to swing into
action! The replacement radiator had still not arrived
yesterday so I flew instead to West Freugh to fix up air
firing facilities for some of our recent arrivals.

The temperature plunged still further this morning, during most of which I struggled to coax a little warmth from a very reluctant coke stove in my office, but failed miserably and only succeeded in filling the room with acrid smoke. By and large the New Year has started in a thoroughly pedestrian fashion, although I am having to spend tonight at readiness as the moon is waxing brightly and Group considers conditions ideal for enemy strikes. None has shown up so far.

January 5th I had twelve aircraft in the air practising formation drill yesterday morning when Red Station was ordered to break off to investigate a plot near Greenock. But it turned out to be a Naval Swordfish which was lost above cloud and we were able to guide it back to Abbotsinch. So, having done our good deed for the day, we resumed the practice which, alas, only showed that most of the new blood will require a lot more training before they can be considered operational.

I left the programme in Micky's hands today as the Lord Provost invited Margaret and me to accompany him to a big orchestral concert being held in the Paramount Cinema to boost the city's war effort. We met up beforehand in the City Chambers where we found Sir Harry Lauder already tucking into the statutory plateful of bacon and eggs. In the event, the concert was a roaring success, the main attraction being Sir Harry himself accompanied, for the first time, by the entire Scottish Orchestra conducted by Warwick Braithwaite. At the end of the show Paddy Dollan made a thank-you speech from the stage, during which he summoned me to take a bow, which meant having to extricate myself from my seat in the dress circle and finding my way through a myriad of dingy passageways to reach the stage where I took my

place alongside the assembled artistes feeling a proper
Charlie. It seems the Lord Provost still has his eyes on me
as the prize exhibit.

But the evening didn't end there, for no sooner had the
final curtain dropped than Margaret and I were whisked
back to the City Chambers in the LP's official car along
with himself and the Lady Provost, to be joined again by
Sir Harry and his niece, Greta. I had not appreciated that
our host and Sir Harry were lifelong friends, having been
down the mines together in Lanarkshire long before
World War One, when they had together done many a
good knock-about turn at local amateur concerts. Thus
began our own private concert when we were treated to
the unlikely due of Sir Harry and our Lord Provost singing
'The Wig-Wig Waggle O' the Kilt' at the tops of their
voices as they cavorted, arm in arm, the full length of the
LP's private office while the City Officer kept the rest of
us acceptably primed with the national beverage.

It was now past midnight so, after I had offered to drive
the LP and his wife back to their flat in the South Side,
the official driver was allowed to go home. Unfortunately
my confidence in the old Vauxhall turned out to be
somewhat misplaced for, when we eventually staggered
into the frosty night air, the wretched car refused to start
and we ended up with the Lord Provost, Mrs Dollan and
my pregnant wife pushing me in the Vauxhall twice round
George Square before its engine reluctantly puttered into
life. And I had been hoping for an early night, as I am
due to record my broadcast for the BBC tomorrow.

January 8th   Had the daunting experience of sitting alone
in a BBC studio on Monday afternoon recording my
prepared talk to an unseen audience, whilst a number of

hazy figures with earphones clamped on their heads glowered at me through the large window separating the studio from the control room. They must be easily pleased, for they seem satisfied with the result, although unable to say when it will be broadcast. 'Probably after one of the news bulletins,' was all I could get from them.

Ayrshire has been enshrouded in heavy mist for the past two days and I'm told it has been a real pea-souper in Glasgow for most of the time. However moves are apparently afoot to make us more warlike up here, for there is now a daily flow of high-ranking visitors coming to inspect progress at Rosemount as well as a new airfield already under construction near the racecourse at Ayr. It seems Fighter Command is unhappy about us sharing a field with ab initio trainers and wants us to move into the new place as soon as possible.

January 11th A slight thaw has had the effect of making the mist even more dense although it thinned sufficiently yesterday afternoon to take Thornton, one of the new lads, for a spot of formation training, in the course of which we were diverted to intercept a bogey which ultimately turned out to be a stray Wellington. However no flying had been possible the day previously and I was treating myself to an extended lunch break when my broadcast unexpectedly came on the air after the One O'clock News. Can't say I recognized my own voice nor, it seems, did the others, for it had no sooner begun when a young pilot officer went to switch off the set with a muttered, 'You don't want to list to this twaddle, do you, sir?' I only managed to stop him in time, although it would probably have been better if I hadn't, for it sounded bloody awful and as if I was speaking with my mouth full of marbles.

Several large convoys have been sailing in and out of the Clyde recently and Control is edgy about their well-being and have us spending long hours on the readiness state in spite of the inclement conditions. In fact we were reinforced yesterday by a flight of Spitfires from 72 Squadron which Desmond Sheen brought over from Drem, although no patrols were called for. Nevertheless one can appreciate Group's concern, as the Germans have recently been making extended use of their navigational beams which are pre-set over intended targets, some of which have been identified over Clydeside. And to emphasize the gravity of the matter, I have just been ordered to send A Flight to Northern Ireland first thing tomorrow morning.

At long last the medicos have managed to scrape the remaining pieces of shrapnel from Glyn Ritchie's legs and he has been pronounced fit for operations again. I shall be glad of his extra experience.

January 14th　The sun has finally shown its face and the local airspace has, since Monday, been full of Spitfires trying desperately to catch up with the training programme. Nevertheless the weather did not clear early enough for A Flight to fly to Aldergrove although I suspect the same conditions must have deterred the enemy, for the special convoy we were due to protect has got off without let or hindrance.

We had an unexpected, but most welcome, visit from John Latta and his wife yesterday. Latta was the first Commanding Officer of 602 Squadron, being appointed in 1925, and this was his first visit to the old unit since handing over to John Fullerton in 1927. Doubtless he went away thinking things aren't what they were in his day!

The better weather has also caused a resumption of the regular flow of staff officers from both Group and Command, ostensibly here to inspect progress at Rosemount and Ayr. Nevertheless it is significant that few leave without first acquiring at least one bottle of scotch, which is apparently more easy to get here than in the south. I was able to oblige Timber Woods in this respect, in return for which he let me fly his Gladiator, a type which has hitherto escaped my attention. I find it pleasant to fly too, although I don't think it would stand much of a chance against a 109E!

Having duly added the new type to my log book, Margaret and I drove to Fairfield's yard in Scotstoun to witness the Lady Provost launching HMS *Oribi*, a new destroyer for the Royal Navy, after which we were entertained to an excellent lunch in the directors' dining room. Unfortunately the occasion proved too much for my wife's interesting condition, for she flaked out in the middle of the standard speeches about launches and lunches, and I had to take her home.

January 17th Intelligence has been reporting greatly increased German beam activity and thinks they may be trying to set a pattern over Glasgow. Consequently the planners have come up with a wheeze to saturate the target area with fighter aircraft from a height of 12,000 feet upwards, leaving the air space beneath for the ack-ack boys to do their worst. We tried it out on Monday, positioning ourselves at intervals of 500 feet from 12,000 to 22,000 feet and found it worked reasonably well, subject to a revision of the take-off intervals. The gunners are slightly annoyed that their upper limit is to be 10,000 feet, but accept the fact that a gap must be left to avoid hitting the fighters flying from 2,000 feet higher. So far so good, but will it work in the dark? At all events, Group Headquarters seems satisfied with the tests and is labelling it 'Fighter Night'.

The Gaiety Theatre in Ayr is one of the few music halls still privately owned and, as most places of entertainment in London have been closed by Government decree owing to the bombing, has been able to present many first-class turns which are seldom seen north of Watford. Eric and Leslie Popplewell, the present owners, are old friends and invited a number of us to see the show on Wednesday. It turned out to be a hilarious evening, as the star of the week is Renée Houston who, being a fellow Glaswegian, was not slow to exploit our presence and soon had me and the others embarrassingly involved in her routine. However we were able to weather the ribbing and were delighted when she later joined us for supper at the Orangefield.

The rest of the week has required my presence in Glasgow, for Paddy Dollan invited me to lunch with the Secretary of State, Sir Archibald Sinclair, yesterday when the latter brought with him a gentleman by name of John Wolfenden, who has been released from his post of headmaster of Uppingham School to rewrite a syllabus for the Air Training Corps. I later spent a most interesting afternoon with Wolfenden, discussing with him a wide range of subjects pertaining to the boys' training before accompanying him and the Lord Provost to the St Andrew's Hall where Sir Archibald gave one of his pep talks to a large audience, in the course of which he had many complimentary things to say about 602 Squadron in general, and Archie McKellar in particular.

Today has been of even greater interest, for Paddy had me as a lunchtime guest in the City Chambers for the second day running, this time to meet the Prime Minister and Mrs Churchill who were visiting Clydeside as part of a nationwide morale-boosting tour. Mr Churchill made a wonderful speech after lunch, although suffering from a heavy cold. Indeed Mrs Churchill confided to me that she was concerned about her husband's health and insisted on his taking a lie-down in the Lord Provost's room which was made available. On this occasion I also had the privilege of meeting Harry Hopkins, President Roosevelt's Special Envoy, who is accompanying the Prime Minister on his tour.

Paddy took me aside while the Prime Minister was resting and showed me an anonymous letter he had received two days ago. It was typed on a page of lined foolscap and referred to the incident outside the City Chambers after Sir Harry Lauder's visit. It read, 'Whilst appreciating the hard work you put into your job, we were nevertheless shocked to see the Lord Provost and the Commanding Officer of Glasgow's Fighter Squadron in George Square on Sunday night at such a late hour, in such a dilapidated car,' and, as if to rub it in to the full, 'and in such a condition!' Paddy's only comment was that maybe the Corporation should subscribe towards a new battery for the Vauxhall.

Am now back at Prestwick, still slightly bemused after such concentrated exposure to the VIPs, although I got my feet partially back on the ground on my way back when calling at Danny Brown's Restaurant to join the sergeants, who were holding their annual dinner.

January 20th   All is quiet on our operational front and we have been able to concentrate exclusively on the training programme, which is coming along famously. On the ground, however, much effort is needed to combat the cold, for the weather, although fine and clear, is well below zero and the wretched stove in my office is playing havoc with both temper and lungs because of its propensity for filling the room with dense smoke instead of calories. Consequently paper work is being neglected in favour of more time in the air where I find the irksome chore of moulding the new boys into fighter pilots infinitely preferable to the discomfort of my office chair.

Lately, my father's eyesight has been deteriorating alarmingly so am taking a few days off to spend them with my parents while the lull lasts. It seems the Old Man is suffering from cataracts in both eyes, although he hopes to begin the remedial treatment soon. Apart from this, both parents are in good heart, although Dad has had to give up his Home Guard activities for the time being, much to Mother's relief, for she tells me he had just managed to wangle a detail which seemed to require frequent visits to his local club.

January 28th   Have had a most enjoyable week, spending half of it at my parents' flat and the other half with Jean and Archie at Uplawmoor, where both are still fully taken up with their ARP duties. Jean has acquired a new tea cosy, this time in a fetching shade of pale blue, which goes well with her dark blue boiler suit. But the weather at Uplawmoor was even colder than at Prestwick and it took several kettlefuls of hot water to unfreeze the Vauxhall's radiator, fortunately without doing it any lasting harm. Margaret understandably has spend much of the week knitting wee woolly hats and things for the little Johnstone, expected in about two and a half months' time.

Micky has been pressing ahead during my absence and has managed to bring several of the tyros up to near operational proficiency. All we need is some enemy activity to put them to the test.

Janaury 31st Two stray barrage balloons were drifting over the airfield when I turned up at the Old Mill on Thursday morning, so took off with Glyn Ritchie to shoot them down. Fortunately they were drifting out to sea, so we were able to attack from above and got both down in next to no time. A tug has put out to salvage what it can. I later drove into Ayr to fetch Charlie Kunz and his son and brought them back to lunch with us at the airfield. Charlie is this week's attraction at the Gaiety and seems to be enjoying a week at the seaside. I couldn't understand why he was so reticent about being allowed to clamber over one of our Spitfires, until he reminded me he is not long out of the internment camp in the Isle of Man where he was being held as an alien internee until his screening formalities could be completed. Fortunately young Gerald Kunz had no such inhibitions.

Rumours are rife again that Germany intends to carry out her threatened invasion, although we think it unlikely at this time of year. However it appears the stories are emanating from America, so maybe we need not give them too much credence. At all events I see no signs of increased panic on this side of the Atlantic.

Was intending to have an early night, but the Ayrshire Farmer's Association is holding a dance in the Orangefield and, as the ballroom is directly beneath my bedroom, I decided to follow the principle of 'If you can't beat 'em, join 'em'. Some of the Land Girls were worth joining too!

1941
February

February 3rd Training, and still more training, is the order of the day for our newer arrivals, but flying for the rest has been largely routine. Micky took his flight to West Freugh yesterday for air firing practice whilst I did a couple of trips to try out new VHF sets recently fitted to our aircraft. But an Anson from the Navigation School failed to return from a sortie on Saturday and we mounted a number of patrols to help in the search. Word eventually reached us that a party of climbers on Goat Fell had spotted wreckage near the summit and I took off to recce the area, but was unable to confirm the report as most of the high ground on Arran was covered by cloud. However our worst fears were confirmed early this morning when a police rescue team reached the spot and found the remains of the aircraft scattered over a wide area and all four occupants dead.

  Indeed it has been a black day all round for Scottish Aviation, for they have just lost their headquarters building. A number of us were walking back to the Mill after lunch when someone spotted a wisp of smoke coming from the centre of the two-storey building on the opposite side of the airfield and, almost before he had time to call it to our attention, there was a sudden 'whoosh' and half the building became enveloped in flames which spread along its entire length in a matter of seconds, sending burning embers high into the air. I ran for my car and, with four others, drove at breakneck speed across the airfield to render what assistance we could, but found help was already at hand.

The station fire services were quickly on the scene and, besides tackling the fire itself, were quickly shepherding staff members to safety or rushing ladders to bring down those trapped in the upper floor. From some of the upstairs windows, we watched a couple of typists hanging from the sills, too frightened to let go until their rescuers reached them and prised loose their grip. Several others were jumping from first-floor offices, some able to limp from the scene under their own steam whilst others less fortunate had to be dragged clear by the band of helpers who had run to the spot. One poor fellow, having leapt to safety, picked himself up and ran off, only to keel over on his way to the sick quarters. When others ran to his assistance, he was found to have died from a heart attack.

It was a nasty scene, and will be a big setback for the company. However the tragedy was not without its moment of light relief for, whilst most of the aircraft parked in the large adjoining hangar were being wheeled to safety without difficulty, we were unexpectedly confronted by what appeared to be a sixteen-legged Anson walking in our direction. Apparently eight worthy fellows had come upon the aircraft, minus its undercarriage, resting on trestles and had decided to carry it to safety on their backs forgetting, of course, they had nowhere to put it down once they got outside. Indeed they were not relieved of their load until the trestles themselves became objects of a rescue operation.

It is too soon to assess the full impact of the disaster, but I understand most of the training records have gone up in smoke together with all the other paraphernalia of a thriving aviation company. At all events, the main building has been gutted and immediate steps will need to be taken to rehouse the organization if the entire training programme is to survive. Not unexpectedly, covetous eyes are already being directed towards the Old Mill and we may have to brace ourselves for a sudden change of scenery. We can but wait and see.

February 6th Awoke on Tuesday morning with the smell of smouldering timbers in my nostrils and drove across to find out from Mac whether we could be of assistance. I found him and his Chief Instructor, Noel Capper, poking through the embers in search of salvageable items, but both in remarkably good humour in the circumstances. It appears they have no immediate intention of trying to oust us from the Mill, having applied instead for an order to requisition the Orangefield Hotel for use as their headquarters until alternative accommodation can be built on the airfield. Whilst a relief in some respects, such a move will deprive us of our favourite venue for fun and games.

In response to a call from Douglo Hamilton, I later flew to Turnhouse in our Magister to discuss with him and his senior controllers their misgivings about the arrangements for Fighter Night operations. We kicked the subject round for well over an hour without coming up with anything better and decided to leave well alone and hope it will work if the need arises. The meeting was no sooner over than a flap developed in the operations room but it soon died down when they discovered the plots were of friendly aircraft. In the meantime the weather had turned nasty, so Douglo invited me to spend the night with him and Betty at Milburn Towers, their temporary home.

It was blowing a blizzard the following morning so, instead of flying back to Prestwick, I borrowed a staff car from Turnhouse and motored to Drem to catch up with

what our Edinburgh colleagues were up to. I also got
Harry Eeles to show me over one of the new Whirlwind
fighters about to be introduced into service. This twin-
engined fighter was originally fitted with contra-rotating
Peregrines which gave the machine an excellent performance, but unfortunately Rolls Royce cannot afford to set
apart a plant solely to manufacture a limited number of
reverse-prop engines and the production aircraft are
therefore fitted with both engines turning in the same
direction. This has produced so much torque that the
Whirlwind is no longer the success it might have been,
which is a shame, for it certainly looks the part.

Snow continued to fall until late last night, so did not
get back to base until this morning, when I found waiting
for me a pile of mail including, among other important
items, a summons to attend an Investiture at Buckingham
Palace on Tuesday week. Also found that Mr and Mrs
Scott, owners of the Orangefield Hotel, have gone to
London to lobby support in their fight to prevent their
business being taken over by Scottish Aviation Limited.

February 10th   A sudden thaw set in towards the end of
the week which has limited the training programme. It
has come at a bad time, for Jake Edy, one of the few
remaining fully trained blokes, has been posted to take
over a flight in 315 (Polish) Squadron. Nor was the
situation improved this evening when Nuts managed to
prang K while landing after a night sortie, fortunately
without doing damage to himself. He says he was temporarily blinded by the exhaust flames. However news from
further afield is better. General Wavell's Desert Army
has suceeded in capturing Benghazi from the Italians!

Am beginning to think a pyromaniac is among us, for
two fires sprang up simultaneously in the Officers' Mess

around midnight. Unfortunately a number of our fellows were in the building at the time, celebrating Jake's posting, when the outbreaks were discovered, and are the prime suspects. Mind you the situation wasn't helped when Pedro Hanbury, in the excitement of the moment, discharged a fire extinguisher over the Chief Flying Instructor and I am not surprised to learn that Capper has placed him, and two others, under close arrest and has called in the police. I have telephoned Douglo Hamilton to put him in the picture and he has promised to fly over tomorrow to try and pour oil on the troubled waters, which is as well, for I now hear that Scottish Aviation has had a change of heart and may, after all, try to get us out of the Old Mill.

February 14th   It obviously pays to have a Duke on one's side, for Douglo has not only managed to divert the company's attention from the Mill, but has persuaded the AOC to release our miscreants from arrest and allow their cases to be dealt with summarily by the station commander. In any case it transpires that someone totally unconnected with 602 Squadron was spotted running from the scene when the fires first started and the CID has been called in to examine whether there is any connection between this fire and the more serious conflagration on the other side of the airfield. Nevertheless the latest schemozzle has done nothing to improve our relations with the parent company, which is hardly surprising as one or two of our chaps were behaving with undue exuberance during the height of the emergency.

In the current strained atmosphere it is fortunate that work on the new airfield is proceeding as well as it is, for the sooner we can relieve Prestwick of our presence, the better. Archie Hope and I drove to Ayr yesterday morn-

ing to find some of the domestic accommodation almost
fit for occupation, although much remains to be done on
the airfield itself. However, I flew there in the afternoon
with Mr Westacott, the resident engineer, as passenger
and landed the Magister on both runways, although I had
to glide under the high-tension cables which still span the
east–west approach. I repeated the performance in a
Spitfire, but the north–south runway is still too short for
normal operations and, of course, the power cables will
have to be taken down.

My faith in the Powers That Be is waning, for no sooner
do we get within sight of becoming operational again than
some of our lynchpins are posted from the squadron.
Posting notices have come in, directing Paul Webb to go
to No 5 FTS and Stow to RAF Ford, and it makes me
wonder whether the Operational Training Units are being
over-stretched and we are being used to make up the
shortfall.

Carried out an unusual assignment this morning when
asked to assess prospects for constructing an airfield at
Turnberry on the site of the golf course, whence aeroplanes had operated during World War One. A strong
onshore wind was blowing when I got there and I experienced a great deal of buffeting on all the approaches,
particularly on the east–west run-in which entailed passing
over the hotel. Certainly I had doubts about its suitability,
particularly as I'm told the place would be used to train
ab initio pilots. Before writing a report, however, I
swapped my Spitfire for the Magister and took Mr Westacott with me to size up the constructural aspects, when
my first impressions were confirmed after landing on one
of the fairways only to be confronted by a stone monument on which were inscribed the names of those who
had lost their lives in flying accidents during its previous

spell as a training aerodrome. The Resident Engineer
supports my belief that it is not a suitable site, and I am
reporting accordingly.

February 6th   The CID has cleared us of any involvement
in either fire, which is a big load off my mind. They have
apparently got a lead on the real culprit but are not
prepared to say who he is. In the meantime a spell of
better weather has boosted flying hours and I was able to
take the entire squadron on an exercise with the Came-
ronians at Androssan, when we carried out a number of
dive-bombing attacks on their troops. I scrubbed the low-
flying details, however, as they would have taken us too
close to the Irvine balloon barrage. Instead I used the
spare time to call the boys in to carry out some unexpected
formation flying in squadron strength and was delighted
when they responded so efficiently.

  Some of us went to the Odeon Cinema in Ayr this
evening to hear Paddy Dollan addressing a large political
gathering which turned out to be a particularly lively
affair. But Mr Dollan is an old campaigner and had little
difficulty in dealing with his hecklers and I thoroughly
enjoyed the experience, as it gave me an insight into the
hurly burly of political life. The Lord Provost and Mrs
Dollan later looked in at the Orangefield for refresh-
ments, but I had to leave them in Micky's hands while I
went to the airfield to deal with yet another problem.
Sergeant Booty had chosen the moment to collide with a
Tiger Moth on landing after a dusk sortie, fortunately
without causing injury to either pilot. But the Tiger Moth
doesn't look so good after its brush with the Spitfire!

February 19th   Much has been happening during the past
three days; so much, in fact, that I hardly know where to
begin.

My driver took me to the City Chambers on Monday morning to join up with the Lord Provost and his wife, who were billed to appear at the same investiture as me, Paddy to receive his knighthood, me to collect a DFC. It seems the Lord Provost had a hand in fixing it so that we could travel together, which was a great stoke of luck for me as the entire trip was organized to the last detail and I was included in the official civic party. Unfortunately Margaret did not feel up to the journey and remained in Glasgow.

A large crowd, including many pressmen, saw us off from Central Station, after which the rail journey was speedy and uneventful, although the Dollans were clearly upset by the extent of the devastation in and around London. Night had already fallen by the time we reached Euston and the air raid sirens sounded while we were being driven in a taxi to the Dorchester Hotel. Neither the Lord Provost nor Mrs Dollan had previous experience of an air raid and asked me what should they do. 'Make for the nearest bar,' I counselled, tongue in cheek. 'That way, the longer the raid lasts, the less one tends to notice it!' Alas, they took my advice and, as the alert was still in force long after midnight, it was an unsteady trio which stumbled to their suites in the early hours of Tuesday morning.

Paddy insisted on turning up at the palace wearing his Lord Lieutenant's uniform which, because of wartime restrictions, is not dissimilar to the uniform of an army general. A problem arose when trying to get the LP properly kitted out, for neither the City Officer nor I had any idea how to assemble a Sam Browne, but fortunately one of the waiters, who had served as a batman during WW I came to the rescue, after which we deemed it safe to present ourselves to the general public. However, our troubles were not yet over for, while waiting outside the hotel for our car to turn up, a young Guards officer passed by and saluted Paddy in true parade ground fashion, to which Paddy responded by lifting his cap.

The ceremony at Buckingham Palace was simple, but impressive, with the King, in the uniform of Admiral of the Fleet, standing on a raised dais whilst a string ensemble from one of the Guards regiments played unobtrusively in the background. Unfortunately I missed the actual moment when Paddy received his accolade, as I was still awaiting my turn in an anteroom along with many others, including Findlay Boyd, Sheep Gilroy and Archie Hope. However I was able to join the Dollans later and watched the rest of the recipients filing past the Monarch before venturing outside to face a battery of press photographers and newsreel cameras, all seemingly hell bent on getting pictures of Glasgow's newest knight.

Several friends of Paddy joined us for lunch, including the Home Secretary, Herbert Morrison, Cecil Weir and Alec King, after which the Home Secretary insisted on taking us back to the Home Office where he conjured up a bottle of whisky from a drawer in one of the filing cabinets. But more was to come for, arising from a previous invitation, we went on to the Prime Minister's temporary residence beneath the Cabinet Offices for afternoon tea with Mr and Mrs Churchill and their daughter Diana. Lady Reading was already there when we arrived, having been invited, I suspect, for Agnes Dollan's benefit as the latter is a leading light in the Women's Institute in Glasgow. Regretfully our time with Mr Churchill was short for, not long after greeting us most cordially, he went off for his afternoon siesta even before the tea trolley was wheeled in. Nonetheless I feel very privileged to have been received by the great man in

the privacy of his own home. Mrs Churchill explained
that they had been made to move into underground
quarters after No 10 Downing Street was damaged in an
air raid but, although a safer haven than their official
house, the Prime Minister didn't like it and preferred to
join the fire watchers on the roof of the building whenever
a raid was on.

It seems one must possess the stamina of an ox to
withstand the rigours of public office for, after leaving the
Churchills', we called at the College of Heraldry for
Paddy to sign on, as it were, then trooped off to Fleet
Street to meet Paddy's boss, Lord Kemsley, at the Allied
Newspapers' Head Office before rushing back to the hotel
to pack. But that was not all, for we put in an appearance
at a reception in the Hungaria Restaurant, where we met,
amongst others, Jack Payne, the dance band leader, and
attended a dinner in the Piccadilly Hotel before finally
catching the night train, which we just did by the skin of
our teeth.

February 20th   I must get out of the habit of referring to
our Lord Provost as 'Paddy' although he is threatening to
kick me out if I don't! At all events, his Knightship
insisted that I breakfasted with him and his new Lady
before I could get away to show my gong to Margaret and
my parents. Corporal Brown later came to the flat to
drive me back to Prestwick when, for the second time in
just over a year, we nearly failed to negotiate the exposed
road over the Fenwick Moor because of heavy snow.

A lot of mail was awaiting my return, amongst it being
a posting notice for Sergeant Whipps, yet another fully
trained pilot, and I was still in the course of opening some
of it when a security bloke was shown into my office,

insisting he see me alone. I didn't much like what he had to say.

Apparently the CID had been called in by a company specializing in breaking up wrecked aircraft for scrap purposes, when one of its workmen came upon two small sticks of dynamite wedged into the casting of the fuel induction system of Spitfire L1019, one of our aircraft which had been salvaged from the sea after being shot down during the Ford action last August. The explosive had not detonated in this instance, but would assuredly have done so if the engine had overheated, and I cannot think how it got there in the first place. Is it an isolated case, or could other unexplained incidents possibly be linked with it? Why, for instance, did Sergeant Whall inexplicably plunge to the ground while accompanying Donald Jack from an action near Arundel or Pat Lyall bale out without previous warning last October? The investigating office has promised to have both cases re-examined.

Was on my way out to my aircraft this afternoon when two Blenheims from the Radio School collided during take-off in formation. One managed to force-land in a neighbouring field but the other crashed into the middle of the airfield and burst into flames. Although we rushed to the scene as fast as we could, the aircraft was a blazing inferno when we got to it and no one was able to get near enough to rescue the two crew members who, in any case, were clearly beyond help. It was a grisly sight and one which I hope never to see repeated.

The Scotts have got their marching orders and have been told to vacate the Orangefield in a month's time, but they will not give up without a struggle and have already got their local Member of Parliament to take up cudgels on their behalf. Nonetheless the place has lost some of its carefree atmosphere, which is a shame.

February 24th At long last we are beginning to see the fruits of our intensive training programme, for Sergeants Booty and Brown have today been declared operational. It seems, too, that Group is beginning to appreciate our problem and has arranged for Sergeant Osborne from 54 Squadron to come to us in exchange for one of our less well trained tyros. Nevertheless everything is not yet beer and skittles, for another Spitfire bit the dust on Saturday when the undercarriage of Francis's aircraft refused to come down, even after he used the emergency air bottle. Luckily he made a safe wheel-up landing, coming to rest next to a Dominie which had earlier overshot and was still entangled in the hedge.

Intelligence reports still point to Clydeside as a prospective target for the Luftwaffe. Not only have more directional beams been identified, but messages from Norway confirm that a crack Bomber *Gruppe* has recently moved to Stavanger, a favourite base from which to launch attacks against targets in Scotland. As a result, a flight of night fighter Beaufighters of 600 Squadron flew in on Sunday evening to reinforce the sector.

Took time off this evening to visit the local cinema where the Gaumont British Newsreel was showing pictures of our recent visit to Buckingham Palace. The cameras were naturally more interested in Sir Patrick and Lady Dollan although yours truly managed to get his mug into one or two of the shots, but I have no idea what the main feature was, for I left before the big picture came on.

* * *

February 28th I must have picked up a chill, for I have been feeling decided groggy for the past few days. I therefore left matters in Micky's hands and joined Margaret in Glasgow, where I knew I would be well looked after. And the treatment worked, for she had me back on my feet by Thursday and I was ready to return to Prestwick although, when I got there, a full gale was blowing, which had not only put paid to flying activities, but had blown down the sign outside the hotel and flattened a number of bordering fences. Our aircraft are still firmly tethered to the ground.

I used the breather to inspect progress at Rosemount and Ayr and found painters putting the finishing touches to the former, whilst at last two dispersal sites could be occupied at Ayr. Unfortunately neither can be used for operational purposes as the Post Office has yet to install the telephone lines, although Loel Guiness has been appointed as the station commander at Ayr and Archie Hope as senior controller at Rosemount.

Was surprised to learn that the Duchess of Rutland was staying at the Orangefield until someone mentioned she is Loel's mother-in-law. It seems Isabel Guiness is expecting a baby at the same time as Margaret and her mother has come north to help with the house-hunting. Indeed this must be the High Society Season, for Douglo unexpectedly turned up this afternoon with Lord Trenchard in tow.

1941

March

March 5th　Latest Intelligence reports must have put Ops on their toes, for we are scrambled whenever a plot appears in our area. Not surprisingly the vast majority turn out to be of friendly aircraft going about their lawful business, although one over the Irish Sea showed more promise. On this occasion the bogey was flying about 25,000 feet, but we never saw it because of heavy cloud cover and it turned south soon after we arrived on the scene. Nevertheless we are fairly piling up flying hours these days, which is no bad thing, as it is giving the new boys plenty of practice.

Had supper on Monday evening with Eric Popplewell before going on to the theatre, where Reginald Foort is appearing at the organ. Although the audience seemed well pleased with the performance and gave the maestro a big hand, Eric is less happy about booking Foort to appear at the Gaiety as he is insisting on the theatre lights being left burning all night in case the temperature should fall and upset the tuning of his organ pipes. It was Eric's turn to fire-watch, so I joined him on the roof after the show, when he continued sucking his teeth about Foort's demand, reckoning the additional charges for electricity will just about negate the week's takings! I left him still muttering.

Am thinking of applying for a 'By Appointment' sign, for have been again rubbing shoulders with Royalty. Paddy was very secretive when he telephoned yesterday morning inviting me to lunch today at the City Chambers to meet, as he put it, some 'Very Special Guests'. I thought I had learned not to be surprised at anything the Lord Provost did, but you could have knocked me down with a feather when I turned up at his office to find myself one of only twelve guests invited to lunch with the King and Queen, who are paying a surprise visit to Clydeside. Thus, seated between Harry Lauder and the Archbishop of Glasgow, I joined this privileged group while it guzzled its way through a simple lunch of broth, mutton and milk pudding, after which I had the honour of meeting Their Majesties, at one time speaking to both together. I was surprised to learn how much the King knew about 602 and its personnel, even remembering the details of Douglas Farquhar's brush with the Heinkel when he landed beside it to stop it being set alight by its crew. Indeed His Majesty must have been expertly briefed for he also remarked on having given me a DFC three weeks ago! I wonder how long it will be before I come back down to earth! At all events, Loel Guiness had turned up to assume command of Ayr in my absence, and didn't seem unduly impressed when I told him what I'd been doing. He is probably more used to that sort of thing.

March 7th   Had some difficulty locating David MacIntyre when I took Loel to meet him yesterday morning, but eventually tracked him down in a small office at the back of the big hangar. This is hardly the type of accommodation in which one would expect to find the managing director of a thriving aviation company and highlights the urgency of rehousing the headquarters as quickly as possible.

Having made the introductions, I left Mac and Loel together and sought out Westacott to fly him round the area in search of a suitable site for yet another fighter airfield. But Ayrshire is not as flat as I had imagined and, in spite of scouring the district from top to bottom, we came up with only one possibility, and that only a few miles north of Kilmarnock, which is probably too close to the existing airfields at Prestwick and Ayr.

A lot of rain has been falling recently and parts of the airfield have become very soft. We found this to our cost when Grant tipped Y on its nose when landing after squadron formation practice this morning and I, too, became hopelessly bogged down and had to be hauled out of the mire with the aid of a tractor. I was therefore not in the best of tempers, having to walk back to the office. But I was in an even worse one after I read the signal lying on my desk, for it was to inform me that Micky has been posted to command No 317 (Polish) Squadron.

March 10th It was a happy coincidence that a full gale was blowing on Saturday and flying had to be scrubbed, for the Glasgow Corporation had laid on a civic luncheon in the squadron's honour. Thus many more were able to attend than might otherwise have been possible. The hospitality was on a generous scale and our hosts made sure their guests, officers, NCOs and airmen alike, were suitably entertained. And many kenspeckle faces were there to join in the fun, the Duke of Hamilton, Sir Robert Bruce and Bobbie Howes among them, to say nothing of my parents, Mother resplendent in a jaunty hat bought especially for the occasion. It was a merry busload of troops which was later seen off outside the City Chambers and I will long remember the loud cheer that went up from the lads as the vehicle drove away and the sight of Mr Moto's cheery face grinning from a rear window with an enormous Havana cigar stuck firmly in the corner of his mouth. It is a marvellous gesture on the part of the City Fathers and much appreicated by everyone in 602.

But we are not neglecting the more serious business of the day. General Walker, recently retired from the Army, has been appointed to command all the Home Guard units in Renfrewshire and Ayrshire and I lunched with him yesterday to discuss our participation in a mammoth exercise he is organizing for the near future. As a start, I am sending one of my officers to his headquarters to help with the planning and, as luck would have it, Colonel Lister and his Commandos have just turned up in the district, fresh from their successful raid on the Lofoten Islands in Norway and when the three of us later got together, it was agreed the Commandos would also take part.

Loel and Isabel Guiness have taken a house on the outskirts of Troon and invited a number of us to dinner this evening. Unfortunately I was not feeling at my best, for I had to leave early to drive Micky to Kilmarnock to catch his train, and have just waved him goodbye. The squadron won't be the same without him.

March 12th   Not much has been happening on the operational front recently, apart from chasing three unidentified plots approaching the Galloway coast last night. This is the first time we've been controlled by Rosemount and it is a pity we could not have opened their account. Alas, the sector is still short of adequate RDF, and the controller was having to rely on information passed by the Observer Corps. In the event I never saw the intruders which, I am told, turned south before they reached Ballantrae.

Have picked up a heavy cold and decided to stay on the ground today to avoid damaging my eardrums. However

I was able to keep a long-standing date to lecture to the ATC lads at Ayr Academy this evening, but just avoided a collision with a tank barrier when driving back in the blackout.

Intelligence says the German beams are actived over Glasgow tonight.

March 13th Was feeling bunged up this morning when accompanying Loel to Ayr to make arrangements for our pending move. However the AOC telephoned at lunchtime with news that his Intelligence chaps were almost certain the Luftwaffe would pay Clydeside a visit tonight and that he was sending his senior ops officer, Group Captain Rogers, to Prestwick to co-ordinate arrangements for the Fighter Night he intended to mount. In the circumstances I put myself back on the flying detail.

Went out to meet the group captain when his Beaufighter was reported overhead and watched the black machine circling out to sea, preparatory to lining up for the final approach. But it did not reappear and, just as I was about to get into my car to find out what had happened, the police from Troon rang to say the aircraft was down in the sea a hundred yards offshore. McDowall and I drove immediately to the scene and arrived just as the ambulance was driving off with the group captain and his navigator inside, only to be told that the former was dead when the rescuers brought him ashore, although his navigator appears to have got off with minor injuries. The AOC was most upset when I broke the news to him.

German signals traffic built up steadily throughout the afternoon, giving added credence to the Intelligence reports. I was therefore not surprised when sent off soon after eight o'clock to patrol a line between Prestwick and

Lanark, but was not long airborne before recalled to refuel, as the Fighter Night was being put into operation.

It has been agreed that the lower height bands would be patrolled by the night fighter Beaus and Blenheims of 600 Squadron from Drem, and that 602 Squadron would operate above them. Consequently I found myself circling over Glasgow at 20,000 feet where the cloud cover was sporadic. Nonetheless I was much more concerned about the other fighters flying 500 feet above and below than concentrating on searching for possible intruders, as the night was very dark and calling for precise instrument flying to preserve the height differential. Indeed I was already having misgivings about the practicability of the scheme. But it was too late to do anything about it, as the controller was already broadcasting a steady stream of information about the progress of the attacking force comprising, he said, some thirty plus aircraft, and which was clearly heading in our direction. Once his flow was interrupted by someone shouting 'Tally-ho', only to break in again soon after to say contact had been lost.

It was not long before the leading raiders reached the target area. I first spotted a number of bomb bursts far off to my right when, all of a sudden, the searchlights were switched on and the clouds all around were illuminated by brilliant beams probing the night sky with pencil-like fingers. Soon the ack-ack opened up and we could see their shells bursting like miniature fireworks well below, whilst fires on the ground began to take hold and spread with alarming rapidity. In next to no time so much was ablaze that it became possible to distinguish the outline of the River Clyde itself. Once I saw the fleeting, but unmistakable, outline of a Heinkel 111 silhouetted against the ruddy background but could not go down to chase it, as we were under the strictest orders not to leave

our designated levels for fear of colliding with other
fighters. One could only try to curb one's frustration and
hope some enemy traffic would come by at a higher level.
But none did, and we had to sweat it out to the limit of
our endurance before landing to refuel, only to be told
the show was over and we were to stay on the ground and
await further orders.

I had often before felt a sense of anger and frustration
when seeing bombs dropping on large towns in the south,
but this is something altogether different. This is my
native city – my birthplace – and somewhere in the midst
of the holocaust is my wife. I can only hope and pray she
is all right, for repeated attempts to get through on the
'phone have met with no success. All telephone lines to
Glasgow are out of order.

And what of the action itself? It appears a Ju88 was
shot down by a Beaufighter of 600 Squadron near Turnberry and the crew taken prisoner and that Pedro Hanbury managed a short squirt at another, but with no
visible success. Nor does it seem the gunners fared any
better. Indeed it is remarkable that the raiders have got
off so lightly with so many British fighters about.

March 14th I thought dawn would never come. The
night seemed interminable, for I had to wait until daylight
before I could stand down and drive to Glasgow to find
out how things stood. My hopes rose when I drove into
the southern outskirts of the city to find few signs of
damage, only to slump again as I got nearer its centre.
Street after street was blocked by fallen masonry and I
had considerable difficulty in reaching the bridge at the
Broomielaw. Indeed, after crossing the river and moving
west, the farther I went, the worse the damage. Great
gaps where blocks of flats used to be; fronts of houses

torn open to reveal the remains of comfortable furnishings
inside; signs of destruction at every turning, often to
buildings and places I have known since childhood. My
heart was in my mouth as I drove into Hyndland Road
but, praise be to God, the solid old tenement was still
standing and, better still, Margaret seemed quite unper-
turbed when she opened the door to find a bleary-eyed
husband standing before her, panting loudly after running
up the stairs, two at a time. 'Oh, it's you!' she exclaimed,
obviously surprised to see me. 'Yes, it was quite noisy
and we've lost the kitchen window. It turned on the sink
tap when it broke!' It was all I could do to hold back the
tears of relief at finding her all in one piece.

Margaret didn't need to be asked twice when I suggested she returned with me to Prestwick and set about
packing a bag whilst I checked on my parents' well-being.
They too were in remarkably good shape, not even having
suffered the inconvenience of a broken window. Their
local balloon was also unscathed although I gather it had
not been raised last night because of the large number of
fighters operating in the area, which is perhaps a pity, for
it couldn't have been any less effective than we were.

The Scotts have made a room available for Margaret in
the Orangefield and I saw her safely installed before
coming back on the night state. Ops are naturally jittery
and insisting on a full turnout, although I will be surprised
if they suggest mounting another Fighter Night! Whatever
is decided upon, however, I hope we will be treated with
gentleness as I have not yet been to bed and am just
about all in.

The reason for last night's fiasco is now the subject of an
inquiry and it is already established that most of the

raiders came over between 10,000 and 12,000 feet. Was this just sheer coincidence, or has someone been talking?

March 16th Have been appointed President of the Board of Inquiry into Group Captain Rogers's accident, so was unable to play an active part in General Walker's exercise. Instead, I have been revisiting the scene with Flight Lieutenant Scarce, and other members of the Board, to gather evidence from eye witnesses and so forth, and we were able to wade out to the wreckage while the tide was low, hoping to spot something of relevance. And spot it we did, for the position of the fuel cocks in the Beaufighter indicated that they had not been switched from the 'Auxiliary' to the 'Main' position, which could have caused both engines to run dry whilst on the final approach. It has certainly given us something to work on, although we must examine all other possibilities before drawing definite conclusions.

Troon itself gave the impression of being a town under siege as the General's men crept furtively from corner to corner in search of an unseen enemy. The exercise was clearly under way, and we were stopped at a couple of road barriers on our way back to Prestwick to have our identities checked, not that I minded as I knew what the Home Guardsmen were trying to do.

The exercise scenario was straightforward. The Commandos were to set out from the Glasgow area with the ultimate objective of capturing the docks in Troon. It was up to the Home Guard to ensure they did not. 602 was to fly continuous reconnaissance patrols over the whole area and report back anything seen. We had already established a R/T link with General Walker's Headquarters for this purpose.

The Commonados were to move off at nine o'clock, but we were not to start flying until ten in order to give them a head start. Rather like a game of hide and seek, when one is required to count to a hundred before shouting 'Coming, ready or not!' However, being a Sunday, our lads flew fairly high for the first two hours to avoid disturbing the churchgoers and so would not have seen much in any case. Our early contribution was further interrupted when both Spitfires participating at the time were diverted to attend to a balloon which had broken loose over Irvine and it was not until that was dealt with could they get down to the job on hand. But, in spite of the excellent weather conditions, with unlimited visibility, no sightings were made. Indeed the only bit of positive information came from Glyn Ritchie who reported he could see the *Glen Sannox* steaming off Clock Lighthouse from as far away as Kilmarnock, the visibility being that good. No doubt he was wishing that he, too, could have been on board enjoying a 'trip doon the watter' instead of flogging the sky in such seemingly fruitless fashion.

By mid-afternoon the General's temper was beginning to wear thin, for he called soon after my return to ask whether I was using blind pilots. 'They must be *somewhere*!' he grumbled. 'Two hundred burly soldiers can't disappear into thin air!' I assured him the lads were searching every nook and cranny. Not long after, he was back on the line. 'You'll never believe this, Johnstone. The blighters are already *in* Troon!' The Sunday trippers had not been alone in appreciating the spell of good weather and Lister had decided to treat his men to a 'sail doon the watter'! The Commandos had boarded *Glen Sannox* at the Broomielaw and merely stepped ashore at Troon when she made her regular call there. Glyn's report had been more relevant than he thought!

* * *

March 20th   The Board of Inquiry has taken up most of my time for the past few days, but it is finally completed and on its way to Group Headquarters. As earlier suspected, the accident must have been caused by pilot error, in that he omitted to switch over to main tanks after taking off from Ouston. In the meantime the wreckage has been recovered and is now on its way to the knacker's yard. However I have developed a heavy cold, no doubt aggravated by wading out, waist deep, to reach the remains of the Beaufighter last Tuesday. Fortunately I felt fit enough to attend the group captain's funeral which took place in the Crematorium in Glasgow on Wednesday.

The squadron is now under considerable pressure to move into its new quarters at Ayr and I spent most of this morning surveying the place with Loel, trying to determine where everything should go. Our deadline is set for Saturday. In the meantime Prestwick continues to be dogged by bad luck, for one of Duncan Somerville's Beauforts crashed into the sea off Troon this afternoon, close to the spot where Rogers came down, killing both crew members.

March 31st   Have been unable to write the diary for the past ten days as my cold developed into a good-going bout of pneumonia, and I have been laid up in the Orangefield ever since, feeling like death warmed up. I am still not sure whether the cure wasn't worse than the complaint, for Doc tried out a new drug on me, something called M and B, which, although helping to hold down the temperature, succeeded in giving me an attack of jaundice, which is surely the most depressing complaint of all. Mr Moto was first to notice it when he insisted on standing by whilst I took a bath. 'I hate to tell you, sir,' he announced, peering gravely through his horn-rimmed spectacles, 'you look like an emaciated Chinaman!'

Happily I am mending rapidly and able to get around. This is fortunate, for a film unit has turned up on the airfield to shoot scenes for a Twentieth Century Fox film entitled *A Yank in the RAF,* starring Tyrone Power and Betty Grable, not that either is likely to show up here, alas. Apparently 602 Squadron is detailed to come off operations to make a number of flying scenes and filming is due to begin as soon as weather conditions allow. I gather we are already nicknamed 'The Glamour Squadron'!

No one is more pleased than Margaret that I am back on my feet, for she will soon have her own problem to contend with, the baby being due in about three weeks' time. Arrangements have been made for her to go into Greystones Nursing Home in Prestwick, where Isabel Guiness is also due to join the production line at the same time. By coincidence both girls are being attended by the same gynaecologist, so it will be a toss-up who secures his services first.

Fortunately things have been quiet during my absence and, apart from making a follow-up recce flight, Jerry has left us alone. Maybe his pictures have convinced him he's already done enough for the time being. I hope so, for he inflicted a lot of damage on areas around Glasgow and Clydebank, which are still groggy after the onslaught. I also found Glyn Ritchie sporting flight lieutenant stripes when I got back.

The move to Ayr has been postponed again. Apparently there is still a shortfall in the matter of telephone lines and, in any case, Group wants us to stay on at Prestwick until filming is completed.

1941
April/May

April 3rd Was somewhat over-optimistic about the speed of my recovery, for I have now developed conjunctivitis on top of everything else and am being kept off flying until it all clears up, not that I am missing anything, as the weather is still foul and no filming has taken place. Also, although keen to get back into harness as quickly as possible, I can do with the extra time to build up strength, as the pneumonia has taken a lot out of me.

My enforced absence from the flights has brought home to me how different the squadron has become since I first joined it, for the turnround of personnel shows no sign of letting up and I keep bumping into fellows I've never met before. Indeed I find I am the only true Auxiliary officer still remaining in 602 Squadron, which I find very sad. But help is at hand, as Hector MacLean arrived at Prestwick today, having been posted to Rosemount for duty as a fighter controller, in the rank of squadron leader.

April 8th The film unit managed to swing into action a couple of days ago and started shooting a number of ground scenes which included shots of a Spitfire being re-armed and of another being started up. But the weather remains obstinately wet and windy and has prevented any shots being done in the air. As a result we have had plenty of time to discuss the programme with the film's director, a delightfully gregarious American with an appetite for large cigars but with no earthly idea of what makes a

Spitfire tick. 'Say, Commander,' he said to me the other day, 'how's about giving us a shot of one of your airplanes coming down in flames and the pilot baling out!'

Nevertheless progress is being made and we spent most of yesterday trotting down the hill, as cameras took pictures purporting to show us running to our aircraft on orders to scramble although, by the time the same scene had been shot, and re-shot, at least ten times, we had long since lost our enthusiasm and the looked-for rush to get airborne had degenerated into something resembling an afternoon stroll in the country. Several shots were also taken of Spitfires taxiing about the airfield, although I have no idea where they are meant to fit into the overall picture.

April 11th The weather has at last improved sufficiently to take a camera into the air in an Anson, the upper gun turret of which has been removed to allow the cameraman freedom of action, although he complained bitterly that it was damned difficult to operate properly while being buffeted by the slipstream. Nevertheless we made several level runs for him, well throttled back to keep down to the Anson's lower speed, and later staged a few peel-offs from an echelon formation. Apparently we can do no more in the air until the director has seen the outcome of today's shooting, although he was able to capture shots of the squadron taking off in formation, which he took from the ground.

Germany invaded Yugoslavia and Greece while we were pretending to be film actors.

April 15th The film unit has now packed up and left. Three consecutive days of fair weather were sufficient for its purposes and we were all relieved when it was over and we could get back to our proper job. By way of recompense a number of us were entertained to a dinner in the Station Hotel at Ayr before the unit finally moved on.

The squadron is about to be denuded still further for, while in the midst of presenting a salver to Nigel Rose to mark his forthcoming wedding, Loel Guiness looked in and drew me aside. 'The AOC has been on,' he whispered in my ear. 'It seems a signal is on its way, posting you from the squadron!' My immediate reaction was one of alarm in case I should have to leave Prestwick before the baby was born.

April 20th Right enough, the AOC's message was on my desk the following morning. I am to be posted to Turn-house for duty as a fighter controller and John Kilmartin, a flight commander in 43 Squadron, is coming to relieve me. Indeed he must be eager to do so, for he turned up that same evening. Fortunately we are being allowed seven days for the handover as we are now in the throes of moving over to Ayr, no easy task, as the place is still in the hands of contractors. It has become a case of waiting outside a door until the painters move out, then moving in to put signs up to 'Mind the Wet Paint'.

In the midst of the hassle Margaret decided it was time she had a share of the action and moved into Greystones on Friday evening, after which I donned the mantle of expectant father and got down to the serious business of biting my fingernails, at the same time ceasing to be of any use whatever to Kilmartin or anyone else. However the suspense ended this morning at three-fifty precisely, when I became the proud father of a bouncing girl weighing 6lbs 9ozs! Am also glad to report that mother and child are both doing well.

Now that the excitement is over I must take a grip on myself and take stock of the future. It will certainly feel strange to be no longer a member of 602 Squadron for, after all, it is the only unit to which I have belonged.

April 29th   The past four days have passed in a whirl of activity, handing over to Killie and seeing the lads into their new quarters. In between dashing between Prestwick and Ayr I found time to fetch my mother and in-laws from Glasgow so that they could come and gloat over their new grandchild. Unfortunately Dad has not yet recovered from his latest eye operation and has had to remain bedridden, not that it has prevented him from making a generous contribution towards ammunition for wetting the baby's head. Indeed, there has been a surfeit of celebrations over the past few days, as Isabel's baby arrived the day after ours.

April 30th   Having concluded I'm likely to live, the Medical Board has passed me fit for full flying duties. Nonetheless it has also seen fit to grant me fourteen days' sick leave as a bonus, which has allowed me plenty of time to spend with Margaret and the babe, now labelled 'Ann'.

In the meantime I completed the handover last Friday when Killie and I put our signatures to the necessary papers, and have since managed to introduce him to the Lord Provost and others I think he should know. I have also spent some time at Rosemount trying to learn something about the gentle art of controlling fighters from the ground.

May 4th   The Luftwaffe has been showing a renewed interest in the Clydeside area and there have been a number of desultory raids during the past few nights, fortunately causing little damage. Nevertheless I didn't like the idea of subjecting the family to unnecessary risk and have brought Margaret and Ann to Uplawmoor for the remainder of my leave, hoping things will have quietened down in Glasgow by the time it is over.

Must admit to having a lump in the throat when I took my final farewell from the squadron, particularly when shaking hands with the grand bunch of airmen who have seen us through thick and thin ever since the war began. But my parting included a moment of real pleasure: Flight Sergeant Connors has been made up to warrant officer.

May 7th Am thankful we came to Uplawmoor, for there have been several heavy night raids in the area and bombs have fallen on Greenock, Dumbarton and Cardross, doing considerable damage. In fact one of my father's shops in Greenock has been completely flattened tonight, which is hardly the sort of present he would have chosen for this, his fiftieth birthday. Maybe it's as well he is still confined to bed.

Archie has just come in after his stint on ARP duty and tells me the gunners have downed a He111 over Glasgow.

I drove Margaret and Jean to Rubislaw Reservoir yesterday to show them where I had come down that night in October 1939 after losing myself in the fog, and found the scars still visible where I had slithered up the slope. However we did not stay for long, as a bull grazing nearby began to take a hostile interest in our presence.

May 11th Dropped off the family in Glasgow on my way through to Edinburgh yesterday afternoon, as I was due to clock on at Turnhouse this morning. Douglo and Betty had invited me to dine at Millburn Towers on my way to the airfield but, in the event, I never got my dinner, as

Douglo had been called away unexpectedly. Instead I went straight to the operations room where I found George Chater and Johnny Johnstone, two of the senior controllers, puzzling over Douglo's trip to Glasgow, for he had apparently rushed off to interview a German airman who had baled out of a Messerschmitt 110 near East Kilbride and who was insisting on seeing the Duke personally. The Me110, they told me, had crossed the east coast, very high up and travelling too fast for Spitfires to catch him, and the pilot had taken to his parachute as soon as a couple of Defiants from Prestwick met him head-on. The German, who has damaged an ankle, says his name is Alfred Horn, but would give no further details about himself. He would speak to the Duke of Hamilton, and no one else. In the meantime he had been picked up by the Army and taken to the military hospital in Maryhill Barracks.

We were still trying to fathom what it was all about when Douglo came into the Ops Room and took George and me into the controller's rest room and shut the door. He was clearly agitated. 'Don't think me mad,' he said, 'but I think Rudolf Hess is in Glasgow!' Beyond that Douglo said nothing, other than that he must fly to London as soon as possible to report his startling news.

George and I realized this was not a matter which could be handled by a junior civil servant, so spent ages on the telephone trying to arrange for Douglo to meet the Foreign Secretary but, when George finally got put through to one of the private secretaries, it was only to be told that such a meeting was out of the question as Lord Cadogan had a heavy list of engagements and could not spare any time in the foreseeable future. We were naturally asked the reason for the request but could only answer that it was not a matter which could be discussed on the telephone; the best we could do was to assure the secretary it concerned something of considerable national importance and that Douglo would present himself at the Foreign Office, willy nilly, by ten o'clock this morning.

Thus we saw Douglo off in a Hurricane borrowed from 213 Squadron shortly before seven, since when we have heard no more. We just hope he has got there safely.

May 14th   I have not chosen the best time to get settled into my new job, for Turnhouse has been buzzing with excitement ever since news of Hess's arrival has become generally known. Douglo flew back on Monday in a Flamingo of 24 Squadron, accompanied by a Mr Ivone Kirkpatrick, who had been on the staff of our Ambassador in Germany and had often met the Deputy Führer. They motored straight to Glasgow where he was able to identify the prisoner as soon as he clapped eyes on him. However it has put the CO on the spot, for the Powers That Be now suspect Douglo of being in cahoots with the Germans and have relieved him of his command for the time being.

In the meantime I have been sitting alongside the duty controllers, trying to learn the ropes, and am fast learning the job is not as easy as I thought. There is much to be assimilated, not only about the technique of actually directing the fighters from the ground, but one must also know how best to interpret information displayed on the plotting table after it has been filtered by a separate co-ordinating team. After all, information on aircraft movements comes from a variety of sources, CH and CHL Stations, the Observer Corps and the Gunners, to name but a few, and each has its own limitations regarding accuracy and speed of passing its information. One can only learn about the idiosyncrasies through experience.

However I will pick up what I can while waiting for my turn to go on a course at the Controllers' Training Unit.

May 17th Have not yet had an opportunity to speak to Douglo, for the poor chap has been ordered to stay away from here until his connections with Hess, if any, can be looked into. I saw him briefly yesterday when he flew off in another of 213's Hurricanes in response to a second summons from London, but he wouldn't speak about his dilemma. I hear he is back in Scotland again, having flown in with another party of big-wigs, and gone straight off to Maryhill Barracks.

May 24th Although still waiting for my course to turn up, I have apparently made sufficient progress to be allowed to take solo watches while things are comparatively quiet. As a result, my life is settling into a definite routine governed by weekly rosters which tell me, days in advance, when I am required to be on duty. Indeed I had my first experience of controlling one of 600 Squadron's Beaufighters two nights ago when a Bogey suddenly popped up on the table shortly before midnight. The intruder unfortunately turned tail before nearing the coast and no interception was possible. We think it was possibly a mine-layer dropping his load in the shipping channel leading into the Firth of Forth and RN minesweepers are now in the area.

Am also able to keep myself in flying trim as Stuart MacDonald is here with 213 Squadron, pending an expected posting to the Middle East, and has loaned me one of his Hurricanes whenever I have asked him. I flew across to Ayr yesterday to visit my old squadron, but picked an unfortunate time to do so for, not long after I landed, Sergeant Brown and John Willy Hopkin collided on take-off. Brown was killed when his Spitfire crashed just short of Prestwick, although Hopkin managed to get his aircraft safely back on the airfield. Apart from that, I found the boys in good heart and seemingly getting on famously without me! I spent most of this afternoon at Turnhouse taking a number of Fettes boys for joy-rides in the Station Magister.

Our Naval Liaison Officer has just told me that HMS *Hood* has been sunk in the North Atlantic. She and HMS *Prince of Wales* were in action against the battleship *Bismarck* apparently, but he has not yet heard how the latter ship fared in the encounter.

May 31st In case any ships involved in the *Bismarck* affair had decided to make for the Clyde, 43 Squadron was moved to Ayr on Saturday to give added support. This may have been a bit of intelligent foresight, for a German recce plane appeared the following day, ostensibly aiming in that direction. I was on duty when the plot first appeared, flying very high, some fifty miles out to sea, off the Northumbrian coast, and I scambled a 213 Squadron Hurricane to go after it. However the raider continued on its westerly course and was clearly going to be too far south for a successful interception by the aircraft scrambled from Turnhouse, so I ordered one of 43 Squadron's aircraft to do its damnest from Ayr. Fortunately the enemy plot was still on the table when Du Vivier's also came up loud and clear, resulting in another Ju88 biting the dust near Hawick. So I was able to claim my first success in the controller's seat although, alas, one is not allowed to paint a small swastika on it to commemorate the victory!

I have been able to rent a flat in Corstorphine and hope to move the family in next week. It's quite on the cards that that is when my troubles will really begin!

1986
Epilogue

Moving the family to Edinburgh was a mixed blessing, as we had hardly time to settle in before I was off the Stanmore for six weeks to be taught the finer arts of fighter controlling. Two months later came my posting to the Middle East, after which I could no longer continue my diary so, in an attempt to tie up a few loose ends, I will append a summary for the benefit of anyone still interested.

HMS *Prince of Wales* and her escorts limped back to Rosyth in early June when the naval liaison officer took me on board while she was still tying up. Consequently I was able to examine at first hand some of the damage inflicted during her action with *Bismarck* – many large jagged holes in the superstructure where shells had struck, splintered planking, and broken boats cradled in their davits. At one point, below decks, there was a series of holes punched clean through the ship from one side to the other where a shell had penetrated without exploding. But most poignant of all was the hefty piece of armour plating embedded in the forrard end, which was all that remained of HMS *Hood*. This chunk of metal had come down on *Prince of Wales* when the battle-cruiser was blown to smithereens a few cable-lengths ahead.

Douglo did not resume command of Turnhouse, although he was quickly cleared of any involvement with the enemy. Loel Guiness took over from him before I left, when Archie Hope also came from Ayr to become the senior controller. Although the circumstances of

Rudolf Hess's extraordinary trip are now well enough known, Douglo remained tight-lipped at the time and it was several years before he told me the full story. Sadly, the Duke died whilst undergoing minor surgery in 1974.

After intensive lobbying, and a considerable amount of in-fighting, the Scotts lost their battle to retain the Orangefield and moved out in August 1941. However they were soon again in business, having acquired a small hotel in Troon, with the RAF continued to rank among its more favoured clientele.

The outcome of our brief acting career eventually appeared on cinema screens during 1942, although no one considered *A Yank in the RAF* to be any great shakes. However the same shots later popped up in such films as *Mrs Miniver*, *Dangerous Moonlight* and *The Battle of Britain*, presumably in the interest of economy at a time when wartime shortages were at their most severe.

In spite of our efforts to dissuade the Powers That Be from building an airfield at Turnberry, runways were laid down and training took place. However I have not yet checked the war memorial to see if any fresh names have been added.

And the review would not be complete without a brief mention of the faithful old Vauxhall, which continued to serve me well until my departure from Edinburgh. It had been parked in a garage which was flattened by a land mine durng the Glasgow blitz yet, when I visited the scene of devastation a few days later, the Vauxhall was the only vehicle salvaged from under the debris, albeit sporting a few extra bumps on the fuselage. Nevertheless it still ran and I was able to sell it for ten pounds more than I had paid for it in 1938.

No 602 Squadron continued to operate with great distinction throughout the rest of the war, flying from bases in the south of England or on the Continent. And it continued to make the headlines when it took on a V2 rocket just as it was being launched from its pad in Germany, and when it was responsible for knocking Rommel's staff car off a French road and injuring the Field Marshal so severely he was unable to take any further part in the war. Nor did it go unnoticed that it was a 602 pilot who first spotted the *Scharnhorst* and *Gneisenau* making their historic dash through the Channel. Indeed 602 was always that sort of squadron and all who served in it did so with a pride reserved only for the very best. What a pity it had to be put into mothballs in 1957.

Glossary

A jargon peculiar to Fighter Command was in general use during World War Two and, for the benefit of those unfamiliar with the terminology, I am appending below a brief description of those in most common use.

ANGELS — Height in thousands of feet. E.g. Angels 5 is 5,000 feet.

VECTOR — Course to steer. E.g. Vector 27 means to steer a magnetic course of 270 degrees.

BANDIT — Hostile aircraft.

BOGEY — Unidentified aircraft.

X-RAID — Unidentified plots.

SCRAMBLE — Take off.

BUSTER — Go at full throttle.

PANCAKE — Return to base and land.

TALLY-HO — Target sighted.

STATES OF READINESS — *Stand-by*. Sitting in cockpits, ready to start up and go.
Readiness. To be able to take off within three minutes.
Available. Fifteen minutes to get airborne.
Released. Stand down. Released from the operational state for a specified period.

CH STATION　　　Chain Home Station (Radar).
CHL STATION　　Chain Home (Low) low-level radar.
VILLA　　　　　　R/T callsign alloted to 602 Squadron.

Index

All these books are available at your local bookshop or newsagent, or can be ordered direct from the publisher.

To order direct from the publishers just tick the titles you want and fill in the form below.

Name _____

Address _____

_____

Send to:
Grafton Cash Sales
PO Box 11, Falmouth, Cornwall TR10 9EN.

Please enclose remittance to the value of the cover price plus:

UK 60p for the first book, 25p for the second book plus 15p per copy for each additional book ordered to a maximum charge of £1.90.

BFPO 60p for the first book, 25p for the second book plus 15p per copy for the next 7 books, thereafter 9p per book.

Overseas including Eire £1.25 for the first book, 75p for second book and 28p for each additional book.

Grafton Books reserve the right to show new retail prices on covers, which may differ from those previously advertised in the text or elsewhere.